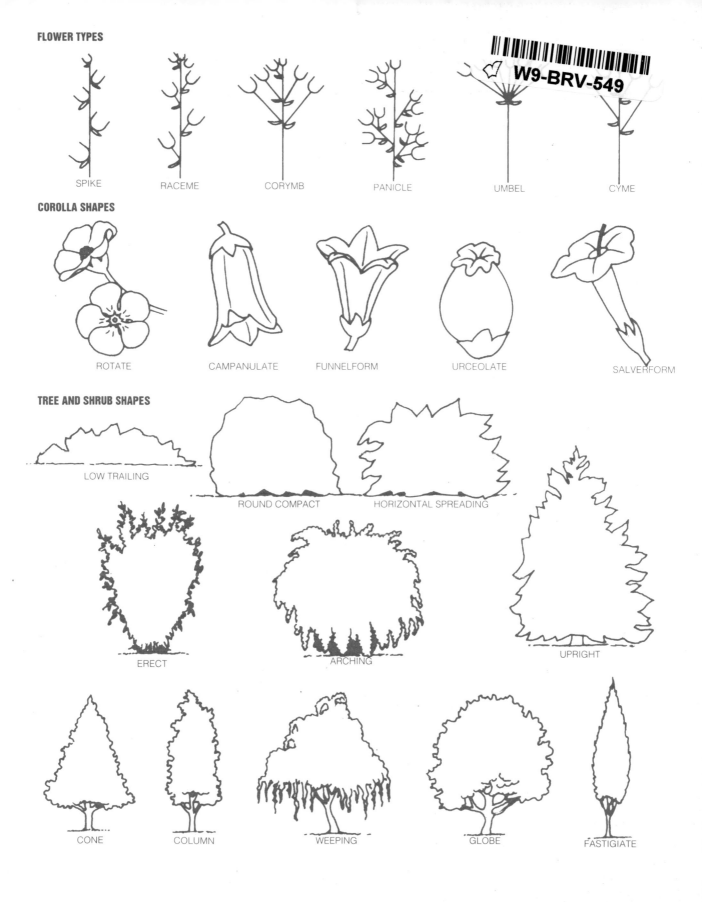

FLOWER TYPES

SPIKE RACEME CORYMB PANICLE UMBEL CYME

COROLLA SHAPES

ROTATE CAMPANULATE FUNNELFORM URCEOLATE SALVERFORM

TREE AND SHRUB SHAPES

LOW TRAILING ROUND COMPACT HORIZONTAL SPREADING

ERECT ARCHING UPRIGHT

CONE COLUMN WEEPING GLOBE FASTIGIATE

shrubs and vines

General Consultants:
Wayne Cahilly, New York Botanical Garden
Dorthe Hviid, Berkshire Botanical Garden, Stockbridge, Massachusetts
Mary Irish, Desert Botanical Garden, Phoenix, Arizona
Richard Isaacson, Minnesota Landscape Arboretum, Chanhassen, Minnesota
Rick Lewandowski, Morris Arboretum of the University of Pennsylvania, Philadelphia, Pennsylvania
James Locklear, Dyck Arboretum of the Plains, Hesston, Kansas
Claire Sawyers, The Scott Arboretum, Swarthmore College, Swarthmore, Pennsylvania
Azalea Consultant, Fred Galle, former director, Callaway Gardens, Pine Mountain, Georgia
Camellia Consultant, Anne Richardson, Huntington Botanical Gardens, San Marino, California
Historical Consultant, Frank Anderson, former curator New York Botanical Garden Library
Botany Consultant, Dr. Lucile H. McCook, former taxonomist, Missouri Botanical Gardens
Enabling Garden Consultant, Eugene Rothert, Chicago Botanic Garden
Design Consultant: Perry Guillot

shrubs and
vines

Chicago Botanic Garden
The Holden Arboretum
Royal Botanical Gardens

Galen Gates

Chris Graham

Ethan Johnson

With Leslie Garisto
Series Editor Elvin McDonald
Principal Photography by Ian Adams

Pantheon Books,
Knopf Publishing Group
New York, 1994

Acknowledgments
This book was created with the help, expertise, and encouragement of a
great many people. We would like to thank all the consultants who con-
tributed so much to it, Leslie Garisto who helped us write it, and Ian
Adams who took magnificent photographs. We also appreciate the
efforts of David Allen, Peter Bristol, Cheryl L. Chapman, David
Gressley, William Isner, and Charles Tubesing at The Holden
Arboretum; Noell Baran at Royal Botanical Garden; and Susan Ralston,
Jennifer Bernstein, Ellen McNeilly, Jennifer Parkinson, Alan Kellock,
Chani Yammer, Albert Squillace, Jay Hyams, Eric Marshall, Kathy
Sammis, Michelle Stein, and Deena Stein.

Project Director: Lori Stein
Book Design Consultant: Albert Squillace
Editorial Director: Jay Hyams
Associate Art Director: Eric Marshall

Library of Congress Cataloging-in-Publication Data
Shrubs and vines gardening / by Galen Gates . . . [et al.] with Leslie
Garisto ; principal photography by Ian Adams.–1st ed.
p.   cm. – (The American garden guides)
Includes indexes.
ISBN 0-679-41433-9
1. Ornamental shrubs–United States. 2. Ornamental climbing
plants–United States. 3. Ornamental shrubs–Canada. 4. Ornamental
climbing plants–Canada 5. Ornamental shrubs–pictorial works. 6.
Ornamental climbing plants–pictorial works. I. Gates, Galen
II. Series.
SB435.5.S48 1994
635.9'76'097–dc20   93-11359
                                               CIP

Manufactured in China

First edition

9 8 7 6 5 4 3 2

Opposite: Rhododendron 'Holden' at the Holden Arboretum .

contents

Ilex verticillata, **winterberry.**

Clematis **'Betty Corning'.**

the american garden guides

The network of botanical gardens and arboreta in the United States and Canada constitutes a great treasure chest of knowledge about plants and what they need. Some of the most talented, experienced, and dedicated plantspeople in the world work full-time at these institutions; they are the people who actually grow plants, make gardens, and teach others about the process. They are the gardeners who are responsible for the gardens in which millions of visitors exclaim, "Why won't that plant grow that way for me?"

Over thirty of the most respected and beautiful gardens on the continent are participating in the creation of *The American Garden Guides*. The books in the series originate with manuscripts generated by gardeners in one or several of the gardens. Drawing on their decades of experience, these originating gardeners write down the techniques they use in their own gardens, recommend and describe the plants that grow best for them, and discuss their successes and failures. The manuscripts are then passed to several other participating gardens; in each, the specialist in that area adds recommended plants and other suggestions based on regional differences and different opinions.

The series has three major philosophical points carried throughout:

1) Successful gardens are by nature user-friendly toward the gardener and the environment. We advocate water conservation through the precepts of Xeriscaping and garden health care through Integrated Pest Management (IPM). Simply put, one does not set into motion any garden that is going to require undue irrigation during normal levels of rainfall, nor apply any pesticide or other treatment without first assessing its impact on all other life—plant, animal, and soil.

2) Gardening is an inexact science, learned by observation and by doing. Even the most experienced gardeners often develop markedly dissimilar ways of doing the same thing, or have completely divergent views of what any plant requires in order to thrive. Gardeners are an opinionated lot, and we have encouraged all participants to air and share their differences–and so, to make it clear that everyone who gardens will find his or her own way of dealing with plants. Although it is important to know the rules and the most accepted practices, it is also important to recognize that whatever works in the long run for you is the right way.

3) Part of the fun of gardening lies in finding new plants, not necessarily using over and over the same ones in the same old color schemes. In this book and others in the series, we have purposely included some lesser-known or underused plants, some of them native to our vast and wonderful continent. Wherever we can, we call attention to endangered species and suggest ways to nurture them back to their natural state of plenty.

This volume was originated by Ethan Johnson of The Holden Arboretum in Mentor, Ohio and Chris Graham of The Royal Botanical Garden in Hamilton, Ontario. The vines section was provided by Galen Gates, of Chicago Botanic Garden. The manuscript was reviewed, and added to, by Claire Sawyers of The Scott Arboretum, Rick Lewandowski of The Morris Arboretum of the University of Pennsylvania, Wayne Cahilly of The New York Botanical Garden, James Locklear of Dyck Arboretum of the Plains in Hesston, Kansas, Dorthe Hviid of Berkshire Botanical Garden in Stockbridge, Massachusetts, Richard Isaacson of The Minnesota Landscape Arboretum, and Robert Bowden, a horticulturist living in Atlanta. The section on camellias was reviewed by Anne Richardson of The Huntington Botanical Garden, and the the section on azaleas was provided by Fred Galle.

Elvin McDonald
Houston, Texas

director's preface

Shrubs are a vital part of our landscape. Can you imagine your backyard without them?

From the earliest blooming witch hazels, to the bounteous yellow of forsythia to the multitude of viburnums, each fulfills an important role in the well-designed landscape. The fragrance of grandma's lilacs at the door are a treasured memory every spring. And who can forget the brilliant coloration of burning bush in the autumn? Planting for winter interest should also be considered. A group of brilliant red-berried sparkleberry hollies against the snow is an unforgettable sight. Shrubs offer beauty and versatility in every season.

The collections of The Holden Arboretum, Mentor, Ohio and The Royal Botanical Gardens, Hamilton, Ontario, feature many highly recommended shrubs, including well-maintained hedge collections at each institution.

Distilling the best of the shrubs for inclusion in this book has been the task of three well-qualified authors: Chris Graham, Manager of Horticultural Service at the Royal Botanical Garden, Ethan Johnson, Plant Recorder at the Holden Arboretum, and Galen Gates, Manager, Horticultural Collections, at the Chicago Botanic Garden. A great deal of study has been necessary to sort through the long lists of lilacs, honeysuckles, mock oranges, roses, and spireas to name just a few groups, to select the best cultivars to illustrate and describe in this book.

The publication of this valuable reference on shrubs and vines helps fulfill the educational role of The Holden Arboretum. A musuem of woody plants, The Holden Arboretum contains 30,000 accessioned plants and encompasses 3,100 acres of plant collections, gardens, woods, fields, and ravines, including 20 miles of interpretive trails.

Use this book for up-to-date information on new and better shrubs and vines for your yard. Consider replacing some of the overgrown material along the back fence with varieties that will offer more interest—flowers, fruit, fall color—in each season. This book with its authoritative text and outstanding photographs will help inspire you to make wise decisions.

C. W. Eliot Paine
Executive Director
The Holden Arboretum

Above: A border of azaleas creates a backdrop for an enormous lawn at Huntington Gardens in San Marino, California. *Opposite top:* Crape myrtle bushes transform a simple staircase into a focal point. *Opposite bottom:* A canopy of wisteria, complemented by rhododendron, is an integral part of the rites of spring.

Preceding pages: The Katie Osborne Lilac Dell at Royal Botanical Gardens.

A bank of forsythia ablaze against the early spring snow, a row of fragrant lilacs, a single, towering holly—shrubs are as diverse as the gardeners who cherish them, and their uses are equally varied. From a purely practical standpoint, shrubs can provide privacy, screen out an unsightly view, or serve as a windblock to protect more vulnerable perennials. Densely planted, a row of bayberry can even muffle the noise of a neighboring highway. Aesthetically, shrubs serve a crucial function, forming the very backbone of the garden. What could be more stunning, after all, than a bed of old-fashioned roses set off by a tightly clipped privet hedge, or a cloud of baby's breath against pendant purple buddleia?

Vines, too, impart drama to the landscape, as anyone who's seen a country wall abloom with climbing hydrangea or smelled the heady fragrance of old-fashioned wisteria can attest. But vines have a lesser-known, utilitarian side as well. Vigorous climbers like trumpet vine (*Campsis radicans*) can mask a drainpipe, disguise an unattractive wall, or cover a stump too large to dislodge. Allowed to twine around flowering shrubs, trees, and roses, abundantly flowered vines like the species clematis can extend the blooming season. And, given sufficient room, vines can make spectacular ground covers.

Vines and shrubs have an additional asset: because of their abundant growth, both provide the shelter necessary to attract nesting songbirds—a significant commendation for anyone who believes the garden should be heard as well as seen.

SHRUBS AND VINES DEFINED Since shrubs and vines are characterized, at least in part, by their diversity, it would be worthwhile to provide a working definition of each. Essentially, a shrub is a low-growing woody perennial that branches from its base. Although it is sometimes difficult to distinguish a mature shrub from a tree, it is safe to say that shrubs don't exceed 25 feet in height and tend not to form the central leaders that become tree trunks. There are, of course, shrubby trees, just as there are treelike shrubs. Certain species of crab apple, for instance, can be pruned to appear bushy, while older rose-of-sharon bushes—especially those that *haven't* been pruned—are very treelike indeed. There are also shrubs that mimic herbaceous perennials, dying back to the ground each winter in the colder zones. For the lay gardener, the definition is often merely a matter of semantics: if it looks like a shrub, and acts like a shrub, for all practical purposes it *is* a shrub.

Vines are somewhat easier to classify, encompassing as a group any climbing or trailing plant, with an elongated stem, that would be incapable of climbing without support. While the definition encompasses most of what we consider vines, it leaves out the climbing roses, which ramble rather than climb. Once again, this kind of distinction means more to horticulturists than to the average gardener, since a vigorous climbing rose can do many of the same jobs as a vine—from dressing up a blank wall to adding vertical interest to a mostly horizontal landscape

CARING FOR SHRUBS As a group, shrubs are perhaps the most adaptable and easygoing of landscape elements. Unlike showy annuals, they won't go to seed just when you're starting to like their looks; they don't require the constant dividing demanded by many of the perennials; like trees, most have sufficiently long root systems to make them resistant to the ravages of drought, while their relatively smaller size keeps them movable for most of their lives. The key to success with shrubs is to choose wisely, making sure to match their needs with the special growing conditions of your area.

Soil As a rule, most shrubs flourish in a well-drained soil that has been generously enriched with composted organic matter. There are, however, several notable exceptions. The aptly named glutton bush grows happily in water, as does sweet gail, which colonizes in ponds. If your backyard runs to the boggy, consider red twigged dogwood, buttonbush, or Virginia sweetspire, all of which are comfortable with wet feet. While the majority of shrubs require a slightly acid soil (pH 6.5—what a good lawn soil should register), some, like lilacs, prefer lime, while others, including all the members of the heath family, are happiest with a markedly acidic soil.

Soils west of the Mississippi are generally alkaline; in the more arid West, they are not only alkaline, but also fairly low in organic matter. A wide range of plants is available to that area; see Chapter 5 for more information on gar-

HISTORICAL NOTES

Hardly had Commodore Perry successfully opened Japan to Western commerce in 1853 than the United States Department of Agriculture began to send plant hunters there. Among the first was Dr. George Rogers Hall, then 35 years old, who had set up a practice in Shanghai after being graduated from Harvard in 1846. However, he soon left medicine in favor of commerce and by 1860 had formed a prosperous nursery garden in Yokohama. From there, he sent back specimens to Parson's Nursery in Flushing, New York, among which were *Wisteria floribunda* and *Magnolia stellata*. The latter was almost simultaneously discovered by a Russian, plus the English firm of Veitch, but Hall won the race, also making it just before the Civil War began.

The USDA remained active in plant exploration and in 1905 sent Frank N. Meyers to North Korea, Manchuria, and northern China to hunt for ornamental and useful plants. He sent back some 2,500 new ones, so he must have kept rather busy. He was also something of a linguist, speaking Dutch, German, English, with a sprinkling of French, Italian, Spanish, and a dash of Russian thrown in. And if that mixture wasn't enough, he was also a Buddhist, but a bad-tempered one, given to fits of depression, often enough quarreling with his helpers. In 1918, while on board a steamer heading down the Yangste to Hankow, he disappeared, and his body was later recovered from the river. He is commemorated by the lilac *Syringa meyeri*.

Another figure connected to many hunters, including Meyers, was Dr. David Fairchild, the famed author of *The World Was My Garden*. He was then in the Office of Seed and Plant Introduction at the USDA and was the man responsible for sending the Austrian plant collector Joseph Rock to the Orient in search of seeds of the chaulmoogra tree, *Gynocardia odorata*, to treat leprosy. In 1920, he was at the University of Hawaii, where he held professorships in botany and Chinese. He found the very hardy species of spruce, the dragon spruce, *Picea asperata*, and over 500 kinds of rhododendron. But much of his exploration was in unproductive territory, sometimes also highly inhospitable. Blamed for a thunderstorm that devastated some crops near Mt. Jambeyong, he was banished from the territory under threat of death and finally turned to ethnology, abandoning further plant hunting at the age of 50.

Somehow, plant explorers seem to attract misfortune, as witness the case of Ernest H. Wilson, keeper of the the Arnold Arboretum. In his numerous trips to China, Wilson never tried to learn a word of the language, relying entirely on interpreters instead. Nor was he a cautious man, plunging ahead in places where the rocks were badly fractured formations of shale. In one such area, on a trail that was too narrow to permit one group to pass another, Wilson was caught in a rock slide that broke his leg in two places. His party improvised a splint out of his camera tripod, for he was using a bulky instrument that held glass plates (a wise choice for mountaineering), when along came a pack train of 50 mules. He had to be stretched out on the pathway so that the animals could step over him, which they did without once planting a hoof on him. Wilson got back to Boston safely, but nearly lost his leg to an infection that left him with a permanent limp. Earlier, he had survived a near drowning and almost starved on a journey into the back country—only to succumb, with his wife, to an automobile crash in the U.S. in 1930. He had received about a hundred horticultural awards and brought back over 1,000 new plants, including *Magnolia wilsonii* and *Hydrangea sargentiana*, but home proved his most dangerous place to be.

About the last of such adventurers was Albert Byrd Graf, working for the New Jersey firm of Roehrs, publishers of that bible of colorful foliage plants, *Exotica*. An unknown host of others still prowls the jungles of Amazonia, searching that tropical treasure trove for the yet undiscovered medicinal and ornamental jewels of that vast storehouse.

Many of the shrubs introduced by the plant hunters form the backbones of our gardens. Vines, too, serve many functions in our gardens. *Rosa wichuraiana*, discovered in Japan in 1861 by the German botanist Max Ernst Wichura, was named the memorial rose and has spread its carpet of white blossoms over walls and embankments ever since.

Darwin once noted, when writing on *The Power of Movement in Plants*, that a vine's herbaceous stem grows at an unequal rate around its support. The cells in the under surface, those in contact with the support, are much shorter than those on the outer side, which automatically forms a continuous coil, wrapping itself around and around like a boa constrictor. As such it is much more welcome in the garden than in the jungle, though it inhabits both.

FRANK J. ANDERSON

dening in the Southwest and specific climates.

Light Nature has felicitously allowed shrubs to grow in a wide variety of environments, from forest floor to open plain: pioneers like junipers, for example, thrive in full sun, while understory plants such as rhododendrons require only dappled sunlight. The individual gardener, then, should have no trouble finding a shrub to fit his own particular landscape. In general, shrubs will tolerate some shade, and many do best under a canopy of trees whose major branches have been pruned to allow in filtered sunlight. A certain amount of shade, in fact, is crucial for broad-leaved evergreen shrubs, which can be damaged even by winter sunlight.

Water Established shrubs, planted in a congenial environment, require very little water other than that provided by nature, except in the case of severe drought. Indeed, some shrubs *never* need to be watered: the New Jersey tea, for example, being native to sandy areas, has an actual taproot that extends several feet into the soil below. The roots of rhododendrons and azaleas, on the other hand, are rarely longer than 3-4 inches, so these plants may need extra help during the predictable dry days of summer. All containerized shrubs should be watered regularly, of course, but even shrubs transplanted from containers should receive a good drenching for the first two growing seasons.

Protection Shrubs are tough by nature, with a healthy tolerance for the elements. Indeed, shrubs are often planted specifically to protect perennials and young seedlings. Wind, therefore, shouldn't be a concern, except in the case of tree peonies, whose blooms are as delicate as they are exquisite. (Some broadleafed evergreens become desiccated by the winds of winter and the heat of summer; these do benefit from a little extra care.) Fortunately, most shrubs are resistant to insects and disease and require very little spraying (except, perhaps, in very humid areas, where a fungicide may be necessary). A few mealybugs on your yews won't detract from the beauty of the garden and are unlikely to do any significant damage to the plants. When real infestations do develop, it's generally the fault not of the plant but the gardener. The presence of black vine weevils on a rhododendron, for example, is an indication that the plant's natural defenses are stressed from a too-alkaline soil (this often occurs when the plants are flush with the house's foundation, which can leach lime).

Space Since most shrubs live to a ripe old age, they need to be allowed a generous space in which to spread their branches and grow. The space allotted by most landscape architects is far too small and represents a gratuitous expense to the homeowner, both in the form of unnecessary plants and additional upkeep (shrubs crowded together will require constant pruning and/or moving). Unless you're planning a hedge, always consider the plant's mature landscape size, which means its diameter and height 10-20 years down the road. And keep in mind that some shrubs are more vigorous growers than others: a single bottlebrush buckeye at the Arnold Arboretum, for example, has spread by suckers to reach a diameter of 50 feet.

There are shrubs for every season. *Berberis thunbergii,* shown above, provides rich green color in spring and summer, vibrant orange, yellow, and brown foliage in the fall, and bright red berries well into the snow season.

CARING FOR VINES Vines can perform wonders. Perennials like clematis and hon-

A BRIEF LESSON IN BOTANY

Plants are living things and share many traits with animals. Plants are composed of millions of individual cells that are organized into complex organ systems. Plants breathe (take in and expel gases) and extract energy from food; to do this they require water, nutrients, and atmospheric gases. Like animals, plants reproduce sexually, and their offspring inherit characteristics through a genetic code passed along as DNA.

Plants, however, can do one thing that no animal can do. Through a process called photosynthesis, plants can capture energy from the sun and convert that energy into compounds such as proteins, fats, and carbohydrates. These energy-rich compounds are the source of the energy for all animal life, including humans.

THE IMPORTANCE OF PLANTS

Because no living animals can produce the energy they need to live, all their energy comes from plants. Like other animals, we eat green plants directly, in the form of fruits, vegetables, and grains (breads and cereals), or we eat animals and animal products that were fed green plants.

The oxygen we need to live on Earth is constantly pumped out of green plants as a byproduct of photosynthesis. Plants prevent the erosion of our precious soils and hinder water loss to the atmosphere.

Plants are also an important source of drugs. Fully one-quarter of all prescriptions contain at least one plant-derived product. Aspirin, one of the most commonly used drugs, was originally isolated from the bark of the willow tree.

THE WHOLE PLANT

Basically, a plant is made up of leaves, stems, and roots; all these parts are connected by a vascular system, much like our circulatory system. The vascular system can be seen in the veins of a leaf, or in the rings in a tree.

LEAVES

Leaves are generally flattened and expanded tissues that are green due to the presence of chlorophyll, the pigment that is necessary for photosynthesis. Most leaves are connected to the stem by a stalk, or petiole, which allows the leaves to alter their position in relation to the sun and capture as much energy as possible.

Leaves come in an astounding variety of shapes, textures, and sizes. Some leaves are composed of a single structure, or blade, and are termed simple. Other leaves are made up of many units, or leaflets, and are called compound (see endpapers).

STEMS

Technically, a stem is the tissue that supports leaves and that connects the leaves with the roots via a vascular system. Stems also bear the flowers on a plant. Therefore, a stem can be identified by the presence of buds, which are the unexpanded leaves, stems, or flowers that will develop later.

A single plant can produce more than one kind of stem; the upright, above-ground stem produces leaves and flowers, while a horizontal, below-ground stem can swell and store food products from photosynthesis. Underground stems can overwinter and produce new plants when conditions are favorable.

The stem of a plant often changes as the plant matures. When a shrub is young, its stems are green and soft; as the shrub grows and ages, however, the stem may develop woody tissues. Woody stems on a shrub or vine are like the wood of a tree trunk–just smaller. Wood is composed of hardened cells that provide strength to the stem and that allow water, gases, and nutrients to move both vertically and horizontally through the stem. Concentric circles inside a woody stem are called annual rings. The oldest wood is in the center of the rings, and the youngest wood is in the outer ring. Light-colored rings, or early wood, are composed of cells that were added early in the growing season of each year; these cells are larger and are less densely packed together. Late wood is darker in color because the cells are smaller and packed more closely. Each set of a light and dark ring represents one year in the life of the growing plant stem. When a plant grows under constant environmental conditions, with no changes in temperature or moisture during the year (like in some tropical rain forests), the wood is uni-

form in color and lacks annual rings.

Bark forms on the outside of woody stems and is made up mostly of dead cells. This corky tissue is very valuable to the stem because it protects the new wood, allows gas exchange into the stem, and lets the stem grow in diameter. All of the bark is not dead tissue, however; the innermost layer is living vascular tissue. If a stem is girdled or the bark is damaged, this vascular tissue, which moves the food products of photosynthesis around in the plant, will be destroyed, and the plant will die.

ROOTS

Although out of sight, roots are extremely important to the life of the plant. Roots anchor a plant in the soil, absorb water and nutrients, and store excess food, such as starches, for the plants' future use. Basically, there are two types of roots: taproots and fibrous roots. Taproots, such as the edible part of a carrot, are thick unbranched roots that grow straight down. A toproot takes advantage of moisture and nutrients far below the soil surface and is a storehouse for carbohydrates. Fibrous roots are fine, branching roots that often form dense mats, making them excellent agents of soil stabilization. Fibrous roots absorb moisture and nutrients from a shallow zone of soil and may be more susceptible to drought. Roots obviously need to come into contact with water, but they also need air in order to work properly. Except for those adapted to aquatic environments, plants require well-drained soils.

VASCULAR SYSTEMS

Plants have a well-developed vascular system that extends throughout the plant body and that allows movement of water and compounds from one part of a plant to another. Roots absorb water and minerals, and the vascular system funnels them to the leaves for use in photosynthesis. Likewise, energy-rich compounds that are produced in the leaves must travel to the stems and roots to provide nutrition for further growth. The vascular system also strengthens plant tissues.

PHOTOSYNTHESIS

A green plant is like a factory that takes raw materials from the environment and converts them into other forms of energy. In a complex series of energy transfer and chemical conversion events called photosynthesis, plants take energy from the sun, minerals

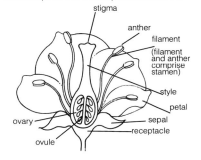

stigma
anther
filament
(filament and anther comprise stamen)
style
petal
sepal
receptacle
ovary
ovule

and water from the soil, and gases from the atmosphere; these raw materials are converted into chemical forms of energy that are used for plant growth. These same energy-rich compounds (proteins, sugars and starches, fats and oils) can be utilized by animals as a source of food and nutrition. All this is possible because of a green pigment, chlorophyll.

Photosynthesis is an extremely complex series of reactions that takes place in the cells of leaves, the byproducts of which are connected to other reactions throughout the cell. The most basic reactions of photosynthesis occurs like this: Energy from the sun strikes the leaf surface, and electrons in the chlorophyll molecule become "excited" and are boosted to a higher energy level. Excited electrons are routed through a chain of reactions that extracts and stores energy in the form of sugars. As a byproduct of electron loss, water molecules (H_2O) are split; hydrogen moves in to replenish the electrons lost from chlorophyll, and oxygen is released, finding its way into our atmosphere. In another photosynthetic reaction, carbon dioxide from the atmosphere is "fixed," or converted into organic compounds within the plant cell. These first chemical compounds are the building blocks for more complex reactions and are the precursors for the formation of many elaborate chemical compounds.

PLANT NUTRITION

Plants require mineral nutrients from the soil, water, and the atmosphere in order to maintain healthy growth and reproduction. Macronutrients, those nutrients needed in large amounts, include hydrogen, oxygen, and carbon –all of which are abundant in our atmosphere. Other macronutrients are nitrogen, phosphorus, potassium, sulfur, and calcium. If macronutrients are in limited supply, growth and development in the plant will be strongly curtailed. Nitrogen is an important component of chlorophyll, DNA, and proteins and is therefore an essential element for leaf growth and photosynthesis. Adding nitrogen to garden soil will generally result in greener, more lush plant growth. But beware of too much of a good thing; too much nitrogen can burn tender plants. Or, you may have large and lovely azalea leaves, but with no flowers! Phosphorus is also used in building DNA and is important in cell development. Phosphorus is necessary for flowering and fruiting and is often

added to garden soil. Potassium is important in the development of tubers, roots, and other storage organs.

LIFE CYCLE

Higher plants (except for ferns) begin life as a seed. Given the right set of conditions (temperature, moisture, light), a seed will germinate and develop its first roots and leaves using food stored in the seed (humans and other animals take advantage of the high-quality food in seeds when they eat wheat and corn, just to name a few). Because of the presence of chlorophyll in the leaves, the small plant is soon able to produce its own food, which is used immediately for further growth and development. As the seedling grows, it also grows in complexity. The first, simple root gives way to a complex root system that may include underground storage organs. The stem is transformed into an intricate system of vascular tissue that moves water from the ground up into the leafy part of the plant, while other tissues transport energy-rich compounds made in the leaves downward to be stored in stem and root systems.

Once the plant reaches maturity, flower initiation begins. Flowers hold the sexual apparatus for the plant; their brilliant colors and glorious odors are advertisements to attract pollinators such as insects or birds. In a basic, complete flower, there are four different parts, given below. However, many plants have incomplete flowers with one or more of these parts missing, or the parts may be highly modified.

1. Sepals. The outermost part of the flower, sepals cover the young floral buds. Although they are often green, they may be variously colored.

2. Petals. The next layer of parts in the flower, petals, are often colorful and play an important role in attracting pollinators.

3. Stamens. Stamens are located next to the petals, or may even be basally fused to the petals. The stamens are the "male"

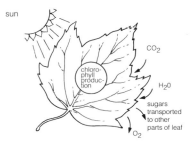

sun

CO_2

chloro-
phyll
produc-
tion

H_2O

sugars
transported
to other
parts of leaf

O_2

reproductive parts of the flower; they produce the pollen. Pollen grains are fine, dust-like particles that will divide to form sperm cells. The tissue at the end of the stamen that holds pollen is called the anther.

4. Pistil. The innermost part of the flower holds the plant's female reproductive apparatus. The stigma, located at the tip of the pistil, is often covered with a sticky substance and is the site where pollen is deposited. The stigma is held by a floral tube, call the style. At the base of the style, the ovary holds one to many ovules, which contain eggs that represent undeveloped seeds.

Pollination is the transfer of pollen from an anther to a stigma and is the first step in the production of seeds. Pollen can be transferred by an insect visiting the flower, by the wind, or even by the splashing of raindrops. After being deposited on a compatible stigma, the pollen grains grow into tubes that travel from the stigma, down the floral tube into the ovary, depositing sperm cells to the ovules. If all goes well, sperm cells unite with the eggs inside the ovules, and fertilization takes place.

After fertilization, the entire floral structure is transformed into a fruit. Fruit can be fleshy, like an apple, or dry like a pea pod. Within each fruit, fertilized eggs develop into seeds, complete with a cache of storage tissue and a seed coat.

VINES

Charles Darwin was so fascinated by how plants move that he spent many years studying how vines climb and how they find supports to climb on. He even published book on his findings, *The Movements and Habits of Climbing Plants.*

To successfully grow a vine, one must understand how the plant climbs. Some vines, like honeysuckle, simple grow upward in a spiral, wrapping, or twining their stems around a support as they grow. Many use their leaves like hooks, holding the vine next to a support until some other method of holding on takes over. English ivy develops roots along the stem that hold the plant tightly to bark or brick. Other vines however, have specialized tissues that grab and hold onto surfaces. Grape vines have modified stems, called tendrils, that wrap themselves around almost anything that gets in their way. Virginia creeper has tendrils that look and act like little suction cups.

Some shrubs can be sheared and pruned for use in formal designs—such as Old Westbury Garden's sculptured silver garden, which uses boxwoods, lavenders, and conifers.

eysuckle will return year after year, becoming ever more bountiful. Annuals, from runner beans to morning glory, need to be grown from seed each season, but they reward the sower tenfold, spiraling upward at a dizzying pace; in addition, annual vines provide instant, if temporary, coverage while the perennial roots are taking their time getting established. Vines as a group have relatively few demands, but those they do—summed up in the paragraphs that follow—should be heeded with care.

Soil Since the roots of most vines, especially the clematis, tend to run deep, the soil they call home should be well drained, to a depth of 18-24 inches; like shrubs, vines do best in soil that has been generously enriched with organic matter.

Light As they evolved, vines found their niche on the forest floor or twining around the trunks of trees, so they can tolerate a fair amount of shade. Nevertheless, most throw off the best color, and the greatest profusion of bloom, in sun. There *are* vines that prefer shade: the pink-striped flowers of the 'Nelly Moser' clematis are more vibrant in shade, as are the silver foliage of *Actinidia* 'Polygama' and the pink leaves of *Actinidia kolomikta*. While the majority of clematis like full or part sun, they prefer cool feet: their roots should be shaded with mulch or low-growing plants.

Water When it comes to hydration, nearly all vines hew to the same guidelines, most requiring about an inch of water a week during the growing season. To keep soil moist, add an inch or two of mulch.

Protection The greatest threat to perennial vines are the eager teeth of mice and rabbits. To make sure the tender base of your vine doesn't become a midwinter snack, keep mulch at least an inch or two away. For additional protection, the base can be wrapped with expanded-metal mesh.

Marginally hardy vines will definitely require a winter mulch and should ideally be sited away from harsh winds—on the east side of a house, for example, beside a boulder in the garden, or close to the foundation where they can benefit from retained heat.

Space One of the most compelling characterizations of vines is their ability to add an enormous amount of visual interest to the garden while demanding very little in the way of space. In fact, most vines are ideally suited to small spaces, where they will happily hug a wall, twine around a lamppost, or clamber up a downspout. Some of the more vigorous climbers, however, refuse to be confined to a corner of the garden: actinidia, for example, can grow with frightening ease to 30 or 40 feet, sending out branches that can easily expand to 8 feet in a single season. Unless you want to make pruning your life's work, consider a vine's mature size and speed of growth before planting.

Structure Unless they're being used as ground cover, all vines require a structure to twine around, ramble over, or adhere to. Depending on the vine and the method it employs to complete its journey skyward, the structure can be a fence, pergola, trellis, arbor, wall—even a small shed. Climbing hydrangea, for instance, does especially well on broad walls of wood and brick (though not on aluminum siding, which retains too much heat), while more delicate annual vines like runner beans and edible pod peas are perfectly content to ascend the slender poles of wooden tepees. The structure need not be manmade, or even inert—shrubs and other vines can provide excellent support for twiners, while offering an appealing visual contrast.

CHOOSING SHRUBS While many shrubs flower—sometimes spectacularly—beauty of bloom is only one consideration among many when planting time comes around. Certainly, there are shrubs whose gorgeous flowers are their sole asset: no gardener with any aesthetic sense would choose a lilac for its foliage, which is undistinguished at best, and downright homely in late summer when it tends to be covered with powdery mildew; but for those 2-3 weeks in spring when the lilacs put on their glorious, fragrant show, nothing can surpass them.

While the blooming period of most shrubs is relatively short, a few are in flower for weeks, and even months; if the flowers of the rose of sharon are less showy than lilacs, they redeem themselves by opening up just when everything else in the garden is beginning to fade—and keeping up the show for months thereafter. Hydrangeas, too, are long-blooming, and many perform the enviable trick of changing colors as the season progresses. PeeGee hydrangeas are especially lovely to behold as their great blowsy heads turn

The graceful rambling flow of azaleas and dogwood trees resembles a natural woodland.

SCIENTIFIC NOMENCLATURE

Botanists and horticulturists use a binomial, or two-name, system to label the over 250,000 species of living plants. Because the names are in Latin, this system crosses both time and language barriers and allows people all over the world to communicate about plants. Occasionally, a scientific name will be changed to reflect additions to our knowledge about plants. A scientific name consists of the genus (singular; genera is plural) and the species—as in the scientific name for grape, *Vitis vinifera*. The genus name is always first and always capitalized; the species name follows and is generally not capitalized.

Cultivated plants are often selected for a particular attribute, such as leaf or flower color or fruit size. These selections are given a cultivar, or cultivated variety, name in addition to the species and genus. Cultivar names are capitalized and surrounded by single quotes, such as *Syringa vulgaris* 'Sensations' or *Acer palmatum* 'Waterfall'. A particular plant may have many common names—Dutchman's pipe and pipe vine are both used for *Aristolachia durior,* for example —but it has only one correct scientific name.

Above: Viburnum trilobum berries.

from green to white to an intense pink-maroon.

What some shrubs lack in blossom, they more than make up for in fruit. Callicarpa, which bears modest lavender flowers in late summer, bursts into its true color in fall when it is covered with great masses of violet-purple berries. The orange berries of pyracantha are breathtaking in fall and early winter. And who could resist the charm of a glistening holly decked with its seasonal fruit?

Most shrubs chosen for their foliage are evergreen, for the obvious reason that they keep the garden looking well dressed all year round. These include conifers like yew and arbor vitae, as well as broadleaf evergreens like rhododendron and mountain laurel. While the broadleaf evergreens tend to bear showy flowers, it is their attractive, glossy foliage that recommends them as perfect four-season plants. Many deciduous shrubs are chosen for their graceful shape, even when bare of leaves, and for their fall color and berries. (See Chapter 5 for more information on using shrubs and vines in the landscape.)

CHOOSING VINES As versatile as they are delightful, vines offer exquisite, often highly fragrant flowers, interesting foliage, and fruit that can be beautiful, edible, or both. In addition, by allowing them to twine, nature has afforded vines a sculptural quality that is often most evident in the dead of winter when little else is around to attract the eye.

The growing popularity of the clematis vines must be due, at least in part, to their absolutely gorgeous flowers. From the spectacular purple of Jackmani clematis to the dazzling white of 'Marie Boisselot' and the white and carmine stripes of 'Carnaby', clematis are typical of vines grown mainly for their bloom. Other bloomers bypass the eye for the nose. While ever-blooming honeysuckle is certainly an attractive vine, its real appeal lies in the seductive fragrance that has sweetened summer nights from time immemorial. And as its name suggests, sweet autumn clematis possesses the twin virtues of a late blooming season and an unforgettable perfume.

Vines grown mainly for their foliage include jasmine and English ivy (two of the few evergreen vines) and Glory vine, whose broad leaves—as large as dinner plates—turn a startling crimson in fall. Boston ivy, too, offers appealing fall foliage, as well as diminutive berry clusters that turn from bright green in summer to deep maroon in autumn.

As with shrubs, many vines produce attractive fruit—but in the case of vines, much of this fruit is edible. Grapes and kiwi are but two among many varieties of vine that would be lovely without fruit but certainly not as popular come harvest time.

THE GARDENERS The main contributors to this book—Ethan Johnson, Chris Graham, and Galen Gates—maintain a daily intimacy with their subjects.

Quite literally raised in a garden (the famous Gwinn estate in Cleveland), **Ethan Johnson** began his horticultural career at Harvard's Arnold Arboretum and has served since 1989 as plant recorder for the Holden Arboretum in Cleveland, keeping track of all that grows among the garden's 3,100 acres. He has a special fondness for shrubs, which he sees as particularly forgiving—"They give a lot for a relatively small input." Though his job requires a certain impartiality, he admits a passion for the bottlebrush buckeye—in part because its huge white flower spikes and dense, bold foliage make for a dramatic summer display, and in part because, like the buckeye, he is a native Ohioan. He is also an enthusiastic proponent of Integrated Pest Management—the idea that by carefully monitoring the life cycle, food preferences, and habits of the pest, you can create the conditions that will best allow the host to protect itself. "Know your enemy" is Johnson's succinct horticultural motto.

Chris Graham, manager of horticulture at the Royal Botanical Garden in Hamilton, Ontario, shares Johnson's enthusiasm for IPM. His first defense against pests is "monitoring like crazy," a tactic followed, if necessary, by biological controls and then—if all else fails—chemical treatments in ascending order of potency. He is also a campaigner for biodiversity, not just in the botanical garden but in municipalities and backyards as well, citing the devastation of the American elm as one argument in favor of planting a variety of species. Crusading against over-hybridization, Graham says, "There's a real danger in breeding to the point where you lose your diversity. We need to keep the gene pool alive." Living and gardening in Canada, Graham has a very practical interest in shrubs, which he admires for their year-round appeal. "With our all-too-short blooming season," he says, "how a plant looks in winter is very important to us. Leaf texture, fruit, bark, interesting branching habit, how the plant looks under snow—these are all serious considerations for Canadian gardeners."

For **Galen Gates**, manager of horticulture collections at the Chicago Botanic Garden, the garden is a place of learning, "a resource from which everyone who visits—children, the gardener, his friends and family—should come away with new insights, new ideas the year round. Because his position has allowed him to spend time in natural areas, where human influence is minimal, he has a personal preference for "informal displays with a more relaxed appearance—spaces that reflect nature's unforced harmony." His mission as a horticulturist is to encourage gardeners to try new approaches, to investigate the use of a broader range of plants; he is, in particular, a booster of native species which not only thrive with relatively little care on their home turf, but give the garden a sense of "regional identity." Above all, he stresses the notion of the garden as ever-changing, a living tapestry whose textures and hues are continually altered by the needs of nature and the gardener.

The reader will, of course, bring his or her own philosophy of gardening to the choosing and cultivation of shrubs and vines, which is very much as it should be. It is hoped, however, that this book will convey, in addition to practical information about planting and culture, some of the wisdom that these gardeners have gleaned from years of work in North America's greatest horticultural treasure troves—her bountiful botanical gardens.

Clematis 'General Sikorsky'

Varieties are arranged alphabeti-
cally, according to their Latin
names; listings for all conifers
follow the main section of the
book; vines follow conifers. (See
the index or contents page for
translations of Latin names.)
Some common shrubs and vines
and their Latin names:
Barberry: *Berberis*
Boston Ivy: *Parthenocissus*
Boxwood: *Buxus*
English Ivy: *Hedera Helix*
Crab Apple: *Malus*
Crape Myrtle: *Lagerstroemia*
Grape: *Vitis*
Heath: *Erica*
Holly: *Ilex*
Honeysuckle: *Lonicera*
Lilac: *Syringa*
Morning Glory: *Ipomoea*
Mountain Laurel: *Kalmia*
Privet: *Ligustrum*
Redbud: *Cercis*
Smokebush: *Cotinus*
Threadleaf Maple: *Acer*
Witch-hazel: *Hamamelis*
Winter Hazel: *Corylopsis*

Though gardening is essentially a hands-on endeavor, some of its greatest
pleasures are vicarious: for most gardeners, nothing surpasses the joy of dis-
covering a new plant. And since more than 5,000 different shrubs and vines
are currently under cultivation—and nurseries, botanists, and private gardeners
the world over are dedicated to finding and introducing more—there will never
be a shortage of horticultural treasures from which to choose.

This chapter is designed to help you sift through those treasures and make
a choice. Our originating gardeners have selected more than 150 shrubs and
vines that work well for them, mixing common, easy-to-find varieties with
others you might not know about, but should; experts from other botanic
gardens around the country then added plants that thrive in their own
regions. Because most of the gardeners couldn't bear to leave out their
favorites, we've included additional recommended plants at the end of many
of the entries; and a brief description of many other shrubs at the end of the
chapter.

The first part of the Plant Selector lists the included varieties according to
size, time of bloom, color of flowers and fruit, and requirements for sun and
water. Following that is the main portion of the chapter—detailed "plant portraits" describing the best conditions for the plants, routine care, propagation,
pest and disease tolerance, and uses in the landscape. Two hundred of the recommended plants are illustrated, with captions noting their mature size and
climate zone.

There are only a few keys to successful gardening; choosing the right plant
is among them. If a well-tended plant refuses to thrive or succumbs to disease,
it probably doesn't belong in its present site. Before deciding on a plant, you
need to understand the special conditions of your own garden. Is it sunny,
shady, or a combination of both? Is rainfall abundant, or nearly nonexistent?
Is the soil sandy, loamy, heavy, well or poorly drained? What is your soil's natural pH? Information on how to answer these questions is located in Chapter
4; your local nursery, botanical garden, or agricultural extension can also help.
But don't forget that your site is unique, with a microclimate of its own created by the contours of the landscape, shade, and natural barriers; it may be different from those next door, let alone at a nursery ten miles down the road.

To help match plant and gardener, each plant portrait includes information
on the following:

Sun Since most shrubs will stay in the same place for many years, you'll need
to consider the future as well as current exposure. A tree growing nearby
might provide more shade than the plant can use in just a few years.

Soil Most soil can be improved to suit the requirements of an individual plant
or amended to make it generally more fertile, but there are limits. If you plant
an azalea in alkaline soil, expect more foliage than flowers year after year;
grow roses in poor soil, and you'll use all your compost keeping them happy.

Water There are plenty of plants that thrive in dry climates—and not all of
them are cacti. Notations throughout this chapter point out plants that are
adapted to dry climates; see pages 208-09 for information on gardening in

dry climates. Since water supplies everywhere are becoming more scarce, all gardeners would do well to heed the basic principles of Xeriscaping: proper garden design, maintenance, and especially plant selection.

Hardiness Consider your area's general climate, but keep in mind too that planting in a protected area might allow you to steal one warmer zone—if you don't mind risking winter damage. See page 212 for information on gardening in cold climates.

Pests and diseases We've noted problems that are common to particular plants; if these pests or diseases are rampant in your area, avoid the plants in question. See pages 203-5 for more information on pests and diseases.

Mature size Information on growth habit and invasiveness is crucial when choosing a plant. Are you willing to prune annually to keep your buddleia from spreading all over the yard? Will you mind when the barberry blocks the sun from your bedroom window?

Whatever your needs—brilliant blooms, fall color, easy maintenance, compact habit, privacy, fragrance, drought-tolerance—there are shrubs and vines to satisfy them. There will, of course, come a time when you fall mindlessly in love with a plant that seems marginally suited to your garden. When that happens, throw all caveats to the wind and try it; the best way to determine if a plant will work for you is to try it—and see if it thrives.

The map below was created by the United States Department of Agriculture. It divides the United States into climate zones. Most nurseries (and this book) use these classifications to advise where plants will be hardy. Although this is a useful system, it is not foolproof; it is based on average minimum temperature, and a particularly cold winter might destroy some plants that are listed as hardy in your climate zone. More often, you will be able to grow plants that are not listed as hardy in your zone, particularly if they are in a sheltered area. There are other climate-zones classifications; the Arnold Arboretum's is also used quite often. The climate zones referred to in this volume are those of the USDA.

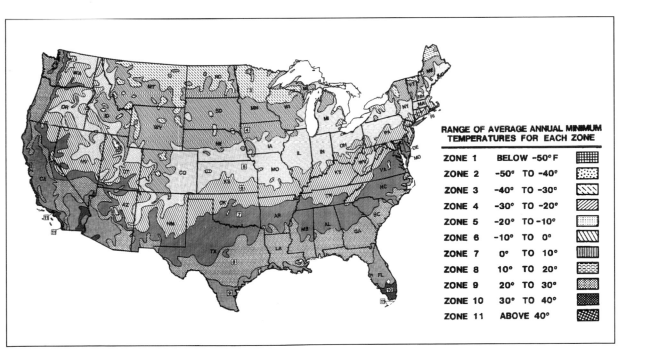

RANGE OF AVERAGE ANNUAL MINIMUM TEMPERATURES FOR EACH ZONE	
ZONE 1	BELOW −50°F
ZONE 2	−50° TO −40°
ZONE 3	−40° TO −30°
ZONE 4	−30° TO −20°
ZONE 5	−20° TO −10°
ZONE 6	−10° TO 0°
ZONE 7	0° TO 10°
ZONE 8	10° TO 20°
ZONE 9	20° TO 30°
ZONE 10	30° TO 40°
ZONE 11	ABOVE 40°

RED BERRIES/FRUITS
Arctostaphylos uva-ursi (bearberry) 33
Aronia arbutifolia (red chokeberry) 35
Berberis species (barberry) 35
Ceanothus species (wild lilac) 46
Cornus species (dogwood) 54
Cotoneaster species (cotoneaster) 60
Daphne species (daphne) 63
Elaeagnus species (elaeagnus) 65
Euonymus alatus (burning bush) 66
Euonymus fortunei (wintercreeper) 153
Ilex species (holly) 78
Lindera species (spicebush) 90
Lonicera species (honeysuckle) 91
Malus species (crab apple) 94
Photinia villosa (oriental photinia) 97
Pyracantha species (firethorn) 103
Rhus species (sumac) 117
Symphoricarpos x chenaultii (coralberry) 129
Taxus baccata (English yew) 145
Taxus cuspidata (dwarf Japanese yew) 145
Viburnum species (viburnum) 134
Vitis species (grape) 165

BLUE/PURPLE BERRIES/FRUITS
Callicarpa species (beautyberry) 39
Chionanthus (fringe tree) 50
Clerodendrum trichotomum (harlequin glory-bower) 53
Gaylussacia species (huckleberry) 70
Lonicera species (honeysuckle) 91
Mahonia aquifolium (Oregon grape) 93
Parthenocissus henryana (silvervein creeper) 161
Symplocos paniculata (sapphireberry) 129
Tropaeolum speciosum (Scottish flame thrower) 169
Vaccinium species (blueberry) 133
Vitis species (grape) 165

BLACK BERRIES/FRUITS
Amelanchier canadensis (shadblow) 32
Gaylussacia species (huckleberry) 70
Ilex species (holly) 78
Jasminum officinale (poet's jessamine) 157
Juniperus conferta (shore juniper) 144
Myrica pensylvanica (bayberry) 94
Raphiolepsis indica (hawthorn) 104
Rhodotypos scandens (jetbead) 117
Ribes odoratum (clove currant) 117
Viburnum species (viburnum) 134
Vitis species (grape) 165

PINK FLOWERS
Arctostaphylos uva-ursi (bearberry) 33
azaleas 111
Buddleia species (butterfly bush) 36
Calliandra eriophylla 39
Callicarpa species (beautyberry) 39
Calluna vulgaris (Scotch heather) 40
Camellia species (camellia) 42
Ceanothus species (wild lilac) 46
Cercis species (redbud) 48
Chaenomeles species (quince) 49
Clematis species (clematis) 149

Clethra species (summersweet) 53
Cotinus coggygria 58
Cotoneaster species (cotoneaster) 60
Daphne species (daphne) 63
Enkianthus species (enkianthus) 65
Hydrangea species (hydrangea) 74
Ipomoea species (morning glory) 168
Kalmia latifolia (mountain laurel) 84
Kolkwitzia amabilis (beautybush) 85
Lagerstroemia indica (crape myrtle) 87
Leucothoe fontanesiana (drooping leucothoe) 88
Magnolia stellata (star magnolia) 91
Malus species (crab apple) 94
Mandevilla suaveolens (Chilean jasmine) 159
Paeonia suffruticosa (tree peony) 96
Pieris species (andromeda) 98
Polygonum aubertii (silver fleece vine) 162
Prunus species 102
Raphiolepsis indica (hawthorn) 104
Rhododendron species 104
Rosa species (rose) 120
Spiraea species (spirea) 124
Symphoricarpos x chenaultii (coralberry) 129
Syringa species (lilac) 129
Tamarix species (tamarisk) 133
Viburnum species (viburnum) 134
Weigela species (weigela) 140
Wisteria floribunda (Japanese wisteria) 167

WHITE FLOWERS
Abelia x grandiflora (glossy abelia) 28
Acanthopanax sieboldianus (fiveleaf akebia) 28
Aesculus parviflora (bottlebrush buckeye) 32
Amelanchier canadensis (shadblow) 32
Arctostaphylos uva-ursi (bearberry) 33
Aronia arbutifolia (red chokeberry) 35
Azaleas 111
Bougainvillea species (bougainvillea) 148
Buddleia species (butterfly bush) 36
Callicarpa species (beautyberry) 39
Calluna vulgaris (Scotch heather) 40
Camellia species (camellia) 42
Ceanothus species (wild lilac) 46
Cephalanthus occidentalis (buttonbush) 48
Cercis species (redbud) 48
Chaenomeles species (quince) 49
Chionanthus (fringe tree) 50
Clematis species (clematis) 149
Clerodendrum trichotomum (harlequin glory-bower) 53
Clethra species (summersweet) 53
Cornus species (dogwood) 54
Cotoneaster species (cotoneaster) 60
Cyrilla racemiflora (swamp cyrilla) 62
Daphne species (daphne) 63
Deutzia gracilis (slender deutzia) 63
Dolichos lablab (hyacinth bean) 168
Elaeagnus species (elaeagnus) 65

Enkianthus species (enkianthus) 65
Erica species (heath) 66
Fothergilla species (fothergilla) 70
Gaylussacia species (huckleberry) 70
Hibiscus syriacus (rose of sharon) 74
Hydrangea species (hydrangea) 74
Itea virginica (sweetspire) 82
Jasminum officinale (jessamine) 157
Kalmia latifolia (mountain laurel) 84
Lagerstroemia indica (crape myrtle) 87
Ligustrum species (privet) 90
Lonicera species (honeysuckle) 91
Magnolia stellata (star magnolia) 91
Malus species (crab apple) 94
Mandevilla suaveolens (Chilean jasmine) 159
Paeonia suffruticosa (tree peony) 96
Passiflora species (passionflower) 161
Photinia villosa (oriental photinia) 97
Physocarpus species (ninebark) 98
Pieris species (andromeda) 98
Polygonum aubertii (silver fleece vine) 162
Prunus species 102
Pyracantha species (firethorn) 103
Raphiolepsis indica (hawthorn) 104
Rhododendron species 104
Rhodotypos scandens (jetbead) 117
Rosa species (rose) 120
Schizophragma hydrangeoides (Japanese climbing hydrangea) 163
Spiraea species (spirea) 124
Stephanandra incisa (cutleaf stephanandra) 126
Stewartia ovata grandiflora (showy stewartia) 126
Symplocos paniculata (sapphireberry) 129
Syringa species (lilac) 129
Tamarix species (tamarisk) 133
Thunbergia grandiflora (sky vine) 169
Viburnum species (viburnum) 134
Wisteria floribunda (Japanese wisteria) 167

RED/ORANGE FLOWERS
Aronia arbutifolia (red chokeberry) 35
Azaleas 111
Berberis species (barberry) 35
Bougainvillea species (bougainvillea) 148
Buddleia species (butterfly bush) 36
Calliandra californica (red fairyduster) 39
Calluna vulgaris (Scotch heather) 40
Camellia species (camellia) 42
Campsis radicans (trumpet vine) 149
Chaenomeles species (quince) 49
Clematis species (clematis) 149
Enkianthus species (enkianthus) 65
Hamamelis species (witch-hazel) 71
Hibiscus syriacus (rose of sharon) 74
Ipomoea species (morning glory) 168
Kalmia latifolia (mountain laurel) 84
Lonicera heckrotti (everblooming honeysuckle) 159

Malus species (crab apple) 94
Mina lobata (crimson starglory) 159
Paeonia suffruticosa (tree peony) 96
Potentilla fruticosa (cinquefoil) 100
Prunus species 102
Rhododendron species 104
Rosa species (rose) 120
Salix species (willow) 123
Thunbergia alata (black-eyed susan vine) 169
Tropaeolum speciosum (Scottish flame thrower) 169
Tropaeplum peregrinum (canary creeper) 169

BLUE/PURPLE/LAVENDER FLOWERS
Akebia quinata (fiveleaf akebia) 146
Amorpha canescens (leadplant) 33
azaleas 111
Bougainvillea species (bougainvillea) 148
Buddleia species (butterfly bush) 36
Callicarpa species (beautyberry) 39
Calluna vulgaris (Scotch heather) 40
Calycanthus floridus (sweetshrub) 42
Caryopteris x clandonensis (bluebeard) 44
Ceanothus species (wild lilac) 46
Cercis species (redbud) 48
Clematis species (clematis) 149
Dolichos lablab (hyacinth bean) 168
Hibiscus syriacus (rose of sharon) 74
Hydrangea species (hydrangea) 74
Ipomoea species (morning glory) 168
Leucophyllum frutescens (Texas ranger) 87
Passiflora species (passionflower) 161
Rhododendron species 104
Syringa species (lilac) 129
Thunbergia grandiflora (sky vine) 169
Wisteria (wisteria) 167

YELLOW/GOLD FLOWERS
Aristolochia durior (Dutchman's pipe) 148
Azaleas 111
Berberis species (barberry) 35
Bougainvillea species 148
Calycanthus floridus (sweetshrub) 42
Clematis species (clematis) 149
Cornus species (dogwood) 54
Corylopsis species (winter hazel) 56
Corylus avellana (corkscrew hazel) 56
Cytisus scoparius (Scotch broom) 62
Elaeagnus species (elaeagnus) 65
Forsythia species (forsythia) 69
Genista pilosa (genista) 71
Hamamelis species (witch-hazel) 71
Hydrangea species (hydrangea) 74
Kerria japonica (Japanese rose) 85
Lindera species (spicebush) 90
Lonicera heckrotti (everblooming honeysuckle) 159
Mahonia aquifolium (Oregon grape) 93
Mina lobata (crimson starglory) 159
Paeonia suffruticosa (tree peony) 96
Physocarpus species (ninebark) 98

CAUTION: SOME BERRIES AND FRUITS ARE POISONOUS

Potentilla fruticosa (cinquefoil) 100
Rhodedendron species 104
Rhus species (sumac) 117
Ribes odoratum (clove currant) 117
Rosa species (rose) 120
Stephanandra incisa (cutleaf stephanandra) 126
Thunbergia alata (black-eyed susan vine) 169
Tropaeplum peregrinum (canary creeper) 169

RED/PURPLE/BRONZE FOLIAGE

Acer palmatum (threadleaf Japanese maple) 28
Berberis species (barberry) 35
Cercis species (redbud) 48
Chaenomeles species (quince) 49
Cotinus coggygria 58
Dolichos lablab (hyacinth bean) 168
Ilex species (holly) 78
Leucothoe fontanesiana (drooping leucothoe) 88
Pieris species (andromeda) 98
Polygonum aubertii (silver fleece vine) 162
Stewartia ovata grandiflora (showy stewartia) 126

SILVER/GRAY/BLUE FOLIAGE

Abies balsamea (balsam fir) 144
Actinidia species (actinidia) 146
Amorpha canescens (leadplant) 33
Calluna vulgaris (Scotch heather) 40
Caryopteris x *clandonensis* (bluebeard) 44
Corylopsis species (winter hazel) 56
Cotoneaster species (cotoneaster) 60
Fothergilla species (fothergilla) 70
Genista pilosa (genista) 71
Hypericum frondosum (St. John's wort) 78
Juniperus conferta (shore juniper) 144
Leucophyllum frutescens (Texas ranger) 87
Mahonia aquifolium (Oregon grape) 93
Parthenocissus henryana (silvervein creeper) 161
Pinus parviflora (Japanese white pine) 144
Potentilla fruticosa (cinquefoil) 100
Rosa species (rose) 120
Salix species (willow) 123
Spiraea species (spirea) 124
Symphoricarpos x *chenaultii* (coralberry) 129

AUTUMN COLOR

Acer palmatum (threadleaf Japanese maple) 28
Amelanchier canadensis (shadblow) 32
Arctostaphylos uva-ursi (bearberry) 33
Aronia arbutifolia (red chokeberry) 35
Azaleas 111
Berberis species (barberry) 35
Callicarpa species (beautyberry) 39
Calluna vulgaris (Scotch heather) 40

Cercis species (redbud) 48
Chionanthus (fringe tree) 50
Clerodendrum trichotomum (harlequin glory-bower) 53
Clethra species (summersweet) 53
Corylopsis species (winter hazel) 56
Cotoneaster species (cotoneaster) 60
Cyrilla racemiflora (swamp cyrilla) 62
Deutzia gracilis (slender deutzia) 63
Enkianthus species (enkianthus) 65
Euonymus alatus (burning bush) 66
Euonymus fortunei (bigleaf wintercreeper) 153
Fothergilla species (fothergilla) 70
Hamamelis species (witch-hazel) 71
Itea virginica (sweetspire) 82
Lagerstroemia indica (crape myrtle) 87
Leucothoe fontanesiana (drooping leucothoe) 88
Lindera species (spicebush) 90
Mahonia aquifolium (Oregon grape) 93
Parthenocissus henryana (silvervein creeper) 161
Photinia villosa (oriental photinia) 97
Rhus species (sumac) 117
Ribes odoratum (clove currant) 117
Schizophragma hydrangeoides (Japanese climbing hydrangea) 163
Stewartia ovata grandiflora (showy stewartia) 126
Vaccinium species (blueberry) 133
Viburnum species (viburnum) 134
Vitis species (grape) 165

**WINTER COLOR -
FOLIAGE/FLOWERS/TWIGS**

Arctostaphylos uva-ursi (bearberry) 33
Berberis species (barberry) 35
Buddleia alternifolia (fountain buddleia) 38
Camellia species (camellia) 42
Cornus species (dogwood) 54
Cotoneaster species (cotoneaster) 60
Euonymus fortunei (bigleaf wintercreeper) 153
Hydrangea anomala ssp. petiolaris (climbing hydrangea) 157
Ilex species (holly) 78
Kalmia latifolia (mountain laurel) 84
Kerria japonica (Japanese rose) 85
Kolkwitzia amabilis (beautybush) 85
Lagerstroemia indica (crape myrtle) 87
Ligustrum species (privet) 90
Lonicera species (honeysuckle) 91
Mahonia (Oregon grape) 93
Physocarpus species (ninebark) 98
Rhodedendron species 104
Schizophragma hydrangeoides (Japanese climbing hydrangea) 163
Stewartia ovata grandiflora (showy stewartia) 126
Vaccinium species (blueberry) 133
Viburnum species (viburnum) 134

SHADE

Acanthopanax sieboldianus (fiveleaf akebia) 28
Acer palmatum (threadleaf Japanese maple) 28
Aronia arbutifolia (red chokeberry) 35
Calycanthus floridus (sweetshrub) 42
Camellia species (camellia) 42
Chionanthus (fringe tree) 50
Clematis species (clematis) 149
Cyrilla racemiflora (swamp cyrilla) 62
Euonymus fortunei (bigleaf wintercreeper) 153
Hedera helix (English ivy) 154
Hydrangea anomala ssp. petiolaris (climbing hydrangea) 157
Itea virginica (sweetspire) 82
Leucothoe fontanesiana (drooping leucothoe) 88
Magnolia stellata (star magnolia) 91
Parthenocissus henryana (silvervein creeper) 161
Rhodotypos scandens (jetbead) 117
Schizophragma hydrangeoides (Japanese climbing hydrangea) 163
Stephanandra incisa (cutleaf stephanandra) 126
Symphoricarpos (coralberry) 129
Viburnum species (viburnum) 134

PARTIAL SHADE

Abelia x *grandiflora* (glossy abelia) 28
Abies balsamea (balsam fir) 144
Acanthopanax sieboldianus (fiveleaf akebia) 28
Actinidia species (actinidia) 146
Aesculus parviflora (bottlebrush buckeye) 32
Akebia quinata (fiveleaf akebia) 146
Arctostaphylos uva-ursi (bearberry) 33
Aristolochia durior (Dutchman's pipe) 148
Buddleia alternifolia (fountain buddleia) 38
Callicarpa species (beautyberry) 39
Calluna vulgaris (Scotch heather) 40
Calycanthus floridus (sweetshrub) 42
Camellia species (camellia) 42
Caryopteris x *clandonensis* (bluebeard) 44
Cedrus deodara (Deodar cedar) 144
Cephalanthus occidentalis (buttonbush) 48
Cephalotaxus harringtonia var. Drupacea (plum yew) 144
Cercis species (redbud) 48
Chamaecyparis obtusa (Hinoki cypress) 144
Chionanthus (fringe tree) 50
Clematis species (clematis) 149
Clethra species (summersweet) 53
Comptonia peregrina (sweet fern) 54
Cornus species (dogwood) 54
Corylopsis species (winter hazel) 56
Cotoneaster species (cotoneaster) 60
Cyrilla racemiflora (swamp cyrilla) 62
Daphne species (daphne) 63

Deutzia gracilis (slender deutzia) 63
Elaeagnus species (elaeagnus) 65
Enkianthus species (enkianthus) 65
Euonymus alatus (burning bush) 66
Euonymus fortunei (wintercreeper) 153
Exochorda (pearlbush) 69
Forsythia species (forsythia) 69
Fothergilla species (fothergilla) 70
Gaylussacia species (huckleberry) 70
Hamamelis species (witch-hazel) 71
Hedera helix (English ivy) 154
Hibiscus syriacus (rose of sharon) 74
Hydrangea anomala ssp. petiolaris (climbing hydrangea) 157
Hydrangea species (hydrangea) 74
Ilex species (holly) 78
Itea virginica (sweetspire) 82
Jasminum officinale (jessamine) 157
Kalmia latifolia (mountain laurel) 84
Kerria japonica (Japanese rose) 85
Leucophyllum frutescens (Texas ranger) 87
Leucothoe fontanesiana (drooping leucothoe) 88
Ligustrum species (privet) 90
Lindera species (spicebush) 90
Lonicera heckrotti (everblooming honeysuckle) 159
Magnolia stellata (star magnolia) 91
Mahonia aquifolium (Oregon grape) 93
Mandevilla suaveolens (Chilean jasmine) 159
Mina lobata (crimson starglory) 159
Myrica pensylvanica (bayberry) 94
Paeonia suffruticosa (tree peony) 96
Passiflora species (passionflower) 161
Philadelphus (mock orange) 97
Picea glauca (dwarf white spruce) 144
Pieris species (andromeda) 98
Pinus parviflora (Japanese white pine) 144
Polygonum aubertii (silver fleece vine) 162
Pyracantha species (firethorn) 103
Raphiolepsis indica (hawthorn) 104
Rhodedendron species 104
Rhodotypos scandens (jetbead) 117
Rhus species (sumac) 117
Ribes odoratum (clove currant) 117
Schizophragma hydrangeoides (Japanese climbing hydrangea) 163
Spiraea species (spirea) 124
Stephanandra incisa (cutleaf stephanandra) 126
Symphoricarpos x *chenaultii* (coralberry) 129
Thunbergia alata (black-eyed susan vine) 169
Tsuga canadensis (hemlock) 145
Vaccinium species (blueberry) 133
Viburnum species (viburnum) 134
Weigela species (weigela) 140

ABELIA X GRANDIFLORA GLOSSY ABELIA *Caprifoliaceae*

With its fine-textured leaves–lustrous deep green during the growing season and purplish in fall and winter–and tendency to form a spreading, dense mass of arching stems, this is an excellent plant for massing. Though far from dramatic, its small white flowers occur over an unusually long period, appearing from late spring until frost. In mild climates, leaves persist.

BEST CONDITIONS Though glossy abelia is tolerant of a wide variety of conditions, it does best in well-drained, moist, acid soil with full sun to partial shade.

PLANTING Balled-and-burlapped and container-grown shrubs can be planted in either spring or fall.

PESTS/DISEASES None serious, but leaf spot can sometimes be a problem.

PRUNING Prune to remove winter damage and to keep the long, arching stems from looking unruly.

PROPAGATION Take softwood cuttings.

USE A natural for massing, glossy abelia also enhances foundation plantings and shrub borders.

ACANTHOPANAX SIEBOLDIANUS FIVELEAF ARALIA *Araliaceae*

The small greenish-white unisexual flowers of this dioecious shrub are less than showy, and since most plants in North American cultivation are female (and thus unpollinated), fruit production is scarce at best. What does recommend this upright grower is its attractive foliage, borne on slender stems that begin to arch as the plant matures. Leaves are bright green and palmately compound, with 5-7 leaflets. Native to the Far East, it is cultivated for medicinal and culinary uses in Japan.

BEST CONDITIONS One of the most easy-to-please shrubs in North America, fiveleaf aralia will adapt to nearly any soil type and pH, is as happy in heavy shade as full sun, and flourishes amid urban pollution and overcrowding.

PLANTING Container-grown plants can be transplanted anytime.

PESTS/DISEASES None serious.

PRUNING Fiveleaf aralia is tough enough to withstand extremely heavy pruning, shearing for a hedge, or renewal pruning for overgrown specimens. It sometimes sends out suckers and may need to be contained.

PROPAGATION Softwood cuttings, taken in summer and treated with a rooting hormone, root easily.

USE Fiveleaf aralia's handsome foliage and lack of floral attributes make it a natural choice for the back of the shrub or perennial border, and its ability to withstand drought, crowding, and pollution qualify it as a first-class urban shrub. Or take advantage of its prunability and prickly stems and use it as a hedge or barrier.

CULTIVAR *A. sieboldianus* 'Variegatus' is a less vigorous grower with leaves attractively edged in creamy white.

ACER PALMATUM THREADLEAF JAPANESE MAPLE *Aceraceae*

A fine-textured shrub with cascading branches and foliage, the threadleaf Japanese maple is used to best advantage as a dramatic focal point in the gar-

ABELIA X GRANDIFLORIA (GLOSSY ABELIA) Mature size: 6 foot tall, 8 feet wide. Deep green leaves turn purple in fall; small white to pink flowers. Full sun is best, tolerates shade; moist, acid soil. Zones 6-9.

ACANTHOPANAX SIEBOLDIANUS 'VARIEGATUS' (FIVELEAF ARALIA) Mature size: 8 feet tall and wide. Bright green leaves, edged in white. Full sun to full shade, any soil type. Zones 4-8.

ACER PALMATUM 'WATERFALL' (THREADLEAF JAPANESE MAPLE) Mature size: 8-10 feet. Leaves deep green in summer, yellow, orange, or red in fall. Moderately fertile loamy soil, full sun to partial shade in North, light to partial shade in South. Zones 5-8.

ACER PALMATUM 'EVER RED' (THREADLEAF JAPANESE MAPLE) Mature size: 12 feet. Deep red foliage. Moderately fertile loamy soil, full sun to partial shade in North, light to partial shade in South. Zones 5-8.

Threadleaf maples supply brilliant color to the garden–rich burgundy, brown, and green in summer, bright orange in fall.

den. Its exquisitely colored foliage varies from deep red to green in summer, and from clear yellow to brilliant orange to scarlet in fall. Look for vigorous plants with well-spaced main branches that don't cross or form V crotches. The choicest specimens have wavy trunks. The species is native to the woods and thickets in the mountains of Hokkaido and Honshu.

BEST CONDITIONS The threadleaf Japanese maple does best in a moderately fertile, well-drained, loamy soil on the acidic side (pH 6.5-4.0). Choose a site with full sun to half shade in the North and ¾-¼ sun in the South. Protection from wind is necessary. *Acer palmatum* is not hardy in Chicago.

PLANTING Plant either in early to mid spring or fall, and space generously, providing a radius of at least 7 feet or an ultimate canopy area of 14 feet or more. Mulch lightly with a fine-textured material.

WATER During the first summer, thoroughly soak the root zone every week or two depending on soil conditions. In successive years, water judiciously during periods of drought.

FERTILIZER Fertilizer should not be applied when planting. After the plant is established, in 1-2 years, you can maximize growth with a moderate, early spring application of slow-release, ureaform or organic fertilizer high in nitrogen.

WEEDING Do not cultivate the soil within the root zone, since the threadleaf Japanese maple's fibrous roots grow close to the surface.

PESTS/DISEASES None serious.

PRUNING The threadleaf Japanese maple has a naturally graceful habit that generally makes pruning unnecessary. If you must prune, do so in late summer or fall to avoid unsightly bleeding.

PROPAGATION Cuttings of the threadleaf Japanese maple don't root easily, and seedlings may not be true to the original plant, so most nurseries graft selected forms onto 1- to 2-year-old seedling rootstocks that are brought into the greenhouse in winter. Plants grown from cuttings are not as vigorous or hardy as grafted specimens.

USE A colorful star performer in the landscape, the threadleaf Japanese maple is set off to best advantage by a backdrop of coniferous shrubs or trees, or planted in combination with birches, which provide light shade. For a striking effect, consider planting it alongside low-growing ornamental grasses, such as Japanese blood grass culivars or *Hakonechloa macra* 'Aureola'.

CULTIVARS Red-leaved varieties of *A. palmatum* sometimes lose color in shade and so need sunny locations. 'Crimson Queen', the nursery standard, is outstanding for its vigor and deep red foliage color that lasts the entire growing season. 'Ever Red' is similar to 'Crimson Queen' except that its late-season color retention is not as good. 'Garnet' fades a bit late in the season but in full sun boasts glorious garnet-hued foliage. 'Red Filigree Lace' offers very fine texture and good color retention.

OTHER SPECIES *A. ginnala*, the Amur maple, has a spreading, open crown and turns bright red or orange in autumn. *A. japonicum* 'Green Cascade' and 'Aconifolium' are hardy in Chicago.

ACER GINNALA (AMUR MAPLE) Mature size: 20 feet tall, 20 feet wide. Ordinary soil, full sun to partial shade. Small leaves, brilliant color in fall. Zones 3-6.

AESCULUS PARVIFLORA (BOTTLEBRUSH BUCKEYE) Mature size: 8-12 feet tall, 15-20 feet wide. White flowers appear in pyramidal clusters in late summer. Full sun with afternoon shade; rich, moist soil; does not do well in drought. Zones 4-9.

AMELANCHIER CANADENSIS (SHADBLOW) Mature size: 25 feet tall, 20 feet wide. Clusters of flowers, silvery leaves turning yellow or orange in fall, small, dark berries. Partial sun; rich acid soil; tolerates other conditions, but not drought. Zones 3-8.

AMORPHA CANESCENS (LEADPLANT) Mature size: 4 feet tall, 4 feet wide. Gray foliage, spikes of blue flowers in early summer. Full sun, well-drained soil, dry conditions. Zones 2-7.

Above: **A threadleaf maple serves as an anchor for a perennial border.**

AESCULUS PARVIFLORA BOTTLEBRUSH BUCKEYE *Hippocastanaceae*

Also called the horse chestnut, this shrub (a favorite of many gardeners) bears cylinders of tiny white flowers. Foliage is coarse-textured and leaves are palmately compound; the overall effect of the delicate bottlebrushes against the dark green foliage fans is dramatic in mid July (early July in Pennsylvania at the Morris Arboretum); it turns an attractive yellow in autumn. Native to the rich moist woods of the southeastern U.S.

BEST CONDITIONS Tolerates full sun but prefers afternoon shade and does best in a moist but well-drained highly organic soil. This is not a plant for hot, dry, or droughty environments. However, an established specimen at the Morris Arboretum does survive these conditions; once the plant has developed an adequate root system, it can tolerate a great deal of stress.

PLANTING Both container-grown and balled-and-burlapped specimens should be planted in early spring and benefit from the application of an organic mulch.

PESTS/DISEASES Remarkably problem-free, especially as compared to other buckeyes.

PRUNING Size may be restricted by selective pruning.

PROPAGATION Propagate by seed, root cuttings, or by removing suckers.

USE This large, rangy, multistemmed shrub tends to colonize by sending up slender upright suckers. Though it is not invasive, its size and habit may preclude its use in most small residential plantings. It is, however, quite effective in shrub borders or as a lawn specimen where it can grow unimpeded. It is a good shrub to use in transitional areas, going from sun to shade, since it does well in both conditions.

CULTIVARS *A. parviflora* 'Serotina' and 'Rogers' are both similar to the species in growth habit. They both bloom 2 weeks later than the species and have pendant leaves. 'Rogers' was selected for its long flower clusters. 'Serotina' has a wonderful cascading effect on the landscape.

AMELANCHIER CANADENSIS SHADBLOW *Rosaceae*

Also called serviceberry. Native to wetlands and coastal areas from Maine to North Carolina, this delicate, graceful shrub–often grown as a small tree–offers year-round interest in the form of spring flowers, summer berries, orange fall foliage, and handsome ascending trunks in winter. In early spring (when the shad are running, according to folk wisdom), it covers itself with clusters of white flowers, which are followed in June by black berries and the birds that love them. Look for balled-and-burlapped plants.

BEST CONDITIONS Shadblow prefers partial sun and an acidic, organic soil with good drainage, but will settle for less-than-ideal conditions (with the exception of drought).

PLANTING Plant in spring (fall for container or balled-and-burlapped plants) and mulch heavily after planting.

PESTS/DISEASES Like any pome-fruited plant, this is subject to fireblight and mites. Borers, witches' broom, and powdery mildew also can be problems.

PRUNING Except for the removal of unwanted suckers, shadblow usually requires very little pruning.

PROPAGATION Propagate from seed, division of the parent plant, and root cuttings, or take softwood cuttings when new growth is several inches long.

USE Shadblow is at its most beautiful when used in a naturalistic setting near the edge of woodlands, rimming a pond or stream, or backed by a stand of evergreens, but it also works very well in the small garden, as a specimen or as part of a mixed-shrub border. Tolerant of salt spray, it's a familiar denizen of seaside gardens.

AMORPHA CANESCENS LEADPLANT *Fabaceae*

Native to the tallgrass and mixed-grass prairies of the Great Plains, this broad, flat-topped shrub makes an attractive, fine-textured landscape plant. The leaves are covered with silvery hairs that lend the plant an appealing gray-green hue, and the purple flowers, appearing in July on dense 6-inch terminal racemes, contrast nicely with the silvery foliage. Leadplant is sometimes considered a subshrub or a semi-woody herbaceous plant.

BEST CONDITIONS Leadplant requires full sun and a well-drained soil and prefers generally dry conditions. This useful plant is tolerant of heat, wind, and slightly alkaline soil.

PLANTING Plant bare-root stock in early spring; containerized shrubs can be planted in spring or fall. Space 2-3 feet apart.

PESTS/DISEASES None serious.

PRUNING Prune as needed to maintain shape and size; hard pruning tends to promote herbaceous growth.

PROPAGATION Take softwood cuttings in late July or propagate by seed. (Seed germination is enhanced by scarification and stratification.)

USE This low grower would be right at home in the rock garden and combines well with herbaceous perennials in beds and borders. Leadplant may be at its best, however, as an accent plant in a mixed-shrub planting.

ARCTOSTAPHYLOS UVA-URSI BEARBERRY, KINNIKINICK *Ericaceae*

Anyone looking for a fine-textured evergreen ground cover would do well to consider the bearberry. Its lustrous, bright green leaves turn a handsome red or bronze in winter, and its white or pink flowers, blooming in late April or early May, take the form of dainty nodding bells. Summer interest is provided by the red fruit, which persists through August. Because of its high salt tolerance, it can be found growing right up to the beach in its native habitat.

BEST CONDITIONS This plant is happiest in infertile, sandy soils, in full sun or partial shade. Like other ericaceous plants, it likes a low pH of 4.5-5.5. It does not do well in Chicago's heavy soil, but can be grown in containers there.

PLANTING Because bearberry doesn't transplant well, it should be planted out only as a container-grown plant. Plant in spring or late summer, spacing plants about 18-24 inches apart, depending on the size of the transplant.

FERTILIZER This is a plant that revels in poor soil; don't fertilize it.

The bottlebrush buckeye derives its name from its large cylindrical panicles, each comprising dozens of tubular flowers with 4 short white petals; the true "bottlebrush" effect is created by the blush-white threadlike stamens, which protrude an inch or more beyond the petals.

ARCOSTAPHYLOS UVA-URSI 'VANCOUVER JADE' (BEARBERRY) Low-growing, spreading ground cover with small evergreen leaves that turn bronze in autumn. Sandy, infertile soils, full sun or partial shade. Zones 2-8.

ARONIA ARBUTIFOLIA 'BRILLIANTISSIMA' (CHOKEBERRY) Mature size: 6-8 feet tall, 3-5 feet wide. White or reddish flowers in mid spring, bright red berries in fall. Best in full sun, tolerates partial shade. Wet or dry soils. Zones 4-9.

BERBERIS X GLADWYNENSIS 'WILLIAM PENN' (Barberry) Mature size: 4 feet high, 8 feet wide. Red and green leaves, extremely thorny. Full sun, moderately fertile and moist soil. Zones 6-9.

BERBERIS THUNBERGII 'CRIMSON PYGMY' (BARBERRY) Mature size: 2 feet tall, 3 feet wide. Reddish foliage. Best color in full sun, moderately fertile and moist soil. Zones 4-7.

PESTS/DISEASES No serious pests, though it does on occasion develop black mildew, leaf galls, and rust.
PRUNING Rarely needed.
PROPAGATION Bearberry can be propagated from seed, but because its seed coat is impermeable and its embryo is dormant, it must undergo acid scarification. A far better method is to propagate from summer cuttings.
USE An outstanding ground cover, bearberry has a fine texture that separates it from most other low growers. It's especially lovely cascading over a low rock wall.
CULTIVAR *A. uva-ursi* 'Vancouver Jade' turns deep purple in autumn.

ARONIA ARBUTIFOLIA RED CHOKEBERRY *Rosaceae*

Red Chokeberry is native to wetlands and wet woods, such as in eastern North America; less frequently found in dry soil.
BEST CONDITIONS This highly adaptable plant is tolerant of both wet and dry soils. Though it grows well in partial shade, expect the best flowering, fruiting, and fall color in full sun.
PLANTING Easily transplanted in spring or fall.
PESTS/DISEASES None serious.
PRUNING Pruning is seldom necessary and, indeed, should be avoided wherever possible, as fruiting and flowering will be affected.
PROPAGATION Softwood cuttings, taken in early summer, root readily. Where only a few plants are required, severing off suckers in early spring is an easy alternative.
USE Because of its suckering and tendency to legginess, this is generally not considered a choice specimen or stand-alone shrub. It is, however, a wonderful plant for the back of the border or for massing where its late-season attributes can be fully appreciated.
CULTIVAR *A. Arbutifolia* 'Brilliantissima' is superior to the species in all ornamental characteristics. It is a tall, slender-stemmed shrub of upright habit that tends to be colonized by suckers. Its small white flowers are borne in mid May in 1½- to 2-inch clusters and are followed by brilliant red fruits that persist well into winter. Additional interest is provided by the glossy, deep green foliage, which turns a dramatic scarlet in autumn.
OTHER SPECIES *A. melanocarpa* (black chokeberry) has similar attributes and attractive black berries; it is quite hardy at the Dyck Arboretum of the Plains.

BERBERIS Species BARBERRY *Berberidaceae*

A popular shrub for hedging, barberry is mainly deciduous, though some varieties are evergreen. Its wood is yellow (sometimes red or nearly black), and its simple leaves grow in small clusters, turning bright orange, red, and yellow in fall. Foliage is dense, clothing arching branches. In spring, small yellow or red flowers appear, followed in fall by red berries. Fastidious gardeners take note: because of its configuration and thorns, barberry tends to collect litter, which is often difficult to remove. Some species, such as *B. koreana* and *B.*

Barberries are useful throughout the year. In the fall, their leaves turn bright yellow or orange, and brilliant red berries form. Their yellow branches are attractive through the winter.

Too recently for comfort, I bought three butterfly bushes: the species, *Buddleia davidii,* whose flowers are small and pallid lavender, and two large-blossomed, well-bred selections, one a rich purple, the other a pleasing pink. Butterflies prefer the common sort. Maybe the nectar of those selected by breeders for their blossoms is too thick for butterflies . . . or maybe they are off-color or off-odor. Or maybe butterflies, like me, are annoyed by stalks so heavy with blossoms that they can't stand up. FROM *NOAH'S GARDEN, RESTORING THE ECOLOGY OF OUR OWN BACKYARDS,* BY SARA STEIN

Above: Buddleia davidii 'White Knight' with swallowtail butterfly.

thunbergii, common in thickets in their native lands, are becoming naturalized in North America as birds disperse their fruits.

NOTE All deciduous species of berberis are prohibited in Canada.

BEST CONDITIONS Color develops best in full sun, though the plant will tolerate light shade. Grow in any ordinary soil of moderate fertility and moisture, with an acid to neutral pH. Protect from wind in cold climates.

PLANTING Plant in spring or fall, spacing 1-2 feet apart for hedges, 4-6 feet apart for massing.

WATER Barberry is sensitive to excess moisture; do not overwater.

PESTS/DISEASES Though barberry is not subject to any serious pests or diseases, it does suffer occasionally from rust, root rot, wilt, and virus mosaic.

PRUNING To keep hedges in shape, prune 2-3 times a season. Remove dead-wood as necessary; ragged specimens can be rejuvenated by cutting back nearly to the ground in late winter.

PROPAGATION Root softwood cuttings in shade, in a moist sandy soil; the cuttings will transplant easily. Semihardwood cuttings can be taken in summer, and hardwood in fall or winter. All cuttings will root in about 4-8 weeks. Barberry can also be propagated from seed.

USE Evergreen varieties especially make for excellent screens and hedges.

SPECIES *B.* x *gladwynensis* 'William Penn', an evergreen variety, boasts the most handsome foliage of any barberry. The habit is dense, low, and spreading. Though the plant produces no fruit, its thorns are formidable. Zones 6-8; 5 with protection. Mature size: 4 feet high, 8 feet wide.

B. koreana, Korean barberry, is a deciduous shrub sporting yellow spring-blooming flowers on 3- to 4-inch racemes; fall foliage is red, as are the fall berries that often persist into winter. Zones 3-7. Mature size: 8 feet high, 8 feet wide.

B. thunbergii, Japanese barberry, includes the cultivars 'Crimson Pygmy', which is a dense, compact, purple-leaved deciduous shrub, and 'Rosy Glow', another red-leaved cultivar that is taller. The cultivar 'Kobold' is deciduous, dense, and compact; like boxwood, it can be pruned topiary-style. Semiglossy dark green foliage. Zones 4-8.

BUDDLEIA Species BUTTERFLY BUSH *Loganiaceae*

The long, arching branches of *Buddleia* support light green willowlike leaves and racemes of tiny flowers (white, pink, red, or blue) that give off a compelling woodsy-sweet fragrance. The flowers are excellent for cutting and for attracting butterflies to the garden. The first plant to return to bombed-out Europe after World War I, *Buddleia* was dubbed "Flower of the Ruins." A good choice for seaside gardens, it also does fairly well at the Desert Botanic Garden in Phoenix and at the Mercer Arboretum near Houston.

BEST CONDITIONS Grow in sun in a relatively light, well-drained soil. *Buddleia* can be grown successfully in comparatively poor, gravelly or sandy, soil and in fact does less well in overfertile soil. It prefers an acid pH of 6.5 or below, but also performs well in soils with a pH of up to 7.8 at Chicago Botanic Garden.

BERBERIS THUNBERGII 'ROSY GLOW' (BARBERRY) Mature size: 1½ feet tall, 2 feet wide. Small bronze-red leaves, dense habit. Full sun, moderately fertile and moist soil. Zones 4-7.

BERBERIS THUNBERGII 'KOBOLD' (BARBERRY) Mature size: 4-6 feet tall and wide. Dense habit, evergreen dark green leaves. Full sun, moderately fertile and moist soil. Zones 4-8.

BUDDLEIA ALTERNIFOLIA (FOUNTAIN BUDDLEIA) Mature size: 12 feet tall, 15 feet wide. Silvery foliage and bark, long spikes of pale purple flowers. Full sun, grows better in poor soils. Zones 5-9

BUDDLEIA DAVIDII (ORANGE-EYE BUTTERFLY BUSH) Mature size: 8-10 feet tall, sometimes up to 15 feet. Upright spikes of purple, pink, white, or red flowers on arching branches in late summer, Full sun, grows better in poor soils. Zones 6-9.

Above: A knot garden, using bayberries and boxwoods. *Top:* The shaping process known as topiary can be used to create simple or elaborate shapes.

PLANTING Above Zone 8, plant anytime; below Zone 8, plant in spring to give it a full season to establish itself before frost.

WATER Water generously, especially in its first growing season.

FERTILIZER In spring apply a complete fertilizer.

PESTS/DISEASES *Buddleia* is rarely troubled. Avoid spraying to protect butterflies.

PRUNING Below Zone 5, cut back to the ground in winter and mulch the crowns with straw or manure; roots will usually survive. For *B. davidii,* cut back to 6 inches every spring.

PROPAGATION *Buddleia* is easy to propagate from softwood or semihardwood cuttings taken in fall; grow in the greenhouse or cold frame.

USE *Buddleia* makes a fine backdrop for the perennial border.

SPECIES *B. alternifolia,* fountain buddleia, with its graceful habit, is more refined than *davidii* and is hardy to Zone 5 without dieback. Native to northwest China; the cultivar 'Argentea' was selected for its silvery-gray foliage color. Blooming on the previous season's shoots, it can be pruned back after the blossoms have faded.

B. davidii, orange-eye butterfly bush, is native to central China, where it is found growing along streams and in thickets. It should be rejuvenated annually in late winter or early spring. Established plants will attain a height of 6-8 feet by late summer. Valuable cultivars include 'White Bouquet', 'Empire Blue', 'Pink Delight', 'Royal Red', and 'Dark Knight,' which grows only 4-5 feet and has purple blossoms that are nearly black.

BUXUS Species BOXWOOD, BOX *Buxaceae*

By far the most popular shrub for hedging and formal borders, boxwood is grown for its dense, glossy evergreen foliage and its easy prunability. Our common garden varieties are natives of central Europe (*B. sempervirens*) and eastern Asia, where they are found in the mountains (*B. microphylla*), often in rocky crevices or along watercourses.

BEST CONDITIONS In northern gardens, grow in full sun to partial shade; in the South, partial afternoon shade is desirable. Box is adaptable as to pH and will thrive in any well-drained garden soil. Protect from drying winds year-round.

PLANTING Spring or fall.

PESTS/DISEASES Not browsed by deer. Male cats commonly spray boxwood to mark their territory. Very susceptible to salt damage. Also susceptible to sunscald, boxwood psyllid, mites, canker, scale, mealybugs, leaf miners, nematodes, and in wet areas, root rot.

PRUNING The quintessential topiary shrub, boxwood responds exceptionally well to trimming and shearing. Use a sharp knife or pruners.

PROPAGATION Though cuttings will root virtually year-round, home gardeners usually find summer cuttings the easiest to propagate.

USE Since the Roman era, boxwood has been the plant of choice for low formal hedging and parterres. Several cultivars, however, will develop into very handsome specimen plants if left untrimmed, giving the effect of billowing clouds.

SPECIES *B. microphylla,* littleleaf box, is a dense, compact, slow-growing shrub that takes a broadly rounded shape as it matures. The species is variable in appearance when grown from seed, and leaf color often fades to an unattractive yellow-bronze, but a large number of appealing cultivars are now available to home gardeners. 'Kingsville Dwarf' is a very slow-growing small-leafed form with a pin-cushion shape. 'Wintergreen' is an extremely hardy shrub that exhibits uniform growth and good winter color. 'Green Velvet' is the best performer in Chicago, providing excellent green color in winter. *B. sempervirens,* common box, is faster and larger-growing than *B. microphylla* but is less tolerant of extreme heat or cold. As with littleleaf box, many cultivars, selected for size, shape, color, and hardiness, are now available. Hardy in Zones 5-8, depending on the cultivar. Mature size: 18 feet tall, 15 feet wide, but cultivars vary dramatically. 'Suffruticosa', often referred to as "edging box," was a favorite in Elizabethan knot gardens. If left untrimmed, it can grow 4-5 feet in height. Not reliably hardy in northern gardens. 'Vardar Valley' forms a flat-topped mound 3 feet tall and 5 feet wide. Zone 5. *Buxus* 'Schmidt' is a new cultivar with dark, glossy, green foliage and an upright habit. Zone 5.

CALLIANDRA CALIFORNICA RED FAIRYDUSTER *Leguminosae*

A native of southern Baja, this evergreen retains some cold sensitivity, as well as great hardiness to desert conditions. It is an evergreen with tiny dark green compound leaves that are a fine background for its brilliant red blooms, which consist mainly of stamens and persist for a very long time—at the Desert Botanic Garden, it is in bloom from March to December.
BEST CONDITIONS This plant needs heat and does not bloom well without intense heat. In very cold climates, it benefits from some protection.
PLANTING Spring or fall; fall is ideal. Never in the heat of summer.
SPECIES *C. eriophylla* is a favorite in native or naturalistic gardens. It has pink blooms and lighter foliage than *C. californica*. It blooms in the spring and then becomes deciduous and does not rebloom that year.

CALLICARPA Species BEAUTYBERRY, FRENCH MULBERRY

Verbenaceae
Though its tiny pink or white summer blossoms exert a demure appeal, *Callicarpa* is largely grown for its small, brightly colored fall berries, borne in dense clusters along the stems. The fine-textured, oppositely arranged foliage turns slightly purplish or yellowish in fall. Native to eastern Asia, where it grows in thickets.
BEST CONDITIONS This adaptable shrub does well in any well-drained fertile soil. Though it tolerates light shade, it flourishes in full sun. Soil pH should be acidic, though it thrives as a half-hardy shrub or perennial in Chicago in soil with pH up to 7.8.
PLANTING Plant in spring or fall, spacing 5-10 feet apart (4-8 feet for masses).
WATER Water during establishment and periods of drought.

TOPIARY

Topiary—the art of training plants into geometrical, figurative, or fanciful shapes—is a horticultural art that dates back at least as far as ancient Rome (Pliny the Younger, Roman statesman and nephew of the famed classical naturalist, boasted an elaborate topiary garden, incorporating fanciful animals, intricate geometric designs, and his own initials cut into shrubbery). From Rome, topiary traveled to Britain, where it found its most extravagant expression in the form of monstrous beasts and wild labyrinths. Though a number of plants is well suited to topiary, boxwood is by far the most popular. Like all the best shrubs for topiary (including Japanese yew and Canadian hemlock), it is dense, finely textured, slow-growing, hardy, and—perhaps most important—evergreen.

Topiary requires an artist's eye, a steady hand, and a patience that approaches the saintly: even so simple a creation as a double ball takes at least five years to mature into the desired form; elaborate figures like running hounds and loping dinosaurs can take over a decade. There are two basic topiary methods: the first is to prune a free-standing plant, over time, into a particular shape; the second is to train the plant over a preshaped wire frame. Both methods require assiduous clipping, which can be done anytime throughout the year, except in fall, when pruning can stimulate tender new growth that may not survive the winter.

Callicarpa dichotoma bears large clusters of lilac berries on graceful arching stems.

FERTILIZER Don't bother with fertilizer, since too rich a soil will only encourage legginess.

PEST/DISEASES None serious.

PRUNING Rejuvenate annually. For the best crop of berries, cut stems to 6 inches from the ground in early spring or late winter. At the Morris Arboretum, gardeners find that shrubs have more structure if pruned every 2-3 years.

PROPAGATION Grow from seed, or take cuttings—softwood in late spring, semi-hardwood in mid to late summer, hardwood in fall or winter.

USE *Callicarpa* makes it best impression as part of a group, and massed plantings ensure cross-pollination. This is an effective "surprise" plant when the leaves drop and expose fall fruit. Unfortunately, fruits don't last long after frost.

SPECIES *C. dichotoma* is most highly recommended by both Holden and Morris arboretums. It is extremely hardy, with graceful arching branches bearing large clusters of deep lilac berries on purplish stems; leaves turn shades of yellow and purple in the fall. 'Issai' is precocious. Zones 5-8.

C. japonica is the hardiest of the *Callicarpas*, with purple berries and yellowish to purplish fall foliage.

C. americana, the native American species, is less hardy than *C. japonica.* It does beautifully in Houston and the rest of the Gulf coastal region. The variety *lactea* has pure white fruits. Zone 7.

C. bodineri 'Profusion' has shiny bluish-lilac berries and pink-purple autumn foliage. Zones 6-8.

CALLUNA VULGARIS SCOTCH HEATHER *Ericaceae*

This low-growing, fine-textured evergreen shrub, most often used as a ground cover, is composed of short upright stems entirely clothed in tiny stalkless green leaves. Flowering begins in mid to late summer, when 1/4-inch bells are produced in 2- to 12-inch terminal racemes, and often extends through mid autumn. Most cultivars flower in shades of pink or white, though deeper shades are also available. Depending on the cultivar, autumn foliage is silver-bronze or red. It is native to Europe and Asia Minor, where it grows in rocky or sandy soil, often overlain with peat and more or less wet.

BEST CONDITIONS Scotch heather favors full sun or light shade, in a slightly acid, relatively infertile, very well-drained soil. Mulch with pine needles to acidify your soil if it tends toward high pH. Avoid planting in areas where hot, dry summers are the norm.

PLANTING Plant in spring, applying a mulch to retain soil moisture.

FERTILIZER It's best not to fertilize, since overly fertile soil tends to produce leggy plants. Supplemental watering is very beneficial, especially during establishment.

PESTS/DISEASES Mites, oystershell scale, and in wet areas root rot.

WEEDING Cultivating the surrounding soil can damage the plant's shallow root system; any weeding should therefore be done by hand.

PRUNING Prune regularly in early spring to keep plants compact.

BUXUS MICROPHYLLA 'KINGSVILLE DWARF' (LITTLELEAF BOX)
Mature size: 1 foot tall, 1½ feet and wide. Slow-growing, small-leaf shrub with pin-cushion shape. Full sun to partial shade; any well-drained soil. Zones 4-9.

BUXUS SEMPERVIRENS 'VARDAR VALLEY' (COMMON BOX) Mature size: 3 feet tall, 5 feet wide. Forms a flat-topped mound with green foliage all winter. Full sun to partial shade, any well-drained soil. Zones 5-7.

CALLIANDRA CALIFORNICA (RED FAIRYDUSTER) Mature size: 3-5 feet tall. Evergreen shrub with compound leaves and brilliant red blooms. Needs heat, full sun. Zones 8-10.

CALLICARPA AMERICANA LACTEA (BEAUTYBERRY) Mature size: 6 feet tall. Small blue flowers, abundant white berries in fall. Full sun is best, tolerates partial shade. Zones 5-8.

ground cover, edging, or rock garden plant. Several cultivars provide excellent fall color, lasting into winter.

CULTIVARS *C. vulgaris* 'County Wicklow' offers a fine prostrate form with dark green foliage and double pink flowers. 'Aurea' has purple flowers and golden foliage that turns red in fall. Grows to 12 inches. 'Alba' has white flowers and gray-green foliage. 'Coccinea' has deep red flowers and green foliage. 'Kersten' grows 8-12 inches tall; its foliage is finely textured and of a beautiful grayish-green color. It has pink flowers in late summer. Zones 5-7.

CALYCANTHUS FLORIDUS SWEETSHRUB, SWEET-SCENTED SHRUB, CAROLINA ALLSPICE *Calycanthaceae*

As its common names hint, *Calycanthus* is grown largely for its spicy-sweet scent. The 2-inch flowers, which bloom from May to July (April and May in the South), are interesting rather than showy and are composed of spiky, brown-to-purple sepals rather than petals. Foliage is a lustrous dark green, and the shrub itself grows to a neat rounded mass. Although it tends to sucker, it is not seriously invasive. Avoid *C. fertilis*, which has little fragrance. Native to rich mountain woods in the eastern U.S.

BEST CONDITIONS An adaptable sort, *Calycanthus* will flourish in either sun or shade, though sun tends to stunt its growth somewhat. Tolerant as well of most soils, it does best in a deep, moist, well-drained loam on the acid side.

PLANTING Plant in spring or fall, enriching the soil with peat moss or leaf mold for maximum moisture retention.

PESTS/DISEASES *Calycanthus* is highly resistant to both insects and diseases.

PRUNING Prune in spring before new growth appears. Renewal pruning can be practiced if plants become leggy and unattractive.

PROPAGATION Propagate from softwood, semihardwood, or hardwood cuttings, or remove and replant suckers.

USE This understory plant is well adapted to foundation, border, or mass planting. To take best advantage of its delightful scent, plant close to the house.

CULTIVARS *C. floridus* 'Athens' has very fragrant yellowish or chartreuse flowers. 'Edith Wilder', a selection named at the Scott Arboretum after its founder, Edith Wilder Scott, is a fine choice for fragrance.

CAMELLIA Species CAMELLIA *Theaceae*

A favorite of Southern gardeners, camellias offer hundreds of species, all boasting glossy, almost leathery foliage and strikingly colored waxlike flowers. Blooms range from the familiar scarlet through the pinks to a pure white.

BEST CONDITIONS Camellias thrive in a moist, well-drained acidic soil (with a pH of about 6.0) that has been well enriched with organic matter. Though they prefer partial shade, they will often tolerate deeper shade as well as full sun.

PLANTING Plant anytime, making sure to provide a layer of mulch to protect the camellia's shallow roots.

WATER Keep evenly moist, especially during establishment.

CALLICARPA DICHOTOMA 'ISSAI' (BEAUTYBERRY) Mature size: 4 feet tall. Graceful arching branches with lilac berries. Full sun is best, tolerates partial shade. Zones 5-8.

CALLUNA VULGARIS (SCOTCH HEATHER) Mature size: 12 inches tall. Low-growing, fine-textured ground cover with tiny flowers; foliage often turns silver-bronze or red in fall. Full sun or light shade; slightly acid, relatively poor soil. Zones 4-7.

CALYCANTHUS FLORIDUS (SWEETSHRUB) Mature size: 9 feet tall. Lustrous dark green foliage, 2-inch flowers composed of spiky sepals, neat, rounded growth habit. Shade or sun, tolerates most soils. Zones 4-9.

CAMELLIA HIEMALIS 'SHISHI-GASHIRA' Mature height: 4 feet tall, 7 feet wide. Medium red flower, semidouble to rose-form double, early in season, compact slow-growing plant, can be pruned low as a ground cover. Tolerates more sun than *japonicas*. Zones 7-10.

Above: Camellia blossoms can be single or double and range in size from 2-5 inches. *Right*: 'Shishi-Gashira' has a spreading growth habit, often reaching 6-7 feet in width.

PESTS/DISEASES Red spider mites; sometimes die-back.
PRUNING Most camellias need little pruning, except to remove faded flower heads; if grown as hedges or espaliers, prune during or immediately after flowering; if grown as foundation plants, prune back annually.
PROPAGATION Propagate by seeds, cuttings, or grafting.
USE Their brilliant blooms and striking foliage make camellias a natural for specimen as well as border plantings, and many make fine hedges. Camellias can also be espaliered against a wall for striking effect.
SPECIES *C. hiemalis,* often grown as a small tree, has pink or white flowers. *C. sasanqua* is grown for its loose habit and small, profusely borne flowers, which range from a pure white to a deep pink and bloom from late fall through early winter; many are fragrant. Zones 7-9; grows from 6-20 feet. *C. reticulata* has rather dull foliage, but its attractive flowers are larger than those of most other species.
C. japonica, an evergreen shrub also known as common camellia, has dark green leaves and flowers ranging in size from miniature (less than 2½ inches) to large (over 5 inches) of white, pink, or red that bloom in mid winter to early spring. Zones 7-9 (can survive in Zone 6 with winter protection); grows to 30 feet or more.
C. saluenensis has bluish-pink flowers and finely toothed leaves.

CARYOPTERIS X CLANDONENSIS BLUEBEARD *Verbenaceae*

Also called blue spirea. The deep blue, delicately fragrant flowers of this compact shrub are borne in small clusters arising from leaf axils at the end of the current season's growth. The leaves are a soft bluish-green above with silvery undersides and yield a spicy aroma when bruised. When most other shrubs have finished their spring and summer performances, the bluebeard is just ready to begin, blooming from early August until first frost. The parent species of this cultivar are natives of dry uplands in eastern Asia.

CAMELLIA JAPONICA 'ADOLPHE AUDUSSON VARIEGATUS' Mature size: 30 feet tall or more. Moist, well-drained soil. Partial shade. Oval leaves, dark green foliage. Semidouble dark red flowers blotched with white, 4 inches in diameter. Zones 7-9.

CAMELLIA JAPONICA 'DEBUTANTE' Mature size: 30 feet or more with vigorous, upright growth. Moist, well-drained soil. Partial shade. Oval leaves, dark green foliage. Full, tight, peony-form pink flowers, 3 inches in diameter. Zones 7-9.

CAMELLIA RETICULATA 'CORNELIAN' Mature size: 35 feet tall or more. Moist, well-drained soil. Partial shade. Large, semi-double to peony-form flowers, 5 or more inches across, red blotched with white. Irregular, wavy and crinkled petals. Zone 7-10.

CAMELLIA SALUENENSIS Mature size: 15 feet tall with dense branching. Moist, well-drained soil. Narrow, pointed leaves. Many single flowers in mid season, white flushed pink to deep rose pink. Zones 7-10.

Blue spirea adds a touch of color to the garden when most other plants are spent.

CONDITIONS Bluebeard will thrive in any well-drained garden soil, in full sun or light shade. At the Morris Arboretum, it is used in dry, open, and extremely hot locations. It is extremely drought-tolerant; indeed, excessive rain or watering causes rotting of crowns. It is hardy at Dyck Arboretum of the Plains as well.

PLANTING Plant in early spring

PESTS/DISEASES None serious

PRUNING Cut back to near ground level each spring before growth begins. After the first year, cut back to just above the first year's pruning for fuller shrubs.

PROPAGATION Softwood cuttings, taken in early summer, root easily, though divisions from naturally occurring layers or occasional suckers are also possible.

USE An effective addition to shrub or perennial borders, bluebeard is also a wonderful foil for 'Annabelle' hydrangea and yellow-flowered potentilla. It is one of the few sources of blue color at Dyck Arboretum of the Plains.

CULTIVAR 'Longwood Blue' was named at Longwood Gardens, Kennett Square, Pennsylvania; it has an attractive growth habit and good flower color. 'Arthur Simmonds' is the hardiest cultivar for the Chicago area.

CEANOTHUS Species WILD LILAC *Rhamnaceae*

The gardener interested in growing *Ceanothus* has an almost bewildering stock to choose among, from 8-inch ground covers to 30-foot trees. In general, this is either a broad-leafed evergreen or a deciduous multistemmed plant, with glossy dark leaves and showy blue, pink, or white flowers that are richly fragrant. Note that some varieties are short-lived.

BEST CONDITIONS Grow only in full sun in well-drained rocky, loamy, or sandy soil. *Ceanothus* is salt-tolerant and therefore a wonderful seaside plant. Tolerant of wind and drought.

PLANTING Plant in spring or fall. Because *Ceanothus* is deeply taprooted it is difficult to transplant.

WATER Water only during establishment.

PESTS/DISEASES Prone to canker disease, *Ceanothus* should be pruned only in the dry summer months. Root rot can be a problem in wet areas.

PRUNING See above (Pests/Diseases); rejuvenate annually.

PROPAGATION Propagate from seed, or by cutting in summer under mist. Old clumps can be divided.

USE Though some of the more dramatically flowered varieties make good specimens, *Ceanothus* is most impressive when planted in large, billowing masses.

SPECIES *C.* x *pallidus* 'Roseus' is a deciduous shrub that forms a 3-by-5-foot mound. Blooming for 3 weeks in late spring to early summer, it produces pale pink flowers that are followed by blush-red seed capsules. Zones 5-8. *C. ovatus* (New Jersey Tea) is a compact shrub native to the eastern United States and less showy than its western cousins. Hardy Zones 3-8.

CAMELLIA SASANQUA 'SETSUGEKKA' (CAMELLIA) Mature size: up to 15 feet tall. Moist, well-drained soil. Leathery, glossy green leaves; small abundant flowers, white, fluted, and semidouble with show of yellow stamens. Zones 7-9.

CAMELLIA X 'FREEDOM BELL' (CAMELLIA) Mature size: 4-8 feet tall. Moist, well-drained soil; partial shade. Small, bell-shaped semidouble red flowers in mid season. Compact upright plant. Zones 7-10.

CARYOPTERIS X CLANDONENSIS (BLUEBEARD) Mature size: 3-4 feet tall. Compact shrub with blue-green foliage and deep blue flowers in late summer. Full sun or light shade, any well-drained soil. Zones 4-9.

CEANOTHUS AMERICANUS (NEW JERSEY TEA) Mature size: 3 feet tall. Small white flowers in late spring. Full sun, well-drained, rocky, loamy, or sandy soil. Zones 4-8.

The doubtfully hardy *Ceanothus* is resolving its doubts in a way I do not like. It may not make it through winter. . . . The grapes are deficient in vigor. The mock orange 'Belle Etoile' has not grown as it should. . . In brief, I am no stranger to the anxieties or disappointments in gardening. . . . And then one bleak day as you blast out the front door in a sprint for the bus, there, by the grace of God, is *Crocus sieberi*. . . . I do say it takes very little to convince a gardener he will make right into spring.
FROM *THE ESSENTIAL EARTHMAN, HENRY MITCHELL ON GARDENING*

C. americanus, closely related to *C. ovatus,* was the first species to be cultivated but is not highly recommended today because it is hard to move. Zone 4; it grows to 3 feet.

Ceanothus cultivars that perform well on the California chaparral include *C. impressus* 'Victoria' (an upright, 9-foot-tall shrub, with dense evergreen foliage and profuse blue flowers in late spring that is hardy in Zones 7-10 and responds well to pruning) and *C. griseus* var. *horizontalis* 'Hurricane Point' (a fast-growing evergreen ground cover with sparse, pale-blue flowers that is hardy in Zones 8-10).

CEPHALANTHUS OCCIDENTALIS BUTTONBUSH *Rubiaceae*

This large, gangly, deciduous shrub is wonderful for naturalizing in wetlands, and especially along the edges of ponds. Its attractive, glossy foliage appears in late spring, followed in midsummer by modest, white, globular flowers that attract butterflies. It is native to the swamps and streamsides of a large portion of North America from New Brunswick to Minnesota and Florida to Mexico.

BEST CONDITIONS Buttonbush thrives in full sun or partial shade, wet soils of acid to neutral pH, and a high humus content.

PLANTING Transplants easily in spring or fall.

PESTS/DISEASES None serious.

PRUNING Cut down close to the ground in early spring for renewal when the plant becomes ungainly or oversteps its bounds.

PROPAGATION Softwood or semi-ripe cuttings in July or August. Seeds germinate without pretreatment.

CERCIS Species REDBUD, JUDAS TREE *Leguminosae*

This large shrub throws off showy clusters of white, pink, or purple pea-shaped flowers in early spring. Flowers give way to 5-inch heart-shaped leaves, which turn yellow in the fall. Avoid bare-root shrubs, which are difficult to transplant.

BEST CONDITIONS Redbud prefers light shade during the hottest part of the day, but will grow in full sun if the soil is kept evenly moist. Does well in many soil types except those poorly drained. Although redbud benefits from protection from excessive wind, several varieties thrive in the windy Great Plains, especially *C. reniformis*. The soil pH can be acid or alkaline.

PLANTING Plant in spring and prune to make up for root loss. Small specimens should be planted with as many roots as possible. Responds well to supplemental watering. Water in well, and keep moist. (Note: Young plants won't blossom for 4-5 years.)

PESTS/DISEASES Redbud is subject to canker, dieback, and wilt; affected areas should be pruned back to a healthy shoot.

PRUNING Though pruning is seldom needed, plants can be pruned for size in winter or spring; severe cutting, however, will result in the loss of a year's bloom.

PROPAGATION Propagation is not easy. Seeds are very hard and need severe treatment if they are to germinate. In spring, file lightly with a nail file and soak in water 150° F. and allow to cool. Redbud can also be propagated by layering, or from softwood cuttings taken in spring.

USE Redbud works well as a specimen or en masse, backed by conifers or close to the house, and is particularly at home in the woodland garden. It makes a felicitous companion to dogwood and can be forced indoors for an early hint of spring.

SPECIES *C. canadensis*, eastern redbud, is native to eastern North American moist woods; specimens found in central Kansas and Oklahoma are adapted to withstand wind and drought. 'Alba' is a white-flowered variety. 'Columbus Strain' is from Columbus, Wisconsin, and is hardy to Zone 5. 'Forest Pansy' has new leaves that are a shiny red-purple changing to purple-green. 'Pinkbud' and 'Wither's Pink Charm' have pink flowers without the purplish cast common to the species. Flower color is identical for these two cultivars. A similar species is *C. reniformis,* Texas redbud.

C. chinensis 'Avondale' is a 12-foot shrub with abundant purplish-pink flowers. Zones 6-9.

C. mexicana, western redbud, is beginning to make an appearance in the Southwest; it does better in shady spots and looks and blooms just like eastern redbud, but has smaller, crinkled leaves. (Desert Botanical Garden)

Redbud Collection, Royal Botanical Garden, Hamilton, Ontario

CHAENOMELES Species QUINCE *Rosaceae*
This rounded, dense shrub is grown for its showy early to mid-spring flowers, which can be red, pink, or white and either single or semidouble. Though the blossoms are profuse, they last only about 10 days. The 1½- to 3-inch leaves

Chaenomeles produces an edible fruit that is sometimes used in preserves; the true quince is produced by a small tree, *Cydonia oblonga.*

are reddish as they expand in spring; the autumn fruits can be used in preserves. Native to Eastern Asia, it has long been cultivated from the wild. Flowering quince inhabits upland woods and pastures.

BEST CONDITIONS Though flowering quince is widely adapted to soil and moisture variations, it requires full sun to flower profusely. Soil should be acid to neutral. Flower buds may be damaged during severe northern winters.

PLANTING Plant in early spring or fall; for hedge planting, space shrubs 2 1/2-4 feet apart.

PESTS/DISEASES Apple scab commonly defoliates many cultivars by late summer. Other problems include scale, leaf spot in wet climates, and chlorosis in highly alkaline soil.

PRUNING Flowering quince is best if left untrimmed and won't tolerate heavy clipping. If necessary, individual branches can be pruned back into the shrub to reduce its size, but wait until flowers have faded, or cut for early forcing inside.

PROPAGATION Propagate from softwood and semihardwood cuttings or root cuttings. *Chaenomeles* can be grown from seed, but expect variation in flower color.

USE Plant in banks or against evergreens. Taller types can be used as a hedge or for espaliering against a wall, where their spring flower show is especially dramatic. Thorny varieties make good barriers.

SPECIES *C.* x *superba* 'Cameo' has profuse double peachy-pink flowers. 'Texas Scarlet' is a relatively compact, spreading shrub with fiery-red flowers; it is reliably hardy at Dyck Arboretum of the Plains. 'Jet Trail' is a white-flowered sport to 'Texas Scarlet'.
C. speciosa, flowering quince, is taller-growing than most.
C. japonica, Japanese quince, is the hardiest of the varieties and can be found as a dwarf or full-sized shrub.

CHIONANTHUS Species FRINGE TREE *Oleaceae*

Grown as a shrub or small tree, *Chionanthus* is prized for its delicate white blooms, borne in spring on long panicles. Male plants produce slightly larger flowers, but only females bear the dark blue grapelike fruit.

BEST CONDITIONS Though *Chionanthus* will bloom in sun or shade, it does best in a bright light in a moist, fertile, slightly acid soil. *C. retusus* tolerates strongly alkaline conditions.

PLANTING Plant in spring or fall from containerized or balled-and-burlapped plants.

PESTS/DISEASES None serious, except for occasional infestations of scale, powdery mildew, or canker.

PRUNING See individual varieties.

PROPAGATION Propagate by layering, cuttings, or seed.

USE These large, striking ornamental shrubs are at their best when grown as individual specimens, or used as anchors or focal points in shrub borders.

SPECIES *C. virginicus* produces lacy, fragrant white flowers on long panicles that

CEPHALANTHUS OCCIDENTALIS (BUTTONBUSH) Mature Size: 15 feet tall. Creamy white round flowers in late summer. Full sun to partial shade;rich, moist soil. Zones 4-10.

CERCIS CANADENSIS (EASTERN REDBUD) Mature size: 20-30 feet tall, 30 feet wide. White, pink or purple pea-shaped flowers, 5-inch heart-shaped leaves turn yellow in fall. Light shade, full sun if soil is kept moist. Well-drained soil. Zones 5-9.

CERCIS CHINENSIS (CHINESE REDBUD) Mature size: 10-15 feet tall. White, pink, or purple pea-shaped flowers, 5-inch heart-shaped leaves turn yellow in fall. Light shade, full sun if soil is kept moist. Well-drained soil. Zones 6-9.

CHAENOMELES JAPONICA (JAPANESE QUINCE) Mature size: 3 feet tall, 4 feet wide. Showy pink, red, or white flowers in mid spring. Full sun, any soil type. Zone 5-8.

CHIONANTHUS VIRGINICUS (FRINGE TREE) Mature size: 25 feet tall, 20 feet wide. Delicate white blooms on long panicles, borne in spring. Sun or shade. Fertile, moist, slightly acid soil. Zones 4-8.

CLERODENDRUM TRICHOTOMUM (HARLEQUIN GLORY-BOWER) Mature size: 10 feet tall, 8 feet wide. Tubular white flowers in late summer, bright blue berries in early fall. Full sun, moist well-drained soil. Zones 5-8.

CLETHRA ALNIFOLIA (SUMMERSWEET) Mature size: 4 feet tall, 4 feet wide. White flower clusters, on spikes, in mid summer, deep green leaves turn yellow in fall. Full sun or partial shade, moist or wet acid soils, high organic content. Zones 5-9.

CLETHRA ALNIFOLIA 'ROSEA' (SUMMERSWEET) Mature size: 4 feet tall, 4 feet wide. Pink flower clusters, on spikes, in mid summer, deep green leaves turn yellow in fall. Full sun or partial shade, moist or wet acid soils, high organic content. Zones 5-9.

appear along with the leaves in late spring. Vivid yellow fall foliage is a plus. Since flowers are borne on old wood, prune to shape immediately after blooming. Grows to 25 or more feet (most specimens stay under 15 feet tall). *C. retusus,* Chinese fringe tree, a large shrub or small tree, boasts small leathery leaves, clusters of white flowers in May and June, and blue fruits, resembling blueberries, in fall. Flowers are borne on new wood, so any pruning to shape should be done in late winter or early spring. Zones 6-8; grows 15-25 feet tall, 20 feet wide.

CLERODENDRUM TRICHOTOMUM HARLEQUIN GLORY-BOWER
Verbenaceae
Native to thickets in Eastern Asia, this die-back shrub attracts butterflies and moths with its tubular white flowers in late summer and early fall. Bright blue berries are displayed against persistent reddish star-shaped calyxes in early autumn. Although many sources list this plant as being hardy only to Zone 6, a specimen has survived at the Holden Arboretum (Zone 5) for the past 60 years.
BEST CONDITIONS Prefers moist, well-drained soil and a sunny site, but is fairly adaptable. Soil pH should be slightly acid to very acid.
PLANTING Plant in early spring.
PESTS/DISEASES Pest-free.
PRUNING Rejuvenate annually in early spring.
PROPAGATION Seed sown in spring, softwood or semi-ripe cuttings, division.
USE Harlequin glory-bower is a fine addition to the shrub border.

CLETHRA Species SUMMERSWEET *Clethraceae*
Native to swamps and woodlands, *Clethra* grows slowly into a broad, oval mass. The white or light pink flower clusters, which appear on spikes in mid summer, scent the air for 4-6 weeks with an intense, spicy fragrance that attracts honeybees. Leaves are deep green, 1½-4 inches long, and turn a vivid yellow in fall.
BEST CONDITIONS Very well adapted to moist or even wet sites, *Clethra* favors full sun to half shade and an acid soil well supplemented with organic matter, peat moss, or leaf mold.
PLANTING Plant in early spring and mulch heavily.
WATER Difficult to establish, *Clethra* requires heavy watering during its first season.
PESTS/DISEASES *Clethra* is pest-free except for infestations of spider mites in dry areas.
PRUNING Though pruning is unnecessary, *Clethra* can be clipped in early spring to keep it in bounds. It can be cut back drastically, but will lose 2-3 blooming years. To keep the plant neat, pick off the messy faded racemes.
PROPAGATION Seeds can be grown in a greenhouse or cold frame, or take greenwood cuttings in summer. Short side-shoots make the best cuttings, with a sliver of the shoot from which they sprang. Divide clump-forming varieties.

Chionanthus virginicus, a close relative of the lilac, blooms around the same time; its leaves appear very late in the spring.

Clethra alnifolia 'Rosea' blossom.

USE Plant *Clethra* waterside or at the edge of woodlands, or use it to pleasant effect in mixed beds.

SPECIES *C. alnifolia,* summersweet, is a native of eastern North America in swamps and wet woods, mostly near the coast. It sports white flowers; the cultivar 'Rosea' has clear pink buds that open to white flowers tinged with pink.'Hummingbird', which was found at Callaway Gardens in Pine Mountain, Georgia, grows to 4 feet, half the size of the species.

C. barbinervis, Japanese clethra, is an upright grower reaching 16-20 feet at maturity. It blooms in July with nodding white flower clusters having little fragrance. Its bark is exquisite, with patches of cinnamon brown, white, and tan. It is less likely to get spider mites in dry areas; at the Morris Arboretum, it has proven to be less tolerant of dry soil than *C. alnifolia.*

C. acuminata, cinnamon clethra, native to the southern Appalachian region, grows 12-18 feet tall and has scentless white flowers in mid summer.

COMPTONIA PEREGRINA SWEET FERN *Myricaceae*

This low, deciduous shrub spreads by shoots sent up by the roots. Its major attribute is its graceful ferny foliage, which exudes a baylike fragrance, especially intense in the early morning when the sun strikes the dew-covered leaves. In early spring, male catkins droop from the branches, followed by inconspicuous female flowers that resemble tiny pinecones. An excellent choice for sunny sites where the soil is poor or has recently been disturbed. Native to eastern North America in dry, often barren, sandy soil.

BEST CONDITIONS Growing well in full sun to partial shade, this shrub prefers an acid pH and a sandy, well-drained soil, but will thrive as well in moist, peaty soils. In Pennsylvania and New Jersey, *Comptonia* is a pioneer species in dry areas along road edges. It prefers to grow in areas where there is little competition for such resources as water and light.

PLANTING Plant container stock in spring or fall; for fall plantings, perform a severe pruning late in the first winter; for spring plantings, renew the following year. Young plants transplant easily; those established for more than 2 years do not.

PESTS/DISEASES None serious.

WATER Water generously during establishment and drought.

PRUNING See above (Planting); to maintain vigor of mature plants, renewal pruning can be performed in late winter or early spring.

PROPAGATION Sow seeds in containers; keep rootball moist when transplanting.

USE A naturalizing shrub border, this low grower makes a fine ground cover, especially on banks. It looks at home in a wild or naturalistic setting and is a good companion for ericaceous plants. Leaves can be used to brew sweet-fern tea.

CORNUS Species DOGWOOD *Cornaceae*

Unlike the familiar tree of the same name, the shrub known as dogwood bears clusters of small creamy-white flowers in spring and white fruits in fall;

in winter, the upright twigs of many varieties are a bright red or yellow.

BEST CONDITIONS Dogwood will thrive in full sun or partial shade (though too much shade will decrease flowering and increase legginess) in any good acidic to neutral garden soil of abundant moisture that has been enriched with organic matter. Although native to wet soils, some of these adaptable shrubs can tolerate dry conditions quite well.

PLANTING Plant in spring or fall. Dogwood is best planted in a mulched bed by a water feature, drive, or path. Plant in a raised bed if the site is excessively wet. Leave a grass-free area around the base.

WATER During periods of drought, water deeply every 7-10 days. At the Morris Arboretum, horticulturists find that redtwig dogwoods perform well during periods of drought with little or no watering.

FERTILIZER Apply a complete fertilizer in early spring or late winter following renewal pruning.

PESTS/DISEASES Prone to many, including scale insects, leaf miners, crown canker, fungus flower, leaf and twig blights, leaf spots, and powdery mildew. To avoid midges, prune in summer.

PRUNING Every 7-10 years, renew in late winter or early spring when stems develop gray bark. At the Morris Arboretum, gardeners remove ⅕-¼ of the oldest stems each year, and the plant produces vigorous shoots every year.

PROPAGATION Take hardwood cuttings, or propagate by layering or grafting.

USE A fine specimen and a pleasing addition to the shrub border, dogwood is a good foil for hollies, viburnums, and bald cypress. It reflects well, and so is often planted near water. These excellent, low-maintenance plants are often used in office or industrial parks.

SPECIES *C. alba* 'Argenteo Marginata' bears tiny white flowers in summer and has silver-edged foliage. It is native to northeastern Asia. 'Coral Beauty' has bright red twigs in winter

C. racemosa, gray dogwood, native to eastern North America, is the species most adaptable to dry sites. It grows to 12 feet at maturity (20 years) and produces clusters of small flowers in late spring, followed by white fruit that never lasts until fall because it is a favorite of every songbird in the East. Zones 3-8.

C. sericea, redtwig dogwood, is native to North America and is found on streambanks and in wet woods. Its variety 'Flaviramea' (yellowtwig dogwood) has yellow twigs; susceptible to canker. 'Cardinal' has brilliant red twigs in winter. 'Silver & Gold', a sport of *C. sericea,* offers variegated foliage, edged in creamy white, and yellow-twigged stems in winter. (Scott Arboretum)

C. mas, cornelian cherry, is native to central and southern Europe and western Asia where it grows on windy, open sites. Typically a large shrub or small tree, it grows to 10-20 feet tall and tolerates dry and hot conditions. In March it is covered with clusters of bright yellow flowers.

C. drummondii, a thicket-forming native shrub averaging 6 feet in height, has terminal clusters of small white flowers in early summer. It is tolerant of full sun and dry soil. (Dyck Arboretum of the Plains)

Cornus species offer much to the gardener wishing to extend his or her garden into four seasons. *C. sericea* produces white berries in late summer, and red or yellow twigs that stand out strikingly against snow.

The pea-shaped blossoms of *C. pauci-flora* are among the first signs of spring.

CORYLOPSIS Species WINTER HAZEL *Hamamelidaceae*

Delicate and refined, winter hazel has smooth gray branches that form a wide-spreading or pyramidal mound. The green to bluish-green foliage can turn yellow in fall. Without dispute, the shrub's most endearing characteristic is its tendency to bloom when the rest of the garden is still in its winter sleep. Though not otherwise showy, the abundant yellow or greenish-yellow flower tassels have a cheering effect when peeking out from beneath a dusting of snow. In southeastern Pennsylvania, the northern edge of its hardiness zone, winter hazel blooms in early to mid April, unless there is snow. Native to the mountains of eastern Asia and the Himalayas in woodlands and thickets, most are hardy in Zones 6-8.

BEST CONDITIONS Growing well in part shade or full sun, winter hazel prefers a light, somewhat sandy acid soil.

PLANTING If possible, plant in a site that provides shelter from wind–against a wall or a bank of evergreens, for example. Space 16 feet or more apart; do not crowd. Supplement heavy soils with peat moss or leaf mold.

WATER In dry weather, water deeply every 7-10 days.

PESTS/DISEASES None serious.

PRUNING If espaliering, prune thinly to shape; otherwise, no pruning is necessary. In northern climates, remove dead branch ends in early spring. At the Morris Arboretum, horticulturists find that many of the larger species (*C. spicata, C. sinensis)* lose vigor as branches age; branches are gradually removed on a 5-year schedule to maintain shrub quality.

PROPAGATION Softwood cuttings, taken in summer, root easily; transplant the following spring. To propagate from seed, collect capsules in fall in a paper bag (to keep the seed from flying away), then sow/stratify.

USE Because of its quiet, less strident spring color, winter hazel is the perfect companion for spring-flowering bulbs, such as *Crocus tomasinianus,* or *Rhododendron mucronulatum*. The flowers are best displayed where the sun will shine on them, but the background should be dark, perhaps the shade cast by conifers.

SPECIES *C. pauciflora* has the shortest and fewest-flowered racemes, but bears them in great abundance on a spreading (6-foot) shrub. It is the finest-textured and most refined variety.

C. glabrescens has delicate yellow flowers; its foliage has a blue-green effect.

C. spicata has 1- to 2-inch flower racemes; shrub is 6 feet tall at maturity. (Scott Arboretum)

C. 'Winterthur' is a hybrid between *C. spicata* and *C. pauciflora*; its foliage and branching are a bit more coarse than *C. pauciflora*, but finer than *C. spicata*. Its flowers are borne on racemes that are longer than *C. spicata.* New from Winterthur Museum and Gardens.

CORYLUS AVELLANA 'CONTORTA' CORKSCREW HAZEL, HARRY LAUDER'S WALKING STICK *Betulaceae*

This nonfruiting cultivar of the European filbert was selected from an English

COMPTONIA PEREGRINA (SWEET FERN) Mature size: 2-4 feet tall and wide. Graceful ferny foliage with baylike fragrance. Full sun to partial shade, sandy, well-drained soil, adaptable to other types. Zones 4-7.

CORNUS SERICEA 'FLAVIRAMEA' (YELLOWTWIG DOGWOOD) Mature size: 12 feet tall, 15 feet wide. Small white flowers, yellow stems. Full sun or partial shade, rich soil. Zones 3-7.

CORNUS MAS (CORNELIAN CHERRY) Mature size: 20 feet tall and wide. Clusters of bright yellow flowers in early spring, shiny green leaves turn reddish-orange in fall. Best in sun, tolerates some shade. Zones 5-7.

CORYLOPSIS PAUCIFLORA (WINTER HAZEL) Mature size: 6-8 feet tall, 4 feet wide. Abundant yellow flowers on short racemes. Full sun or partial shade, light soil. Zones 6-8.

'Royal Purple' smokebush is an integral part of an exquisite arrangement of colorful shrubs and perennials at The New York Botanical Garden. Its deep color contrasts beautifully with silver gray artemisia, bright lythrum, and white clary sage.

hedgerow for its curiously curled and twisted stems—highly prized by floral designers for their sculptural quality. In early spring, Harry Lauder's walking stick produces long, bright yellow catkins, transforming its contorted appearance. The large twisted leaves, which some gardeners have unkindly compared to wilted cabbage, mask the stems completely in summer. Native to Europe, where it is found in woodlands and ravines especially in association with ash *(Fraxinus excelsior)* and maple *(Acer campestre)*.

BEST CONDITIONS Grow in full sun, in a well-drained, acid to neutral soil.

PLANTING Both container-grown and balled-and-burlapped plants can be planted in early spring.

PESTS/DISEASES None serious. Japanese beetles sometimes attack the plant, but it usually recovers.

PRUNING Suckers from the understock must be removed regularly. A judicious pruning of the crown just as the leaves emerge will help retain this shrub's unique character.

PROPAGATION Almost always accomplished by grafting species understock, a task best left to a professional propagator.

USE This shrub is most often used as a specimen pruned to resemble a small tree and underplanted with ground covers or annuals. It is definitely at its best during the dormant season, especially when silhouetted against snow.

SPECIES *C. americana* is a deeply branched thicket-forming shrub that grows 14-16 feet tall. It is loved by wildlife, particularly turkeys and squirrels. *C. cornuta*, beaked filbert, grows 6-8 feet tall, and is native to eastern North America, as is *C. americana*.

COTINUS COGGYGRIA 'ROYAL PURPLE' 'ROYAL PURPLE'
SMOKEBUSH *Anacardiaceae*

A large upright shrub whose form is more compact than most of the smokebushes, 'Royal Purple' has deep purple foliage and small yellowish flowers that come and go unnoticed in June. The "smoke" in its common name is derived from the pink, haired flower stalks that fade and often persist until early autumn. It is native from southern Europe to central China on dry banks, rocks, and open woods in alkaline soil.

BEST CONDITIONS Plant in full sun in any well-drained garden soil; avoid an overly wet environment.

PLANTING 'Royal Purple' transplants easily; plant anytime in season from container.

PESTS/DISEASES None serious.

PRUNING A hard cutting-back each spring will produce vigorous new growth, but 'Royal Purple' requires nothing more than routine removal of the oldest stems to maintain vigor.

PROPAGATION Softwood cuttings, taken in early summer and treated with IBA, root easily; take care, however, not to disturb the rooted cuttings or plant them out until the following spring.

USE With its deep maroon foliage, this is an effective accent plant for the

CORYLUS AVELLANA 'CONTORTA' (CORKSCREW HAZEL, HARRY LAUDER'S WALKING STICK) Mature size: 10-20 feet tall, 15 feet wide. Twisted, curled stems, long bright yellow catkins in early spring. Full sun, well-drained soil. Zones 3-8.

COTINUS COGGYGRIA 'ROYAL PURPLE' ('ROYAL PURPLE' SMOKEBUSH) Mature size: 15 feet tall, 12 feet wide. Compact upright shrub with deep purple foliage. Full sun, any well-drained soil. Zones 5-8.

COTONEASTER DAMMERI 'CORAL BEAUTY' (BEARBERRY COTONEASTER) Mature size: 2 feet tall, 6 feet wide. Wide-spreading shrub with small white flowers followed by red fruit. Full sun or partial shade, any soil. Zones 6-9.

COTONEASTER GLAUCOPHYLLUS (BRIGHTBEAD COTONEASTER) Mature size: 3 feet tall, 4 feet wide. Shiny small dark-green leaves turn reddish purple in fall; bright red berries. Full sun, any well-drained soil. Zones 6-8.

Cotoneaster apiculatus, one of several prostrate species of this genus, which also includes many upright shrubs.

shrub border; the "smokey" flower stalks add welcome late-summer interest. It provides quality foliage and color for dry areas.

SPECIES *C. obovatus,* American smoketree, an outstanding but little-used species, is native to the southeastern United States; it reaches 20-30 feet in height and can become a full-sized tree if not pruned. It has attractive foliage that develops striking shades of yellow, salmon and orange. (Scott)

COTONEASTER Species COTONEASTER *Rosaceae*

These fine-textured spring bloomers, some of them evergreen, bear small white or pinkish flowers that give way to handsome black or red berries in the fall. Native from the mountains of central China to the Himalayas in thickets and open rocky ground. Cotoneaster comes in a wide range of varieties, including ground covers and tall shrubs.

BEST CONDITIONS Adaptable to almost any garden soil, cotoneaster does well in either full sun or partial shade.

PLANTING Since this is usually grown and sold in containers it can be planted anytime; transplant in the garden in early spring.

PESTS/DISEASES Fire blight, aphids, and mites in some varieties.

PRUNING A spring tidying of winter-damaged tips is usually necessary in the North.

PROPAGATION Softwood cuttings, taken in early summer and treated with IBA in talc, root easily.

USE See individual varieties.

SPECIES *C. dammeri,* bearberry cotoneaster, with its cultivar 'Coral Beauty', is among the most popular of the cotoneasters. It is a wide-spreading shrub that throws off small white flowers in late May, followed by coral-red persistent fruit. The lustrous, dark green leaves are evergreen in the South. Prostrate and supple when young, 'Coral Beauty' mounds in on itself with age, as the arching branches become stiff and interwoven; it makes an excellent ground cover, particularly useful on slopes or draped over low walls. Space 3-5 feet apart. Cut back severely every 6-8 years. Mature size: 2 feet tall, 6 feet wide. Zones 6-9.

C. horizontalis, rockspray cotoneaster, has small dark green lustrous leaves that turn reddish-purple in autumn. The branchlets are borne in a fishbone pattern. The small pink flowers in late May and early June are followed by bright red fruit that persists into October. Its architectural quality makes it an exceedingly useful and versatile shrub. Ethan Johnson of the Holden Arboretum recommends backing it with purple sand cherry and pagoda dogwood and fronting it with low-growing junipers for a wonderful, year-round informal effect. Deciduous in the North but evergreen elsewhere. Mature size: 3 feet tall, 4 feet wide. Zones 5-8.

C. apiculatus, cranberry cotoneaster, is similar to rockspray cotoneaster but has cascading branchlets that go every which way. This species is more tolerant of mid-continental extremes of soil and climate than most.

C. glaucophyllus, brightbead or gray cotoneaster, is similar to *C. horizontalis,* but

CYRILLA RACEMIFLORA (SWAMP CYRILLA) Mature size: 15 feet tall and wide. Produces slender racemes of delicate, fragrant white flowers. Full sun to heavy shade, well-drained, slightly acid, organic soil. Zones 6-10.

CYTISUS SCOPARIUS (SCOTCH BROOM) Mature size: 5 feet tall, 7 feet wide. Showy bright yellow flowers in early June. Full sun, any soil type, including sandy, dry, or infertile. Zones 5-8.

DAPHNE X BURKWOODII 'CAROL MACKIE' Mature size: 3 feet tall, 4 feet wide. Abundant small pinkish flowers, dark green leaves banded in creamy white. Full sun to partial shade, well-drained soil high in organic matter. Zones 4-8.

DEUTZIA GRACILIS 'NIKKO' Mature size: 2-4 feet tall. Small white flower, foliage turns deep burgundy in fall, low compact habit. Tolerates very dry soil, partial shade. Zones 5-8.

its foliage is gray to blue-green. A welcome alternate to the horizontal junipers, it boasts vivid berries in winter and is highly tolerant of drought.

CYRILLA RACEMIFLORA SWAMP CYRILLA, LEATHERWOOD

Cyrillaceae

In its natural state, swamp cyrilla's habit is large and spreading, but creative pruning can transform it into a small tree whose broad, twisting branches add an architectural note to the landscape. In summer, it produces slender racemes of delicate, fragrant flowers. The glossy dark green leaves turn orange and red in autumn and may be quite persistent, especially in the South.

BEST CONDITIONS Though swamp cyrilla is particular about its growing medium—preferring a well-drained, slightly acid, organic soil—it can be grown under almost any light conditions, from full sun to quite heavy shade.

PLANTING Spring or fall.

PRUNING Pruning is seldom required, except when using as a small tree, and then only to remove suckers and lower branches.

PROPAGATION Softwood cuttings, taken in summer and treated with IBA, root easily. Sow seed in the autumn when ripe.

USE A natural for informal designs—especially those featuring native plants—swamp cyrilla is the perfect border shrub for larger gardens. In smaller landscapes, try pruning it to tree form.

CYTISUS SCOPARIUS SCOTCH BROOM *Fabaceae*

This broad, rounded deciduous shrub sports erect, slender bright green stems with small trifoliolate leaves of a similar shade. Showy bright yellow flowers are borne abundantly along the stems in early June. Scotch broom is native to Europe in heaths and in open woods.

BEST CONDITIONS Scotch broom needs full sun, but is less picky about soil and will tolerate dry, sandy, infertile soil quite well.

PLANTING Plant container stock in spring or fall.

PESTS/DISEASES Leaf spot or blight; this is a short-lived shrub.

PRUNING To keep the plant tidy, prune regularly after flowering.

PROPAGATION From cuttings taken in summer, or from seed.

USE Because of its large size and tendency to become ratty with age, ordinary scotch broom is a difficult plant to integrate in home gardens. Its primary use, owing to its ability to thrive and colonize on even the poorest of soils, is as a soil stabilizer along highways.

SPECIES *C.* x *beanii* 'Golden Carpet' grows no more than 3 feet tall. The most reliably hardy broom for northern gardens, it dependably produces a profusion of yellow spring blooms as far north as Ottawa, Canada.

DAPHNE Species BURKWOOD DAPHNE *Thymelaeaceae*

Some of the most beautiful of the garden plants, these dense, rounded shrubs produce highly fragrant, white, pink, or lilac blossoms in dense terminal clusters. Flowers appear in late May and early June, before the lanceolate leaves have fully unfolded. The individual tubular flowers are star-shaped, ½ inch in diameter, and have a waxy, almost artificial appearance. Foliage remains handsome throughout the growing season, and some varieties are evergreen. The small red fruit that appears in early summer is poisonous.

BEST CONDITIONS Choose a site in full sun to half shade, and a well-drained soil high in organic matter. Some winter protection is desirable, as the weight of snow and ice can split the rather brittle branches. Soil pH should be neutral.

PLANTING Plant in early spring or fall; fall plantings thrive at Holden Arboretum. Container plants are best for transplants. It can be slow to establish; expect occasional failure. Very difficult to transplant once established.

PRUNING Does not respond well to heavy pruning.

PROPAGATION Take softwood cuttings in early summer and treat with IBA.

USE This is a superb accent plant, particularly effective when combined with low-growing junipers and spring-flowering bulbs near a building, or backed by yews in a shrub border.

SPECIES *D.* x *burkwoodii* 'Carol Mackie' is an outstanding cultivar, with green-and-white-striped foliage. 'Somerset' is a vigorous green-leaved form with deeper, rosy-pink flowers.

D. caucasia offers delightfully fragrant white flowers over May and June and sporadically thereafter until frost. It reaches 4 feet in height and does best in sun and well-drained soil.

D. cneorum, rose daphne, is an excellent rock-garden plant, forming an 8- to 12-inch-tall spreading ground cover and producing profuse rosy-pink flowers in mid spring. Zones 4-7.

D. odora, winter daphne, is the most fragrant of the daphnes and has small rosy-purple flowers. It is a rounded evergreen that grows to 6 feet tall and wide at maturity. It requires partial shade and is hardy in Zones 7-8.

Daphne x *burkwoodii* 'Somerset' is a particularly prolific bearer of rosy pink flowers.

DEUTZIA GRACILIS SLENDER DEUTZIA *Saxifragaceae*

The most widely cultivated of all the deutzias, *gracilis* derives its name from its graceful, slender stems—a recommendation, certainly, but this deutzia is most beloved for the bounty of pure-white flowers, borne in profuse clusters, that appear just before the leaves in mid spring.

BEST CONDITIONS Deutzia performs well in sun or partial shade (some afternoon shade will prolong the blooming period) in well-drained, moist, relatively fertile and humus-rich acid soil. For most abundant flowering, grow in full sun.

PLANTING Easily transplanted, *Deutzia gracilis* can be planted virtually anytime, though spring is preferable. Space 2-2½ feet apart for hedging.

PESTS/DISEASES None serious.

PRUNING Thin drastically, removing old wood and shortening stems immediately after flowering. Cut off winter-killed stems in early spring.

PROPAGATION Softwood cuttings, taken as the new growth hardens (about the first of June at the Morris Arboretum) root easily. Deutzia can also be propagated by layering, hardwood cuttings, divisions, and seed.

USE Deutzia is often used for banks, borders, or hedges. To show it off to best effect, group it in front of evergreens.

CULTIVAR *D. gracilis* 'Nikko', native to Japan, is tolerant of both very dry soil

ELAEAGNUS PUNGENS 'FRUITLANDII' (THORNY ELEAGNUS) Mature size: 12-15 feet. Fast-growing hedge plant with silvery flowers in mid autumn. Tolerates most soil types, seaside conditions, sun to partial shade. Zones 7-10.

ENKIANTHUS COMPANULATUS 'SHOWY LANTERN' (REDVEIN ENKIANTHUS) Mature size 12-15 feet. Upright shrub with pink flowers, red foliage in fall. Full sun to partial shade. Well-drained peaty soil, rich in organic matter. Zones 5-9.

ERICA CARNEA 'SPRINGWOOD PINK' (HEATH) Mature size: 6-8 inches tall. Spreading ground cover with pink flowers in winter and early spring. Full sun, well-drained, relatively infertile soil. Zones 5-8.

EUONYMUS ALATA 'COMPACTUS' (BURNING BUSH) Mature size: 8 feet tall. Grown for foliage, which turns brilliant scarlet or pink in autumn. Needs full sun for best color, relatively moist well-drained soil. Zones 4-8.

and partial shade. In May it arrays itself with small white flowers. Fall foliage is a deep burgundy. With its low, compact habit and slender erect branches, this is an excellent ground cover. 'Nikko' is very easy to propagate from cuttings. The plant benefits from some afternoon shade in hotter climates.

ELAEAGNUS ELAEAGNUS *Elaegnaceae*

The genus *Elaeagnus* contains both deciduous and evergreen shrubs, prized mainly for their decorative, often edible fruit and handsome foliage.

BEST CONDITIONS Tolerant of wind, heat, and drought, elaeagnus does well in full sun to partial shade, in virtually any garden soil. Indeed, its ability to fix nitrogen from the atmosphere allows it to positively thrive even in poor soils.

PLANTING Spring or fall.

PRUNING To tame its tendency toward legginess, prune heavily once a year in mid summer.

PROPAGATION Soft- and hardwood cuttings root easily, as do root root cuttings, taken in spring. Elaeagnus can also be propagated by layering; seeds must be stratified before sowing.

USE A good shrub for difficult situations, most varieties make good hedges.

SPECIES *E. pungens,* thorny elaeagnus, is a longtime favorite of southern gardeners, valued for its gardenialike fragrance. Dense and thorny, it makes an excellent windbreak and a nearly impenetrable hedge.

E. umbellata, autumn elaeangus, is a spreading shrub with fragrant yellow-white spring flowers and silvery fall berries that eventually turn red.

ENKIANTHUS ENKIANTHUS *Ericaceae*

This neat, deciduous shrub has fine-textured foliage carried on layered, whorled branches and bears clusters of white, pink-edged, or red bell-shaped flowers in mid to late spring.

BEST CONDITIONS Provide full sun or partial shade (shade in hot climates) and well-drained, peaty soil, moist but not wet, rich in organic matter. Soil pH should be moderately acid–6.0 and below.

PLANTING Plant in spring or fall and apply an organic mulch, ½-1 inch thick; transplant with care.

PEST/DISEASES Infrequently suffers from mites.

PRUNING Enkianthus rarely requires pruning, though overgrown specimens can be rejuvenated.

PROPAGATION Enkianthus roots easily from cuttings taken in late May and June; do not transplant until the following spring. For best results, provide extended lighting to rooting cuttings.

USE Enkianthus lends itself to massing, plantings near buildings, or incorporation into the shrub border. It blends well with other ericaceous plants and evergreens, especially rhododendron.

SPECIES *E. campanulatus,* redvein enkianthus, native to the mountains of Japan, is an upright shrub with a rich, layered effect, sometimes compared to a pagoda. *E. perulatus,* white enkianthus, also a native of Japan, produces showers of pure white flowers in spring, and brilliant red fall foliage; a stunning shrub.

Enkianthus' horizontal branches can be espaliered against a wall or trellis. See page 203 for more information about how to create an espalier.

plant selector

Above: Euonymus fortunei, which is often grown as a vine (see vines section), has a very different habit from E. alatus

ERICA Species HEATH *Ericaceae*

Mostly evergreen, the heaths are compact, low-growing, often prostrate shrubs with needlelike foliage and dainty flowers produced profusely in spring and summer.

BEST CONDITIONS Heaths require full sun for at least ⅔ of the day, along with very well-drained, relatively infertile soil—half sand (if possible, volcanic) and half peat moss is best. Soil pH should be acidic—6.0 or less. Avoid drought and clay soil, and protect from winter sun and wind in the North. In continental climates, cover with evergreen boughs from New Year's through mid winter.

PLANTING The best times to plant are early spring and early to mid autumn. Before planting, clear out any perennial weeds—heaths are shallow-rooted, and cultivating the surrounding soil can do serious damage. Dig some well-rotted manure, leaf mold, or compost into the planting hole, and mulch well on the surface. If you have clay soil, don't dig; create a raised bed of one part sand and one part peat.

WATER Water during establishment.

WEEDING Do not cultivate the surrounding soil; remove any weeds by hand.

PESTS/DISEASES Heaths are subject to *Phytophthora cinnamomi,* a soil-borne fungus that thrives in wet conditions and usually kills the plant. It is best avoided by ensuring good drainage.

PRUNING Trim after flowering to prevent plants from becoming straggly. Don't cut back into the old wood unless you have *E. arborea* or *E. vagans.*

PROPAGATION Take cuttings of young wood; provide proper ventilation.

USE Heaths make fine ground covers, especially for wind-swept sites (but see BEST CONDITIONS above). A natural choice for the rock garden, they pair perfectly with slow-growing dwarf conifers and low ericaceous shrubs like *Vaccinium vitis-idaea* and dwarf rhododendrons and azaleas.

SPECIES *E. carnea (E. herbacea)*, spring heath, is a native to the Mediterranean and the mountains of central Europe, growing in pastures, rocky slopes, and the edges of pine woods. This species tolerates shade, salt, and limy soil. 'Springwood Pink' is 6-8 inches tall, vigorous, and has shell-pink flowers in winter/early spring. 'Springwood White' is 8 inches tall, vigorous, and has white flowers in winter/early spring. 'Pink Spangles', a strong grower, is 9-12 inches tall, with two-tone pink flowers in winter and early spring.

EUONYMUS ALATUS BURNING BUSH *Celastraceae*

(See vines section for *E. fortunei*)

E. alatus, also called winged euonymus, is native to northeastern Asia in woods and thickets in lowlands and mountains. It has brilliant scarlet or pink foliage in autumn; color is best in a sunny spot. Though immune to insect pests, burning bush is a favorite with deer and mice. An excellent plant in the landscape, it has naturalized in eastern woodlands in the past years. Grown for its foliage, which is smooth and oppositely borne, the deciduous burning bush has brilliant fall color, showy red-orange fruit, and insignificant flowers. At Chicago Botanic Garden, this plant is used in the Sensory Garden, where

EXOCHORDA X MACRANTHA 'THE BRIDE' (PEARLBUSH) Mature size: 5 feet tall, 5 feet wide. Long arching branches with pearlescent flower buds. Full sun or partial shade, any well-drained soil. Zones 5-8.

FORSYTHIA X INTERMEDIA 'ARNOLD DWARF' (FORSYTHIA) Low-growing drought-resistant shrub with pale yellow flowers. Full sun or light shade, any soil (deep loam is best).

FORSYTHIA 'NORTHERN SUN' Mature size: 10 feet tall, 10 feet wide. Deep yellow flowers on long, arching branches. Full sun or light shade, any soil (deep loam is best). Zones 5-8.

FORSYTHIA 'MEADLOWLARK' Mature size: 10 feet tall, 10 feet wide. Vigorous, cold-hardy variety, with deep-yellow flowers. Full sun or light shade, any soil, drought-tolerant (deep loam is best). Zones 4-8.

Forsythia is particularly attractive in mass plantings.

the visually impaired can appreciate its intense color. The corky wings on the twigs add winter interest.

BEST CONDITIONS *E. alatus* will do well in full sun to ¾ shade and thrives in relatively moist, well-drained acid to alkaline soil. Unexpected early frost can kill this shrub.

PLANTING Plant in spring or fall. Easy to transplant. For hedging, space 2-3 feet apart. Cover with a thin (1-2-inch) layer of organic mulch.

PESTS/DISEASES Pest-free.

PRUNING Pruning is not only unnecessary, but will destroy this shrub's pleasing natural shape if not done properly.

PROPAGATION Take semihardwood cuttings or sow seeds.

USE Tall varieties work well at the back of the shrub border. Use burning bush for hedging, foundation planting, or as a specimen; excellent when planted near water.

VARIETIES *E. alatus* 'Compacta' is full-sized, but the corky wings on the branchlets are not as pronounced, giving the plant a finer texture in winter.

EXOCHORDA X MACRANTHA PEARLBUSH *Rosaceae*

Pearlbush's common name is derived from the pearlescent expanding flower buds that develop along the previous season's growth in May. A hybrid of species native to the mountains of Asia it has long, graceful, arching branches and a rounded outline.

BEST CONDITIONS Choose a site in sun or partial shade in any well-drained garden soil. The pH should be acid to alkaline.

PLANTING Transplants easily in spring or fall.

PESTS/DISEASES None serious.

PRUNING Prune to shape immediately after flowering.

PROPAGATION Softwood cuttings, taken in summer, root easily.

USE A real attention-getter when in bloom, this is a fine backdrop during the rest of the season. Plant it where it can be easily admired in May.

CULTIVAR 'The Bride' has a dense, compact habit and grows to 6 feet tall.

FORSYTHIA Species FORSYTHIA *Oleaceae*

Vitually synonymous with spring, forsythia is one of the first shrubs to bloom; in the South, it actually beats the spring by a month, throwing off its abundant yellow flowers in February. For even earlier bloom, forsythia is extremely easy to force. Habit is upright and spreading, with arching branches. The attractive green leaves are held well into fall and sometimes turn maroon. Numerous cultivars are available, all in some shade of yellow. Most garden varieties are descended from eastern Asia species found in thickets or on moors and cliffs.

BEST CONDITIONS Plant in full sun or light shade, in any soil (though deep fertile loam is best); flower buds die in temperatures below -10° F. with most species.

PLANTING Plant in spring or fall, leaving plenty of room to spread. For hedging, plant 2 feet apart.

WATER Forsythia is one of the first shrubs to show drought stress; water well during dry periods.

FERTILIZER Fertilize well and often.

PESTS/DISEASES Though forsythia is very resistant to most pests and diseases, it is sometimes susceptible to stem gall, leaf spots, and nematodes.

PROPAGATION While some forms of forsythia (including dwarf forms) require more care during propagation, most can be easily propagated by harvesting stems that are at least pencil-thick and 2 feet long during autumn and planting them where desired. By spring, these stems will develop roots and will flower in 1-2 years.

PRUNING Almost frighteningly vigorous, forsythia benefits from frequent pruning; for best results, cut off ⅓ of the oldest canes at ground level immediately after flowering, or prune to the ground in late winter.

USE A good city plant, forsythia is handsome when massed against evergreens and makes a fine border background for informal gardens. Massed plantings of forsythia are particularly attractive when viewed from a distance.

SPECIES *F. mandshurica* 'Vermont Sun' is an early blooomer, growing 4-5 feet

FORCING BRANCHES

You don't have to wait until your forsythia decides that it is time to bloom. You can hasten springtime by several weeks by cutting branches and "forcing" them indoors. Choose branches with abundant flower buds (the flower buds are usually plumper and less pointy than the leaf buds). Cut 1- to 2-foot lengths; if you can, soak them in the bathtub or a tub of warm water overnight or for several hours (they will probably bloom even if they are not soaked). Then place them on a sunny windowsill in containers of lukewarm (but not hot) water. Don't give up on them if they don't burst into bloom right away; it can take up to 4 weeks, but you will usually be successful. Other shrubs that can be forced include *Cornus mas, Chaenomeles,* magnolia, winter hazel, and witch-hazel.

Fothergilla is prized as much for its striking fall color as for its creamy white flowers.

tall and hardy to -25° F. 'Meadowlark' is vigorous, drought-tolerant, and hardy to -35° F.—the best cultivar for northern climates. 'New Hampshire Gold' is hardy to -35° F. 'Northern Sun' is hardy to -30° F. Other species are not hardy in Chicago.

F. x *intermedia* 'Arnold Dwarf' is drought-tolerant, pest-resistant, and low growing, often used effectively as a ground cover. Its deep foliage is more impressive than its pale yellow flowers. 'Spectabilis', a spreading heavy bloomer, grows 10 feet tall; Zones 5-8.

F. 'Spring Glory' has flowers of a slightly paler yellow than most.

F. suspensa var *sieboldii,* weeping forsythia, will drape its long branches straight down for 20 feet or more if planted at the top of a wall.

F. viridissima 'Bronxensis', Bronx forsythia, is a dwarf variety, sometimes only 1 foot tall, that was originated in The New York Botanical Garden.

FOTHERGILLA Species FOTHERGILLA *Hamamelidaceae*

The fragrant creamy-white flowers of this deciduous shrub are borne in mid spring and expand with the dark green foliage, which turns an arresting yellow, orange, and red in the fall. Neat and rounded in habit, fothergilla tends to form clumps. Native to the southeastern U.S.

BEST CONDITIONS Easy to care for and not at all particular as to soil, fothergilla requires an acid soil pH of 6.0 or below and full sun to half shade (more sun in the North). It performs well in Chicago in soil with pH up to 7.8.

PLANTING Plant in spring or fall, adding organic matter to the soil before planting and mulching with an additional 1-2 inches of organic matter.

WATER Keep moist during dry periods.

PESTS/DISEASES Pest-free; no serious diseases. Rabbits sometimes feed on stems in winter.

PRUNING Unnecessary.

PROPAGATION Softwood cuttings, taken is summer, root easily. As with many shrubs in the related witch-hazel family, cuttings should not be disturbed following rooting. Sow seeds in late summer. Pick seed capsules before seeds are ejected and store in a paper bag.

USE An easygoing plant, fothergilla blends nicely with most other shrubs and so is well-suited to the shrub border.

SPECIES *F. gardenii* has broad, wedge-shaped leaves and white flowers. Mature size: a dwarf variety, it grows to only 3-4 feet. Native to the coastal plains in sandy swamps. 'Blue Mist', a Morris Arboretum introduction, is noted for its blue-green leaves; at maturity, it reaches 3 feet in height.

F. major matures to a height of 7-10 feet. Native to Blue Ridge and Appalachian Mountains in rich moist woods.

GAYLUSSACIA Species HUCKLEBERRY *Ericaceae*

Named for the French chemist Louis Gay-Lussac, this is a large group of deciduous and evergreen shrubs, all spreading by runners, and many having a tendency to form colonies. Berries are black or blue.

BEST CONDITIONS Grow in partial shade in a sandy or peaty acid soil—huckleberry will die in soil that is too alkaline.

PLANTING Spring or fall.

FERTILIZER Huckleberry requires a permanent mulch of peat, compost, or other organic material.

PESTS/DISEASES None serious.

PRUNING Prune in late winter or early spring to shape.

PROPAGATION Sow seeds in peat moss, or propagate by division.

SPECIES *G. brachycera,* box huckleberry, is a neat evergreen creeper with leathery, glossy green, fine-toothed leaves, well-suited to rock gardens, sunny borders, and native or naturalistic gardens. Zones 6-7.

G. baccata is a spreading deciduous plant growing to 3 feet high. It bears modest white urn-shaped flowers, rimmed with pink, carried on racemes. Plant in a sunny spot; drought-tolerant. Zones 3-7.

G. dumosa, dwarf huckleberry, is a deciduous plant growing to 1 1/2 feet high, especially useful in wet-sandy or peaty soils. Zones 6-9.

GENISTA PILOSA GENISTA *Fabaceae*

This low, spreading evergreen shrub forms a dense undulating mound of arching gray-green stems and small bright green leaves. In May it produces a blanket of golden-yellow flowers that brightens the garden for a full month. *G. pilosa* is native to Europe, found on semiarid stony hillsides, heaths, and thickets.

BEST CONDITIONS Genista needs full sun and very well-drained soil. Chris Graham of Ontario's Royal Botanical Garden has had significant difficulty finding an appropriate site for this plant in Hamilton and believes that dependable snowcover would be an advantage in gardens at the northern limit of hardiness.

PLANTING Container-grown specimens can be planted anytime throughout the growing season.

PESTS/DISEASES None serious.

PRUNING Genista rarely requires pruning.

PROPAGATION Softwood cuttings, taken in summer, root easily.

USE An excellent plant for the smaller garden, genista can be used in foundation plantings and rock gardens or as a ground cover. In colder areas, try growing it in pots on the patio or balcony, and moving it indoors in cold weather.

CULTIVAR 'Vancouver Gold' is among the best cultivars.

HAMAMELIS Species WITCH-HAZEL *Hamamelidaceae*

The simple, toothed leaves and spidery flowers of this upright or spreading shrub are far from dramatic, but witch-hazels are beloved of gardeners for their unusual period of bloom—autumn or winter/early spring depending on variety. The flower petals can be yellow, orange, or red and curl into a ball under frost and then unfurl again when the temperature rises—a trick that

Above: One of the few plants that actually blooms in snow, witch-hazel puts forth its small yellow flowers in late autumn or early spring, depending on the variety.

PROPAGATING WITCH-HAZELS

Seed capsules should be harvested in early autumn, before seeds are ejected, and placed in paper bags to open. When the seeds are extracted, they can be planted immediately outside. When planted fresh, seeds will germinate the following spring. However, if seeds are stored for any length of time, they will develop a complex dormancy that may require up to 5 months of warm followed by 3 months of cold and finally a second period of warm stratification to induce germination.

Almost all cultivars of witch-hazel are grafted. The most common understock is *H. virginiana.* Grafting is established during January and February and results in a high rate of success. However, gardeners should be wary of sucker sprouts from the base of the plant. Cutting propagation has been inconsistent, and so far most plants perform poorly on their own roots.

allows them to survive temperatures that would fell other, less hardy blossoms. The flowers of many cultivars have an appealing spicy fragrance, and the foliage, which is a clear, bright green in season, sometimes turns yellow or burnt orange in mid autumn.

BEST CONDITIONS Witch-hazel does best when provided with at least partial shade and will grow in any slightly acid, ordinary soil, supplemented with well-composted organic matter. In Chicago, witch-hazel sometimes exhibits chlorosis (leaf yellowing) at a soil pH of about 7.3.

PLANTING Plant in fall or early spring; in clay soils, plant high in a shallow hole. Take special care when choosing a site. Once established, witch-hazels are fairly difficult to move because of their coarse, deep root system. However, many witch-hazels are grafted onto *H. virginiana,* and the fibrous root system of this species makes transplanting considerably easier.

WATER Water well during establishment, especially the first 2 summers.

FERTILIZER Fertilizing witch-hazel is not only unnecessary but can be harmful to a plant under stress.

PESTS/DISEASES Very disease-resistant, though gall-forming and leaf-folding insects are occasional problems, as are leafspot diseases.

PRUNING Prune weak V-crotches. For an early hint of spring, prune late-winter bloomers in winter and force the flowers into bloom in a vase. But beware: the fragrance is heavy indoors.

USE Witch-hazel makes an effective screen or backdrop, but is also popular as a specimen to brighten the late-winter garden. The plant is especially at home in a woodland setting, where its vigorous habit can be more naturally accommodated, or close to the home where its flowers can be appreciated. It contrasts well with evergreens.

SPECIES *H.* x *intermedia* 'Arnold Promise' produces the showiest yellow flowers of all the hybrids; they appear in January and February in the South and February and March in the North. A vigorous grower, it can reach 20 feet in height. Zone 5. 'Feurzauber' has rich orange flowers. 'Pallida' and 'Primavera' are floriferous selection with bright yellow flowers.

H. vernalis, vernal witch-hazel, grows to a height of 6-10 feet, throwing off blooms in January and February. 'Sandra' is a popular cultivar that usually displays fall color ranging from yellow to reddish purple in Chicago; *H. vernalis* ssp. *carnea* is a red-flowered form. Zones 4-8.

H. virginiana, or common witch-hazel, a native shrub, is the hardiest of the species, producing an abundance of yellow flowers in November and December (October and November in the northernmost zones and often yellow fall color in Chicago). Mature size: 6-10 feet tall. Zones 4-9.

H. mollis, Chinese witch-hazel, the most fragrant of all witch-hazels, flowers in early spring (February-March in the North, January-February in the South). Hardy Zones 5-9; mature size: 15-25 feet tall. 'Early Bright' was named at the Scott Arboretum for its bright yellow flowers that open earlier than other *H. mollis* cultivars.

FOTHERGILLA MAJOR (FOTHERGILLA) Mature size: 3-10 feet tall. Creamy white flowers in spring, dark green foliage turns yellow, red, or orange in fall. Full sun to partial shade, any soil. Zones 5-9

GAYLUSSACIA BRACHYCERA (BOX HUCKLEBERRY) Evergreen creeper with glossy green leaves. Full sun. Zones 6-7

GENISTA PILOSA 'VANCOUVER GOLD' (GENISTA) Mature size: 1 foot tall, 3 feet wide. Arching gray-green stems, small bright green leaves, golden-yellow flowers in mid spring. Full sun, very well-drained soil. Zones 5-8.

HAMAMELIS X INTERMEDIA 'ARNOLD PROMISE' Mature size: up to 20 feet tall. Showy yellow flowers in winter. Partial shade, slightly acid soil. Zones 5-8.

Despite its fragile-looking flowers, *Hibiscus syriacus* can withstand city pollution and often lends a fresh natural charm to a busy city street. It blooms in mid to late summer in the North, even longer in the South.

HIBISCUS SYRIACUS ROSE OF SHARON *Malvaceae*

Grown as a sizable shrub or small tree, rose of sharon (also known as shrub althea) is prized mainly for its large flowers, which range in color from pure white to deep red and lavender blue. Otherwise, the 3- to 5-inch leaves are quite coarse, and the shrub itself tends to look unkempt no matter how assiduously it is pruned. What does recommend this shrub is its long-lived display of blooms up to 4-inches in diameter.

BEST CONDITIONS Rose of sharon will grow in full sun or partial shade. Though it prefers a moist, well-prepared soil, it performs well in a variety of soils, except those that are very wet or dry. Adaptable as to pH, this is a shrub that truly revels in hot weather. Very severe cold can cause damage.

PLANTING Plant anytime, enriching the soil with well-composed organic matter. Space 6-8 feet apart.

WATER Water as necessary to provide the preferred moist conditions.

PESTS/DISEASES None serious.

PRUNING As necessary. Rigorous pruning to tree form is one way to tame this plant.

PROPAGATION Take cuttings in mid to late summer and add rooting hormone. Seedlings grow readily, but may not be color-true.

USE Because of its leggy habit, it is effective used in a small group as a backdrop to a perennial or small-shrub border.

VARIETIES 'Diana', a tetraploid that produces no seed, has 4-inch white blooms.

HYDRANGEA Species HYDRANGEA *Saxifragaceae or Hydrangeceae*

Few flowers are as consistently showy as those of the deciduous or evergreen shrubs in the genus *Hydrangea*. Dozens of small blooms are carried in large flat-topped or pyramid-shaped clusters in colors that range from pure white to intense pink and nearly pure blue. With their impressive flower heads and a tendency to spread, hydrangeas are among the most dramatic denizens of the American garden.

BEST CONDITIONS Grow in half shade to full sun in a fertile, porous soil. Avoid overly dry or waterlogged soils. Soil pH should be slightly acid–from 5.0-7.0; soil over pH 7.5 will produce chlorotic (yellowed) flowers. The exact flower color depends on both the pH and the aluminum content of the soil.

PLANTING Plant in early spring or fall, keeping the rootball intact. If planting *H. macrophylla* or *H. quercifolia*, add well-composted organic matter in moderation–an excess will produce foliage at the expense of flowers. All varieties, however, will benefit from a surface mulch of organic matter.

WATER As their name implies, hydrangeas are water-loving; water well to keep them from wilting during dry spells.

FERTILIZER Supply a complete fertilizer in spring.

PESTS/DISEASES Hydrangeas are susceptible to a number of afflictions, including aphids, rose chafers, scale, nematodes, bud blight, botrytis, leaf spot, and powdery mildew. In temperatures above 100° F., tree-form hydrangeas can develop chlorosis. *H. paniculata* and *H. quercifolia* are quite problem-free in the

HAMAMELIS VIRGINIANA (COMMON WITCH-HAZEL) Mature size: 6-10 feet tall. Native species produces abundant yellow flowers in late fall or winter. Partial shade, slightly acid soil. Zones 4-8

HIBISCUS SYRIACUS 'HELENE' (ROSE OF SHARON) Mature size: 10-12 feet tall, 10 feet wide. Coarse, rangy shrub produces large flowers, up to 4 inches in diameter. Full sun or partial shade, any soil but very wet or very dry. Zones 5-9.

HYDRANGEA ARBORESCENS 'ANNABELLE' Mature size: 3 feet tall, 5 feet wide. Dense mounding shrub with large flower clusters. Full sun to partial shade, fertile, well-drained soil. Zones 4-8.

HYDRANGEA MACROPHYLLA 'BLUE BILLOW' (BIGLEAF HYDRANGEA) Mature size: 3 feet tall. Lacy, intensely blue flowers, compact plant. Full sun to partial shade, fertile, well-drained soil; good in seaside locations. Zones 6-8.

Hydrangea macrophylla will produce blue flowers if the soil pH is below 5.5; above it, the flowers will be pink. If you want to adjust the pH of your soil, add iron sulfate to the area around the hydrangea. This is a quick method for adjusting soil pH; see page 186 for more information about soil amendments.

Chicago area and at the Chicago Botanic Garden.

PRUNING For *H. paniculata*, remove inflorescences (which are superb in dried arrangements) in September; prune in winter or spring, removing all crowded shoots and shortening those remaining to 1-3 inches. To renew *H. arborescens,* prune in early spring. Prune *H. macrophylla* directly after flowering. Cut back all winter damage severely, but leave at least 2 or 3 sets of buds above ground level to obtain bloom the next season.

PROPAGATION Propagate from cuttings taken almost anytime during the growing season, or sow seed in pots or flats, covered and shaded in a greenhouse; transplant when seedlings are large enough to move.

USE Hydrangeas make excellent accents in the border, singly or in groups. They are often used in foundation plantings. *H. quercifolia* can be placed at the edge of a woodland area, or naturalized.

SPECIES *H. arborescens,* hills-of-snow, is a dense, mounding shrub that is covered in blooms from early to mid summer. Hardy Zones 4-8. Mature size: 3 feet tall, 5 feet wide. 'Annabelle' bears large flower clusters, 8 or more inches in diameter, composed almost exclusively of sterile flowers.

H. macrophylla, bigleaf hydrangea, has an upright, rounded habit and flowers prolifically; it is one of the few shrubs that flourishes in a seaside environment. For southern planting, select a relatively cool and moist site. If soil pH is below 5.5, *H. macrophylla* will produce blue flowers; at a pH of 6.0-6.5, blooms will be pink. It reaches a height of 3-5 feet, depending on region and pruning. 'All Summer Beauty' produces rich, clear blue flowers in acid soil, and pink/blue flowers in near neutral soil. Mature size: 3 feet tall. 'Blue Billow' bears lacy, flat-topped intensely blue flowers in June and July; plants are compact in habit. Mature size: 3 feet tall.

H. paniculata, panicled hydrangea, produces large white flower clusters in mid to late summer. Prune in late winter or early spring to restrict size and enhance flowering. Hardy Zones 4-8. Mature size: 20 feet tall. 'Grandiflora', commonly known as PeeGee hydrangea, is widely planted, and justifiably so. Its mostly sterile flowers resemble huge, pyramidal snowballs and mature from snowy white to ivory-tinged burgundy in the fall. 'Praecox' has mostly fertile flowers and begins blooming almost 3 weeks earlier than the species. 'Tardiva' is the top performer at the Chicago Botanic Garden.

H. quercifolia, oakleaf hydrangea, is grown equally for its bold, oaklike foliage and its lovely white summer flowers. It can tolerate a fair amount of shade, but will not bloom if shade is too dense. Sensitive to heavy clays, it tolerates alkaline soil and prefers a pH of 4.5-8.5. If planted in a sunny area, it produces splendid rose and maroon color in autumn. 'Snowflake' produces showy, sterile inflorescences 1 foot or more in length. 'Snow Queen' offers the bonus of deep-red autumn color. The many-flowered white inflorescences are borne upright and turn pink as they mature. It sometimes dies back in cold winters in Chicago.

HYDRANGEA QUERCIFOLIA (OAKLEAF HYDRANGEA) Mature size: 5 feet tall, 5 feet wide. Bold, oaklike foliage, white summer flowers. Full sun or light shade, tolerates wide pH range in soil, but not clay. Zones 4-8.

HYPERICUM FRONDOSUM 'SUNBURST' (ST. JOHN'S WORT) Mature size: 3-4 feet tall. Brownish-red bark, shiny, blue-green foliage, 2-inch golden yellow blossoms in late spring to early summer. Full or filtered sun, heavy to dry soils. Zones 4-8.

ILEX AQUIFOLIUM (ENGLISH HOLLY) Mature size: up to 50 feet tall, 25 feet wide. Glossy dark green leaves, bright red berries. Full sun or partial shade, any moist, acid, fertile soil. Zones 7-10.

ILEX CORNUTA (CHINESE HOLLY) Mature size: 8-12 feet. Rounded glossy leaves, Christmas-tree shape. Full sun to partial shade, any moist, acid, fertile soil. Zones 7-10.

HOLLY AND CHRISTMAS

Though hollies hail from three continents and present themselves in a wide variety of forms, both evergreen and deciduous, the variety most intimately associated with Christmas is *Ilex aquifolium,* or English holly (a misnomer, since its origins are actually in southern Europe). With its glossy evergreen leaves and bright red, berrylike fruit, English holly found what may have been its first festive use in ancient Rome, where it was gathered to celebrate the solstice feast known as Saturnalia. Later the Celts appropriated the practice in ceremonies of their own; when English monks adapted the pagan rituals to the Christian calendar, holly became an intrinsic, if secular, element of the Christmas celebration. An ancient myth has holly springing from the footsteps of Christ on the road to Golgotha—the red berries symbolizing his blood, and the spiny leaves his crown of thorns. Whatever its mythic origins, the venerable evergreen is now part and parcel of the American Christmas celebration, and the branches that were harvested in the wild by ancient hands are now cultivated for profit in the nurseries of Oregon and Washington State.

HYPERICUM FRONDOSUM ST. JOHN'S WORT *Guttiferae*

Adaptable to a wide variety of adverse environmental conditions, this is a shrub of considerable appeal that deserves to be planted much more widely. The brownish-red exfoliating bark provides a fine foil for the shiny blue-green foliage, and the 2-inch golden-yellow late-spring-to-early-summer blooms offer great color at a time when the rest of the landscape may be lagging. If this isn't enough, it is supremely easy to grow. Choose container-grown specimens with stiff upright stems.

BEST CONDITIONS This adaptable shrub will thrive in heavy and dry soils, in full or filtered light, and can tolerate a range of pH from 5.0-7.5.

PLANTING Plant in spring, spacing 4-6 feet apart. Mulch to maintain even moisture.

PESTS/DISEASES None.

PRUNING Prune as needed to maintain shape.

PROPAGATION Softwood cuttings, taken in early summer, root easily.

USE Blends beautifully in perennial gardens and provides early color.

CULTIVAR 'Sunburst' is recommended for its wonderful mounding habit.

ILEX Species HOLLY *Aquifoliaceae*

With their well-shaped leaves and showy, berrylike fruit, hollies are among the most popular of shrubs. Never mind that their flowers range from inconspicuous to nonexistent—evergreen hollies are the heart and soul of many a winter garden. Since the ancients, the word *holly* has been virtually synonymous with the holiday season. The ever-festive Romans decked their Saturnalia gifts with it, and the Druids considered it a "holy" plant—which may explain the derivation of its common name. There are both evergreen and deciduous hollies; evergreen varieties are slower growing. Hollies bear male and female flowers on separate plants, and both should be present to obtain fruit. Plant 1 male for every 5-7 female plants.

BEST CONDITIONS Hollies do well in full sun to half shade in any moist, fertile, acid soil (pH can range from 4.0-6.0). *I. verticillata* produces healthy green at Chicago Botanic Garden in soil with a pH of 7.0.

PLANTING Spring planting is best, but fall is fine in warmer climates. Prepare the ground fully before planting; if the soil is high in clay content, dig a hole twice as big as the rootball and add well-composted organic matter plus a conditioner like coarse sand, brick, or rubble to improve aeration. Make sure the earth is firm before you plant. Mulch immediately and stake as needed.

WATER Water well the first year and in periods of drought.

FERTILIZER Fertilize generously, particularly evergreens, with a high-nitrogen (10-6-4) fertilizer or manure.

PESTS/DISEASES Hollies are susceptible to leaf miners, holly midges, aphids, scale, red spider mites, root nematodes, and leaf spot. Good siting and culture are essential to maintaining health and vigor. At Chicago Botanic Garden it is usually problem-free except for chlorosis and leaf spot.

PRUNING Pruning is not necessary, but if you wish to restrict size, prune once or

Holly foliage. *Left row, top to bottom: Ilex pedunculosa, I. opaca, I. x meserveae, I. crenata. Right row, top to bottom: I. aquifolium, I. aquifolium 'Ebony Magic', I. cornuta, I. glabra.*

ILEX GLABRA (INKBERRY) Mature size: 8 feet tall, 10 feet wide. Dark shiny leaves, small black berries. Full sun to partial shade, any moist, acid, fertile soil. Zones 5-9.

ILEX X MESERVEAE 'BLUE PRINCESS' (MESERVE HOLLY) Mature size: 12 feet tall. Purplish-green spiny leaves, abundant red fruit. Full sun to partial shade, any moist, acid, fertile soil. Zones 5-8.

ILEX OPACA (AMERICAN HOLLY) Mature size: 20-40 feet tall. Duller leaves, bright red fruit. More tolerant of clay soils than other hollies. Zones 5-9.

ILEX OPACA 'MARY NELL' (AMERICAN HOLLY) Mature size: 20-40 feet tall. Duller leaves, bright red fruit. More tolerant of clay soils than other hollies. Zones 5-9.

twice a year, in early spring or just before Christmas, but unless espaliering or using as a hedge, maintain the shrub's natural shape.

PROPAGATION Propagate by cuttings, layering, or grafting. It is possible to obtain results from seeds, but you'll need to stratify, and germination can take up to 18 months.

USE Evergreen hollies make fine, dense hedges, and many varieties lend themselves to espaliering. Eminently useful at the back of the shrub border, hollies—especially those with a pyramidal habit—make fine specimen plants as well.

SPECIES *I. aquifolium*, English or European holly, has lustrous dark green leaves and bright red fruit. Evergreen. Zones 6-10. Grows 15-20 feet or more in the South.

I. cornuta, Chinese holly, has rounded, glossy leaves and a Christmas-tree shape. Evergreen. Hardy Zones 7-10. Grows 8-12 feet.

I. crenata, Japanese holly, is an evergreen with a neat, rounded form and lustrous green leaves. It makes a good hedge, background shrub, or foundation plant. Mature height: 8-12 feet. Zones 6-8, 5 for some cultivars. 'Black Beauty' has lustrous dark green foliage, hardy to Zone 5. 'Convexa' foliage bears a similarity to boxwood and is large and broad-spreading.

I. decidua, deciduous holly or possum-haw, is a large native shrub or small tree up to 15 feet tall. It has attractive dark green foliage and red fruit that remains on the tree until late winter in some areas of the country.

I. glabra, inkberry, is evergreen, bears black berries, and does well in wet soil but languishes in heavy clay. Inkberry is native to the eastern seaboard (Nova Scotia to Florida) in swamps, bogs, and wet woods. Zones 5-9. Its cultivar 'Compacta' grows 5-7 feet tall, 7-9 feet wide. It has a relaxed, graceful, rounded habit and small, shiny evergreen leaves. An excellent background plant, it is tolerant of wet soils and heavy pruning. 'Nordic' is a northern selection.

I. laevigata, smooth winterberry, is a deciduous holly that sets fruit without pollination. Zones 4-8. Grows to 10-12 feet.

I. x meserveae, meserve holly, is an evergreen shrub with purple twigs and purplish-green spiny leaves. Zones 5-8. Grows as wide as tall. 'Blue Boy' matures at 10-15 feet. 'Blue Maid' grows to15 feet; red fruit. 'Blue Stallion' has leaves that are not spiny; 15 feet tall. 'Blue Prince' grows to12 feet. 'Blue Princess' (Chicago's best performer in this group) has abundant fruit red. 'China Girl' has lustrous green leaves that are not as dark as the "Blue" series; fruit red; 10 feet at maturity. 'China Boy' matures at 10 feet.

I. opaca, American holly, has duller leaves. American holly is native to the eastern seaboard and the southern states, in sandy soil, but is more tolerant of clay soils than many other species. It will grow to a 20- to 40-foot tree. Among the best selections are 'Old Heavy Berry', 'Jersey Knight', 'Wyetta', and 'Jersey Princess'. 'Wyetta', which has luminous dark green leaves and showy fruit, grows 15-20 feet tall and 7-10 feet wide. It is faster growing than the species and attains a pyramidal form. Zones 5-9.

FRUIT DEVELOPMENT

When buying plants, it is important to know whether the plants are male (staminate), female (pistillate), or both. Plants are said to be dioecious when the staminate and pistillate flowers are on separate plants; plants with unisexual flowers--staminate and pistillate on the same plant--are monoecious. Dioecious plants require male and female plants for fruit development (males don't bear fruit), so you'll need to plant both in your garden to have fruit. When buying plants, be sure that you are getting some of each sex; not all nurseries are diligent in providing this information.

I. verticillata, winterberry, a deciduous holly, bears an abundance of red fruit that is a beacon to birds in winter and early spring. Good in wet, swampy soils. Mature size: 10 feet tall. Zones 4-9. 'Red Sprite' reaches 5 feet at maturity and has larger fruit. 'Dwarf Male' is a slow-growing mate for 'Red Sprite', a compact form, growing 3-4 feet tall, with glossy dark green foliage and an abundance of fruit. 'Shaver' is a southern type with large orange-red fruit. 'Winter Red' is more upright than most winterberry hollies and produces the most spectacular bright red fruit; it is sometimes so laden with fruit that its branches bend almost to breaking. 'Ebony Magic' grows to 20 feet tall and 10 feet wide, with dark green spiny leaves, bright orange-red fruit; Zones 6-9. Pollinator 'Ebony Male'. 'Emily Brunner' grows to 20 feet, abundant red fruit, dark evergreen foliage; Zones 7-9. 'James Swan' is a pollinator for 'Emily Brunner'. Both have spiny leaves.

I. verticillata x *I. serrata* is a hybrid that offers large, deep red fruit. Its cultivar 'Sparkleberry' is somewhat taller and leggier than winterberry with smaller fruit (a trait of *I. serrata,* from Japan). 'Apollo' is the pollinator of 'Sparkleberry'; both are U.S. National Arboretum introductions.

I. vomitoria, Yaupon holly, is more tolerant of alkaline soils and drought and is therefore popular in the southeastern U.S; dwarf forms are popular for low clipped hedges. Evergreen. Zones 7-10. Grows 10-20 feet.

ITEA VIRGINICA SWEETSPIRE, VIRGINIA WILLOW, VIRGINIA SWEETSPIRE, TASSEL-WHITE *Saxifragaceae*

Grown for its showy flowers and brilliant maroon-red fall foliage, this clump-forming shrub is tolerant of a host of adverse conditions, including salt, heat, and soil compaction. In early summer lovely white flowers, borne on spikes that can be either upright or drooping, sit atop the plant's many slender stems. Native to the eastern U.S. in swamps and wet woods, along the coastal plain and in the Mississippi valley. It provides great color in autumn.

BEST CONDITIONS *Itea* flourishes in sun or shade (except in hot climates, where it requires at least light shade) and does best in slightly acid, wet to moist soils. It tolerates seasonally dry soil, which will produce a more compact plant with brighter foliage.

PLANTING With its shallow fibrous roots, this shrub is easy to transplant and can be planted in spring, summer, or fall.

WATER/FERTILIZER A good plant for the compulsive caregiver, *Itea* responds well to high levels of moisture and nutrients.

PESTS/DISEASES None serious.

PRUNING *Itea* can be pruned severely in late winter; retain as many strong, branchless stems as possible, since these will bear the current season's flowers.

PROPAGATION Propagate by cuttings, seeds, or division.

USE Use this versatile shrub near walls, in shrub borders, or near water in low, poorly drained spots, or try naturalizing it in a woodland setting. Companions include winterberry and inkberry hollies, clethra, swamp azalea, willow, bald cypress, and river birch.

ILEX VERTICILLATA 'WINTER RED' (WINTERBERRY) Mature size: 8 feet tall, 6 feet wide. Deciduous shrub with serrated oval leaves, abundant bright red fruit. Full sun to partial shade, wet, swampy soils. Zones 3-8.

ITEA VIRGINICA (SWEETSPIRE) Mature size: 5 feet in North, 10 feet in South. Produces spikey white flowers on slender stems in summer. Sun or shade (needs some shade in South), slightly acid wet to moist soils. Zones 5-9.

KALMIA LATIFOLIA 'REDBUD' (MOUNTAIN LAUREL) Mature size: 7-15 feet (under 7 in North). Partial shade, well-drained soil, rich in organic matter. Zones 5-9.

KALMIA LATIFOLIA 'CAROUSEL' (MOUNTAIN LAUREL) Mature size: 7-15 feet (under 7 in North). Partial shade, well-drained soil, rich in organic matter. Zones 5-9.

Kalmia is perfect for natural settings, or at the edge of woodlands.

CULTIVAR *I. virginica* 'Henry's Garnet', named at the Scott Arboretum, produces a profusion of spikey white, highly fragrant flowers that are larger than the species. Great color lasts into late fall.

KALMIA LATIFOLIA MOUNTAIN LAUREL *Ericaceae*

This slow grower starts out dense and rounded but becomes open and gnarled as it ages. The appealing foliage, alternate or whorled (and highly toxic, should you feel the urge to taste it), is evergreen, but the shrub's real attraction is its spectacular flowers, white to deep pink, blooming in late spring or early summer. Native to eastern North America, mostly in acid soil.

BEST CONDITIONS Grow in partial shade in a well-drained, acid soil high in organic matter. It does not perform well in the Chicago area.

PLANTING Mountain laurel transplants well (but take care not to break the brittle branches) and can be planted in spring or early fall. In poorly drained soils, plant in raised beds. A thin layer of mulch will help protect the shallow root system.

WATER Water sparingly at first; once established, the plant rarely needs more water than nature affords.

PESTS/DISEASES Subject to leaf-spot disease in some localities, mountain laurel is relatively pest-free with the occasional exception of leaf spot.

PRUNING Removal of faded flowers discourages fruiting and encourages better flowers the following year.

PROPAGATION Sow seeds on peat. Provide supplementary light to seedlings. Cuttings can be very hard to root. Most cultivars in commerce have been propagated by tissue culture.

USE Often used as a specimen, mountain laurel is also a fine companion for azaleas and rhododendrons and works well in both wild and formal settings.

CULTIVARS *Kalmia latifolia* 'Olympic Fire' has deep red buds that open to white flowers. Cuttings root easily. 'Sarah' has red buds that open to pink flowers. 'Silver Dollar' has pink buds that open white, large flowers. 'Fuscata' (banded laurel) has flowers with a maroon band inside the corolla 'Elf' is ½-⅓ the stature of the species, flowers slightly smaller, pink in bud and opening white. 'Pink Charm' has pink flowers; roots from cuttings; 'Snowdrift' has pure white flowers on a compact mound-shaped plant. 'Star Cluster' has white flowers with a maroon "band"; selected at the Holden Arboretum, it is adaptable to clay soils. 'Shooting Star', from the wilds of North Carolina, has distinctive white flowers, reflexed and deeply divided; it blooms a week later than the species.

KERRIA JAPONICA KERRIA, JAPANESE ROSE *Rosaceae*

This dense, rounded suckering shrub has bright green foliage and stems and bright yellow five-petaled flowers that appear for a week in early or mid spring. The leaves occasionally turn yellow in autumn; in winter the slender green twigs provide excellent winter interest in a naturalized setting. Native to Japan and China, common in the foothills and the mountains.

BEST CONDITIONS Though kerria prefers partial shade, it will grow in full sun and dense shade as well. However, flowers will fade quickly in strong sun. Plant in a well-drained, acid to neutral soil. The soil shouldn't be excessively rich; indeed, kerria is tough enough to grow in almost any soil and will do nicely enough in poor soil. In cold climates, protect the tips from killing frost.

PLANTING Plant in spring or fall.

PESTS/DISEASES None serious.

PRUNING If necessary, remove winter-killed tips in spring, but save major pruning till after the flowers fade, since they form on new growth. Cut back any main stems that aren't branching freely, and thin old wood at least every few years. One guide for pruning is to remove wood that changes from green to brown; this ensures that the plant retains its interesting twig character.

PROPAGATION Softwood cuttings, taken in spring, root easily. Kerria can also be propagated by layering and division.

USE Kerria is best used in groups. Force indoors in late winter or early spring.

CULTIVARS 'Pleniflora' produces double flowers with overlapping petals that resemble golden balls. Its loosely branched form sometimes makes it difficult to use in the landscape. 'Picta' has attractive white-edged foliage and single yellow 'buttercup' flowers. Occasionally produces shoots with green leaves that must be removed. It should be grown in the shade, for sun burns its leaves. Grows 3-5 feet, with equal spread. Zones 5-10. (Berkshire)

KOLKWITZIA AMABILIS BEAUTYBUSH *Caprifoliaceae*

This old-fashioned, fast-growing deciduous shrub has a broad, arching shape and in late May is covered in clusters of perfect-pink, yellow-throated trumpet flowers. Native to Central China, it is rare and endangered in its rocky mountainside habitat.

BEST CONDITIONS Grow in full sun in any well-drained garden soil (partial shade

Above: Kolkwitzia amabilis 'Pink Cloud' has darker pink flowers than the species.

KERRIA JAPONICA (JAPANESE ROSE) Mature size: 3-5 feet tall. Dense, rounded shrub with bright green leaves and bright yellow flowers in mid spring. Partial shade is best, well-drained acid to neutral soil, not very rich. Zones 5-9.

KOLKWITZIA AMABILIS (BEAUTYBUSH) Mature size: 8 feet tall, 8 feet wide. Broad, arching shrub produces clusters of pink trumpet flowers in mid to late spring. Full sun, any well-drained soil. Zones 4-8.

LAGERSTROEMIA INDICA (CRAPE MYRTLE) Mature size: 15-20 feet tall, 15 feet wide. Exfoliating bark, vivid fall color, attractive flowers. Full sun, hot weather, well-drained soil. Zones 7-9.

LEUCOPHYLLUM FRUTESCENS (TEXAS RANGER) Mature size: 4-8 feet tall. Evergreen shrub produces rosy-purple bell-shaped flowers and silvery foliage. Full sun or partial shade, well-drained soil. Zones 8-10.

is ok in the South). Thrives in both acid and alkaline conditions, a remarkably adaptable plant.

PLANTING Plant in early spring.

PESTS/DISEASES None serious.

PRUNING To shape, prune after flowering. Regular removal of the oldest branches to ground level will help maintain vigor.

PROPAGATION Softwood cuttings, taken in early summer, root easily.

USE A plant of unsurpassed beauty in flower, beautybush fades into the background for the remainder of the year. Though its size precludes its use in many residential landscapes, it makes an effective backdrop for larger shrubs or perennial borders, especially when planted with May appreciation in mind.

CULTIVAR 'Pink Cloud' is a particularly beautiful variety.

LAGERSTROEMIA INDICA CRAPE MYRTLE *Lythraceae*

Grown either as a large shrub or small tree, summer-flowering crape myrtle offers the gardener a wide selection of floral colors, including red, white, pink, and salmon. As attractive as its flowers may be, the shrub's most appealing characteristics are its wonderful exfoliating bark–similar to that of the sycamore tree–and its first-rate fall color. This is one of the best plants for the southern garden. Look for container-grown or balled-and-burlapped plants.

BEST CONDITIONS Adaptable as to soil type and pH, crape myrtle likes full sun and hot weather, but is decidedly negative about wet feet and cannot tolerate hard freezes.

PLANTING Plant in spring or fall, adding a good mulch to maintain soil moisture.

FERTILIZER Apply a general-purpose fertilizer in spring.

PESTS/DISEASES Powdery mildew can be a real problem on many varieties; the best defense, if possible, is to select resistant varieties.

PRUNING Prune after flowering to promote continuous bloom. It comes back from the roots and blooms on new wood.

PROPAGATION From root sprouts, seeds, or leaf-bud cuttings taken in July.

USE A fine specimen, crape myrtle should be planted where its eye-catching winter bark can be appreciated up close.

VARIETY 'Natchez' boasts pure white flowers and fine brown-gray bark and is resistant to the powdery mildew that afflicts so many other varieties. Many excellent varieties have been introduced by the late Dr. Donald Egolf through the National Arboretum.

LEUCOPHYLLUM FRUTESCENS TEXAS RANGER *Scrophulariaceae*

This evergreen shrub flourishes in its native Southwest, producing an abundance of rosy-purple bell-shaped flowers in summer and holding on to its silvery foliage throughout the year (though the leaves tend to yellow out somewhat during the winter). It has been less successful in other areas of the country, particularly where humidity and night temperatures are high.

BEST CONDITIONS Texas Ranger loves the hot, arid conditions that prevail in its

Above: Crape myrtle's display of flowers in summer is only one facet of this valuable shrub's appeal; it also offers beautiful exfoliating bark and dazzling fall color.

I know well a stretch of road where nature's own landscaping has provided a border of alder, viburnum, sweet fern, and juniper with seasonally changing accents of bright flowers or of fruits hanging in jeweled clusters in the fall. . . . But the sprayers took over and the miles along that road became something to traverse quickly, a sight to be endured with one's mind closed. . . . But here and there authority had somehow faltered and by an unaccountable oversight there were oases of beauty in the midst of austere and regimented control—oases that made the desecration of the greater part of the road the more unbearable. . . . Such plants are weeds only to those who make a business of buying and selling chemicals.

FROM *THE SILENT SPRING*, BY RACHEL CARSON

namesake state, admirably tolerating drought, hot weather, and high winds. Though it also takes well to high alkalinity, the soil must be extremely well drained; this is not a shrub that enjoys wet feet. Grow in full sun or partial shade.

PLANTING Best planted in fall. No special soil conditioning or amendments are necessary or recommended.

PESTS/DISEASES Very susceptible to root rot if overwatered; the first symptom is leaf drop.

WATER Water deeply but infrequently, even in summer.

PRUNING None necessary.

PROPAGATION Cuttings root easily.

USE Texas Ranger makes a fine informal hedge, as well as an arresting specimen. Because of its silvery foliage, it works well in the mixed-shrub border when set against plants whose leaves are a darker green. It is often used in street plantings and public areas because of its low care requirements.

CULTIVARS Named cultivars of *L. frutescens,* all developed at Texas A&M Research Station: 'White Cloud', a medium-sized (6 feet tall, 4 feet wide) variety, with a gray-to-whitish leaf that is hairier than most Texas Rangers. 'Green Cloud' is the largest cultivar, very dark green with a nearly purple bloom. Because its blooms often occur after rain, it is known as "barometer bush." 'Compacta' is a smaller version, usually about 4 feet tall, with whiter leaves and blue-purple flowers.

OTHER SPECIES *L. zygophyllum* is a small shrub with silver white leaves and stunning dark purple flowers. Its irregular shape gives it an informal look. *L. laevigatum,* known as Cenizo, is also somewhat informal in shape, with small green leaves and masses of dark blue blooms. (Desert Botanical Garden)

LEUCOTHOE FONTANESIANA DROOPING LEUCOTHOE Ericaceae

With its long, graceful, arching branches and leathery long-tipped leaves, this is a supremely elegant shrub. In spring, pendant 3-inch clusters of white bell-shaped flowers emerge from the axis of the leaves, spreading their fragrance throughout the garden. Unfortunately, in northern areas, it tends to look ragged in spring before new growth comes in.

BEST CONDITIONS Drooping leucothoe demands a well-drained but moist, highly organic and acidic soil and prefers ½-¾ shade in the North and deep shade in the South.

PLANTING Plant container-grown shrubs in spring.

PESTS/DISEASES Sunscald and drought stress open the door for leaf blights. Leaf spot fungi can be devastating.

PRUNING Very little pruning is required. In northern areas, prune back dead branches in early spring.

PROPAGATION Softwood cuttings, taken in mid summer and treated with IBA, root easily.

USE This is a wonderful companion plant for rhododendrons and azaleas; colored-leaf forms add brightness to shady gardens.

LEUCOTHOE FONTANESIANA (DROOPING LEUCOTHOE) Mature size: 3-5 feet tall. Arching branches, long-tipped leaves, white bell-shaped flowers. Partial shade, well-drained, moist soil. Zones 5-8.

LIGUSTRUM OBTUSIFOLIUM VAR REGELIANUM (REGEL PRIVET) Mature size: 10-12 feet tall, 12-15 feet wide. Rounded, untoothed leaves, profuse creamy white small flowers in spring. Full sun or partial shade. Any well-drained soil. Zones 4-8.

LINDERA OBTUSILOBA (SPICEBUSH) Mature size: 10-15 feet tall. Lobed leaves, large flowers, excellent yellow color in fall. Needs shade, coarse to moderately fine acid soil. Zones 5-9.

LONICERA FRAGRANTISSIMA (FRAGRANT HONEYSUCKLE) Mature size: 5-10 feet tall, 8 feet wide. Stiff leathery leaves, small, white, lemon-scented flowers in early spring. Full sun, loamy soil. Zones 5-9.

Above: Lindera benzoin's spicy, fragrant flowers.

CULTIVARS *L. fontanesiana* 'Rainbow' earns its name in spring, when new leaves emerge in eye-catching color combinations of white, pink, bronze, gold, and green. 'Scarletta' has scarlet foliage in spring that matures to a deep lustrous green and then turns burgundy in the fall.

LIGUSTRUM Species PRIVET *Oleaceae*

This fine-textured, adaptable, and vigorous shrub produces clusters of small, creamy-white, strongly scented (sometimes malodorous) flowers in late spring. Leaves are oval and untoothed. Privet will happily tolerate drought, wind, pollution, and heavy pruning. A note of caution: This plant has escaped cultivation and is naturalizing in woodlands; gardeners concerned about this problem should avoid *L. amurense* and *L. obtusifolium*.

BEST CONDITIONS Grow in full sun or partial shade in any well-drained garden soil; privet is tolerant of most conditions, but dislikes wet feet.

PLANTING Easy to transplant; look for bare-root plants. For hedges, space 1- 2 feet apart.

PESTS/DISEASES Privet is subject to aphids, thrips, and privet weevil, as well as powdery mildew and anthracnose twig blight.

PRUNING To avoid flowers, prune in early spring. Hedges should be sheared twice a year, in early spring and again in early summer; to maintain the shrub's natural habit, remove deadwood only.

PROPAGATION Take softwood or semihardwood cuttings.

USE Commonly clipped into hedge form or used as a screen or divider, privet also makes an attractive specimen when allowed to grow naturally.

SPECIES *L. obtusifolium* var *regelianum*, or regel privet, is a broad-spreading shrub that produces a profusion of flowers in spring. Growing 10-12 feet tall and 12-15 feet wide, it looks best unpruned.

L. amurense, amur privet, has small leaves and is excellent for hedges; highly cold-resistant.

L. japonica, Japanese privet, is one of several evergreen varieties; it does best in southern gardens.

LINDERA SPECIES SPICEBUSH *Lauraceae*

This shrub throws off masses of tiny yellow flowers in early spring, followed by small red fruits in autumn. The large bright green leaves turn yellow in fall. Leaves or stems give off a strong spicy aroma when crushed. A dioecious shrub, spicebush requires male and female plants for fruit development. A note of caution: Spicebush possesses compounds that tend to cause some plants to do poorly when situated near it.

BEST CONDITIONS Spicebush prefers light to medium shade and a moderately coarse to moderately fine acid soil supplemented with leaf mold or peat moss. Grow in wet to average conditions.

PLANTING Plant in early spring or fall. Because spicebush develops a deep, coarse root system, it is difficult to transplant. When it becomes well established, it sometimes forms large colonies.

PESTS/DISEASES None serious.

PRUNING Prune after the flowers fade in spring. Spicebush can be rejuvenated.

USE Because the blossoms coincide with many of the Northeast's and Midwest's native wildflowers, this is a perfect understory shrub for naturalistic landscapes.

SPECIES *L. benzoin,* native to the eastern United States, has a dense habit with spicy fragrant flowers that appear in early spring; when crushed, the twigs and foliage are also spicy. Best in moist soils.

L. erythrocarpa can grow to a 30-foot tree with lustrous dark green foliage that turns golden yellow in fall. It is tolerant of dry soils as long as it is grown in partial shade. (Morris Arboretum)

L. salicifolia is especially attractive in winter because it holds its leaves after they turn salmony brown. (Scott Arboretum)

L. obtusiloba is an irregular, rounded shrub that grows 10-15 feet tall and produces very large flowers in mid spring and turns an exquisite yellow in fall. Its lobed leaves are different from other spicebush species.

LONICERA Species HONEYSUCKLE *Caprifoliaceae*

These upright shrubs, part of a large family that includes the better-known honeysuckle vines, bear fragrant tubular flowers in shades of white, pink, yellow, or red. The profuse blooms are followed by ornamental berries, many of which are so beloved of the birds that gardeners may never get to see them.

BEST CONDITIONS *Lonicera* prefers full sun, but will tolerate partial shade as well, in any loamy soil. Though they do best with even moisture, they abhor overly wet conditions.

PLANTING Extremely easy to establish and to transplant, *Lonicera* can be planted in spring or fall.

PESTS/DISEASES None serious.

PRUNING *Lonicera* can withstand heavy pruning. See individual varieties.

PROPAGATION Propagate by seed or cuttings.

USE Many varieties make fine hedges; the taller forms are splendid in shrub borders, especially where their ornamental fruit can be admired close up.

SPECIES *L. fragrantissima*, fragrant honeysuckle or winter honeysuckle, has stiff, leathery leaves and bears small, white early spring flowers with an intense lemon fragrance. The bright red fruit appears in mid spring, but may be obscured by dense new growth. Prune to shape after flowering. Drought-tolerant. Zones 5-9; grows to 5-10 feet tall, 8 feet wide.

L. pileata, privet honeysuckle, is prized for its horizontal-branching habit, glossy green leaves, creamy white flowers, and violet-purple berries. Evergreen or semievergreen, it tolerates shade better than many other varieties. Zones 5-9

MAGNOLIA STELLATA STAR MAGNOLIA *Magnoliaceae*

Grown as a large shrub or small tree, star magnolia blooms with the daffodils in very early spring. The fragrant 3- to 5-inch flowers of delicate shell pink

Its very name comes from the Latin word that gives us "privacy," and it's easy to understand why the common privet is the most widely used plant in America for hedges. . . . All the standard books on gardening agree that it has an amiable tolerance for conditions that would drive less sturdy plants to destruction. . . . Above all, privet is submissve to human beings wielding pruning shears, even if their knowledge of the art of pruning is so rudimentary as to be well-nigh nonexistent.
FROM "IN PRAISE OF PRIVET" BY ALLEN LACY

LONICERA PILEATA (PRIVET HONEYSUCKLE) Mature size: 12 feet tall. Horizontally-branched, glossy green leaves, creamy white flowers, violet-purple berries. Tolerates shade; loamy soil. Zones 5-9.

MAGNOLIA 'ANN' ("LITTLE GIRL" MAGNOLIA) Mature size: 12 feet tall. Deep pinkish-purple flowers, somewhat later than most magnolias. Full or partial shade, moist, loamy soil. Zones 5-9.

MAGNOLIA SOULANGIANA (SAUCER MAGNOLIA) Mature size: 20 feet. Large, pure white flowers, graceful branches that face the ground. Full or partial shade, moist, loamy soil. Zones 5-9.

MAHONIA AQUIFOLIUM (OREGON GRAPE) Mature size: 3-6 feet. Low-growing broadleaf evergreen, compound dark green leaves, bright yellow flowers in mid spring, clusters of deep blue berries in early fall. Zones 5-8.

open before the foliage. Leaves are dull green and up to 5 inches long. Though the shrub's floral display is enchanting, its wonderful open habit would recommend it even if it failed to bloom.

BEST CONDITIONS Tolerant of northern cold and southern heat, this agreeable shrub will thrive in full sun or partial shade in moist, peat and loamy soil with a pH of 6.0-6.5. It does, however, require careful siting–strong winds can shatter the delicate flowers, and south-facing buds can open too soon, leaving them susceptible to frost damage and discoloration, particularly in cold climates.

PLANTING Magnolia roots are fragile; transplant carefully in spring.

PESTS/DISEASES None serious.

PRUNING Remove dead wood after flowering.

PROPAGATION From seeds, cuttings, layers, or grafts.

USE This shrub looks lovely as a specimen plant, set off from others, particularly evergreens.

SPECIES *M. stellata* 'Centennial' has pure white flowers, each sporting 5-30 narrow petals.

The "Little Girl" series ('Ann', 'Susan', 'Betty', 'Jane', 'Jody', etc.) is a group of hybrids of *M. liliiflora* 'Nigra' and *M. stellata* 'Rosea' developed at the National Arboretum and named for the daughters of the staff and thus known as the "Little Girl" series. These lovely slow-growing shrubs bloom several weeks later than *M. stellata* and are therefore not as susceptible to frost damage.

MAHONIA AQUIFOLIUM OREGON GRAPE *Berberidaceae*

This low-growing broadleaf evergreen has stout, upright stems and few side branches, with pinnately compound dark green leaves comprised of 5-9 stiff, glossy, leathery leaflets. In early to mid spring its terminal racemes carry bright yellow, mildly fragrant flowers, followed in early fall by clusters of deep blue berries. Autumn fruit is set off nicely by the foliage, which turns a purplish bronze. In Chicago, the foliage remains through mid winter when planted in a protected site, presenting a kaleidoscope of reds, oranges, and yellows. Plants tend to be stoloniferous, forming irregular colonies over time.

BEST CONDITIONS Oregon grape prefers partial shade and in northern areas needs protection from winter sun and wind. Plant in a well-drained, slightly acid soil high in organic matter.

PLANTING Both container-grown and balled-and-burlapped plants will do best when planted in spring.

PESTS/DISEASES None serious.

PRUNING Pruning is seldom necessary, except to remove unwanted suckers.

PROPAGATION Cuttings taken in early autumn will root, but for home gardeners looking to propagate a small number of plants, the easiest method is to divide suckers from the parent plant in early spring.

USE Try this shrub in a border or foundation planting, especially in shady areas.

Above: **Fruit from *Malus* x 'Callaway'.
Crab apples are distinguished from
eating apples by being less than 2
inches in diameter.**

SPECIES *M. bealei,* leatherleaf mahonia, has coarse unbranched stems with 7-11
blue-green leaflets. It blooms early in spring and is highly fragrant; in summer it produces very effective bluish-black grapelike fruit.
M. japonica is similar in shape, flowers, and fruit to *M. bealei,* but forms a
graceful mound.
M. repens, creeping mahonia, is an attractive woody ground cover with beautiful foliage, flowers, and fruit, native to sites in the western mountains. It is
drought-tolerant and grows best in light shade. (Dyck Arboretum)

MALUS SPECIES CRAB APPLE *Rosaceae*

Although the genus *Malus* encompasses both apples and crab apples, only
crab apples are sufficiently compact to be considered shrubs. (Indeed, most
crab apples are categorized as trees, though several varieties have the compact,
mounded habit that qualifies them as shrubs.) Say "crab apple," and most
people think of showy spring flowers, but in fact crabs are equally valuable for
their attractive red or yellow fall fruits, which often persist well into the winter and even up to the following spring if the birds aren't overly greedy.
Flowers are generally small, in shades of white, pink, and red, and bloom in
mid May, just after the early cherries and just before the late ones.
BEST CONDITIONS Though crab apples will do fairly well in almost any soil, they
prefer a well-drained soil of moderate acidity. Full sun is a must for abundant
flower production.
PLANTING Easily transplantable, crab apples can be planted in spring or fall.
FERTILIZER Apply a balanced fertilizer once or twice a year, but only if the
plant's rate of growth seems sluggish.
PESTS/DISEASES Borers, scales, apple scab, cedar apple rust. Since many vari-
eties—especially the Oriental hybrids—are highly pest- and disease-resistant, it's
wise to choose crab apples carefully.
PRUNING Most crab apples require little or no pruning, except to remove suckers, waterspouts, and crossing branches, which can be done anytime of year.
PROPAGATION Take softwood cuttings in early summer.
USE These highly showy shrubs are often planted as specimens, but given sufficient room they can be massed for splendid effect.
SPECIES *M. sargentii,* sargent crab apple, is prized not just for its fragrant,
showy pure white flowers and dark red fruits, but for its superb disease resistance as well. Its dense, mounded habit makes it the "shrubbiest" of all the
crab apples. Zones 4 -8; it has a dwarf (6-10 feet tall, 10 feet wide) spreading
growth habit unique for a crab apple.
M. x 'Callaway' is one of the best shrub crab apples for southern gardens.

MYRICA PENSYLVANICA BAYBERRY *Myriaceae*

This deciduous-to-semievergreen shrub has a very irregular, loosely upright
habit. When crushed, its leathery leaves are pleasantly aromatic. The unprepossessing flowers are followed by attractive small, gray, waxy berries, borne
in clusters along the stem. Persistent fruit and an interesting habit make bay-

MALUS 'SNOWDRIFT' (CRAB APPLE) Mature size: 15-20 feet tall, 20-25 feet wide. Dwarf form with a profusion of white flowers followed by small reddish fruit. Full sun, almost any soil. Zones 5-8.

MYRICA PENSYLVANICA (BAYBERRY) Mature size: 5-7 feet tall and wide. Loosely upright shrub, with leathery leaves and small waxy berries. Sun or partial shade, sandy soil. Zones 2-8.

PAEONIA SUFFRUTICOSA 'AGE OF GOLD' (TREE PEONY) Mature size: 4-5 feet tall. Very showy double flowers, bright gold, in mid summer. Morning sun, afternoon shade, well-drained, friable soil. Zones 5-8.

PAXISTIMYA CANBYI (CANBY PAXISTIMA, RAT-STRIPPER) Mature size: 12 inches. Low-growing evergreen ground cover, narrow dark green leaves. Best in full sun, tolerates some shade; well-drained, peaty, sandy soil. Zones 3-8.

berry a pleasing winter specimen. Because bayberry lacks a fibrous root system, container grown plants are recommended for transplanting.

BEST CONDITIONS Though very adaptable, bayberry prefers a sandy, slightly acid
soil, in sun or partial shade.

PLANTING Plant in spring. To ensure good fruit production, plant both male
and female plants. (A caveat: Most nurseries don't "sex" their plants, so it's
hard to tell which is being purchased unless you buy them in the fall when
they have fruit.)

PESTS/DISEASES None serious.

PRUNING Bayberry usually requires no pruning.

PROPAGATION Propagation is best achieved from seed collected in October.
Remove the waxy coating to extract the seed from the fruit, then stratify the
seed in damp sand at 40° F. for 90 days before sowing.

USE Bayberry is one of the most versatile of landscape plants, equally at home
in mass plantings, shrub borders, or informal foundation plantings, where it
combines well with evergreens; it is a good choice for seaside locations. The
berries can be boiled to extract the wax, which is used to make aromatic bayberry candles. When established, this plant can "move" about the garden
with its suckering root system, sometimes creating a colony; this can happen
even in heavy clay soil like that of the Chicago area.

PAEONIA SUFFRUTICOSA TREE PEONY *Ranunculaceae*

Contrary to popular opinion, the tree peony is a surprisingly easy shrub to
grow, as long as its basic needs (see below) are met. Very free flowering, it
bears large, sweetly fragrant flowers, either single or double, in a wide range
of colors, including yellow, red, white, or pink.

BEST CONDITIONS Morning sun, but some afternoon shade in a rich, well-
drained, friable soil, pH 6.2-7.0; in Chicago a soil pH of 7.6 does not present
a problem. Avoid extreme heat, wet feet, and hot afternoon sun, and protect
from winter exposure.

PLANTING Bare-root shrubs should be planted in the fall; container-grown specimens can be planted anytime. Space 4 feet apart, making sure the scion is 4-
6 inches below ground level (2-4 inches in the South). Mulch well to keep
roots cool.

WATER Keep moist, but not wet.

PESTS/DISEASES Tree peony is susceptible to botrytis and anthracnose.

PRUNING Unnecessary.

PROPAGATION Not recommended.

CULTIVARS 'Age of Gold' blooms in mid summer and boasts creamy-yellow
semidouble flowers with raspberry flares. Many excellent varieties have been
introduced by Klehm nurseries.

PAXISTIMA CANBYI CANBY PAXISTIMA, RAT-STRIPPER *Celastraceae*

Native to the rocky slopes of Virginia, West Virginia, Kentucky, Pennsylvania,
and Ohio, this low shrub has long, rooting branches that qualify it for use as a

ground cover. Its evergreen leaves are a lustrous dark green and narrow enough to give the plant a fine needlelike texture. Look for container-grown plants.

BEST CONDITIONS Paxistima thrives in well-drained, peaty, sandy soil on the alkaline side. Though it tolerates a certain amount of shade, it will be fuller and more compact when grown in full sun.

PLANTING Plant container-grown shrubs in spring or fall.

FERTILIZER Fertilize sparsely.

PESTS/DISEASES Leaf spot and scale can be problems.

PRUNING Rarely requires pruning.

PROPAGATION Easy to propagate from divisions or cuttings, it can also be propagated from seed.

USE A good ground cover, especially when used with broadleaf evergreens, paxistima can also be used as a low hedge or a facer for larger shrubs. It is valued in Chicago, where few evergreen ground covers are available, even though it may be somewhat difficult to establish.

PHILADELPHUS Species MOCK ORANGE *Saxifragaceae*

The only real reason to grow this generally unprepossessing shrub is for its fragrance. Foliage is ordinary, turning an unremarkable yellow in autumn; the fruit is a dry seed capsule; and the single or double flowers are pretty but hardly dazzling. It is, however, an easy plant to grow and so recommends itself to the otherwise busy gardener.

BEST CONDITIONS Mock orange will grow in any garden soil, in full sun to partial shade.

PLANTING Plant in early spring, making sure to emend the soil with generous amounts of peat moss or other moisture-retentive organic matter.

PESTS/DISEASES Nearly pest- and disease-free.

PRUNING Prune annually after blooming to keep the plant bushy.

PROPAGATION Semihardwood cuttings, taken in early summer, root easily, as do soft- and hardwood cuttings. Or propagate by division, layering, or seed.

USE Site to make the most of its fleeting fragrance: by a path, porch, or stairway.

SPECIES *P. coronarius,* sweet or common mock orange, has long been popular for its enchanting fragrance and tolerance of dry soils and droughty conditions. When choosing plants, make sure they are highly fragrant; many nursery specimens are inferior, and some possess little if any fragrance at all. Takes well to yearly renovation-pruning. Hardy Zones 5-9; grows to 10-12 feet high. 'Dwarf Snowflake' is a first-rate dwarf variety, highly fragrant, cold-hardy (Zones 3-8), and rarely if ever exceeding 4 feet in height.

PHOTINIA VILLOSA ORIENTAL PHOTINIA *Rosaceae*

This hardy shrub is grown for its flat clusters of small white flowers that appear in late May, its bright-red fall berries, and especially, its striking autumn foliage, which can range from yellowish-red to red-bronze to pure scarlet.

plant selector

Above: Pieris japonica's blossoms, which appear in early spring.

BEST CONDITIONS Photinia requires full sun and a well-drained soil that has been generously amended with well-composted organic matter.

PLANTING Plant in spring or fall, making sure to emend the soil with generous amounts of peat moss or other moisture-retentive organic matter.

WATER Water generously and often, especially during establishment.

PESTS/DISEASES Fireblight, often exacerbated by allowing water to splash onto leaves, can be a serious problem. Water at the roots only. Also susceptible to aphids and scale.

PRUNING Prune to keep in bounds and to remove any branch tips blackened by fireblight; when pruning diseased branches, make sure to sterilize tools between cuts.

PROPAGATION Take soft- or hardwood cuttings, or propagate by layering. Seeds can be sown but require stratification.

USE Use photinia as a free-standing specimen or as an accent plant in a mixed-shrub or shrub-and-perennial border.

PHYSOCARPUS Species NINEBARK *Rosaceae*

With its ovate toothed leaves and clusters of white, or off-white, early summer flowers, this hardy deciduous shrub—more often than not found growing as a single specimen in the wild—resembles the better-known spireas. A winter plus is the exfoliating bark, which peels in strips.

BEST CONDITIONS Becoming open and leggy in shade, ninebark prefers a sunny spot in a reasonably fertile, acid to neutral soil that is deeply worked. It will tolerate conditions that range from somewhat wet to somewhat dry.

PESTS/DISEASES Ninebark is extremely resistant to disease. If you live in the Northeast or Colorado, check the flowers for rose chafers, beige insects with sharply spined legs that resemble Japanese beetles.

PRUNING Lateral-flowering branches die back after several years, but the shrub can be easily renewed by cutting it to the ground in late winter.

PROPAGATION Seeds, division, and cuttings are all effective methods of propagation. Softwood cuttings work well in mist, in a greenhouse or cold frame; hardwood cuttings also root easily.

USE Ninebark makes an effective low screen.

SPECIES *P. opulifolius* 'Dart's Gold' is a compact variety with particularly good yellow color. 'Nana' is a smaller form, well-suited to the scale of the home landscape.

PIERIS Species ANDROMEDA, PIERIS *Ericaceae*

A broadleaf evergreen, this justifiably popular shrub has an upright habit and gracefully arching branches. Its fine-textured foliage, yellow-green or reddish when new, turns a deep green in summer. During its spring blooming season, andromeda produces clusters of delicate white or pink flowers. Excellent in mass plantings, this slow grower is also a fine accent plant for the border or rock garden.

BEST CONDITIONS Andromeda does well with half a day of sun, or in part sun

PHILADELPHUS 'DWARF SNOWFLAKE' (MOCK ORANGE) Mature size: 4 feet tall or smaller. Highly fragrant shrub with double flowers. Full sun to partial shade, any soil. Zones 3-8.

PHOTINIA VILLOSA (ORIENTAL PHOTINIA) Mature size: 15 feet tall. Clusters of small white flowers in mid spring, bright red berries and colorful foliage in autumn. Full sun, well-drained soil, rich in organic matter. Zones 5-8.

PHYSOCARPUS OPULIFOLIUS (NINEBARK) Mature size: 5-7 feet. Clusters of off-white, early summer flowers, exfoliating bark. Full sun, fertile soil. Zones 3-6.

PIERIS JAPONICA (ANDROMEDA, PIERIS) Mature size: 3-10 feet. Drooping flower clusters, good fall color. Partial shade, well-drained, humusy soil. Zones 6-9.

Above: Prunus triloba blossom.

with dappled shade. It prefers a humus-rich, well-drained, somewhat sandy acid soil (through a pH above 6.0 can cause chlorosis). Once established, it is quite drought-tolerant as long as it is not exposed to hot sun.

PLANTING Prepare a shallow hole in a site that is protected from excessive sun and wind. If drainage is a problem, plant high or in a raised bed. Because of its shallow root system, andromeda will benefit from a mulch to keep the soil cool and moist.

WATER New transplants should be kept evenly moist, and all plants—especially in the South—should be watered during prolonged periods of drought.

PESTS/DISEASES Lace bugs and mites, which hide on the underside of leaves, can be a problem, but less so in sites with adequate moisture. If soil is badly drained or excessively wet, however, andromeda may be plagued by phytophthora or dieback.

PRUNING Prune in spring, immediately after flowering. To enhance next year's bloom, deadhead spent blossoms.

PROPAGATION Andromeda can be propagated by seeds, layering, or from cuttings taken in July and August or from mid October to late November.

USE With its delicate foliage, andromeda is a perfect foil for needle-leafed evergreens.

SPECIES *P. floribunda*, mountain andromeda, is found in the mountains of the southeastern United States. With a mature height of 3-6 feet, it is shorter than *P. japonica* but often wider. Its white, upright-spreading flowers appear slightly later than those of *japonica*.

P. japonica, Japanese andromeda, whose mature height ranges from 3-10 feet, sports drooping flower clusters that can be either white or pink. 'White Cascade' has abundant, long-lasting white flowers. 'Dorothy Wycoff' has red buds in winter that open pink and then turn white. 'Variegata' is a slow grower with narrow, white-margined leaves and relatively fewer flowers. 'Red Mill', vigorous and hardy in Zone 5, has white flowers and red-hued new foliage. 'Valley Valentine' has attractive pink flowers. 'Brouwer's Beauty' is the best performer at Chicago Botanic Garden, where the soil is well drained and has a pH of 7.5

POTENTILLA FRUTICOSA CINQUEFOIL *Rosaceae*

A dense, bushy shrub with slender upright branches, cinquefoil boasts yellow (and sometimes orange or red) flowers, 1¾ inches in diameter, set off by fine-textured grayish-green foliage. The first flush of bloom is in June, with flower production continuing until frost. In hot regions, avoid red- or orange-flowered potentilla, as the blooms will invariably bleach to an unattractive rusty yellow.

BEST CONDITIONS Grow in full sun, in any well-drained garden soil. Cinquefoil is tolerant of drought and alkaline soils. It is an excellent shrub in most parts of the Great Plains.

PLANTING A very fibrous root system makes transplanting easy at any time.

PESTS/DISEASES Spider mites can be a problem in very hot, dry areas.

POTENTILLA FRUTICOSA 'PRIMROSE BEAUTY' (CINQUEFOIL) Mature size: 3 feet tall and wide. Dense, bushy shrub with fine-textured foliage and small yellow flowers. Full sun, well-drained soil. Zones 2-7.

PRUNUS LAUROCERASUS (CHERRY LAUREL) Mature size: 6-10 (and up to 25) feet tall, 10 feet wide. Evergreen shrub with dense foliage and creamy-white flowers. Full sun or partial shade, well-drained soil, neutral pH. Zones 6-9.

PRUNUS TRILOBA (FLOWERING ALMOND) Mature size: 10 feet tall and wide. Showy double pink flowers. Full sun or partial shade, well-drained soil. Zones 4-8.

PYRACANTHA 'MOHAVE' (FIRETHORN) Mature size: 6-18 feet tall. Showy white flowers in spring, abundant red-orange fruit in fall. Full sun or partial shade, any soil that is not too wet or too dry. Zones 6-10.

PRUNING Renewal pruning can be achieved in one of two ways: removal of ⅓ of the oldest canes each year, or an occasional cutback to the ground of the entire plant in winter.

PROPAGATION Softwood cuttings, taken in early summer, root easily.

USE This shrub's fine texture, refined size, and extended period of bloom make it useful for shrub and perennial borders. Water-wise gardeners choose it for its hardiness and drought-resistance.

CULTIVARS 'Primrose Beauty' is a hardy and most attractive yellow cultivar. 'Abbotswood' has fine-textured, clean blue-green foliage and lovely, long-blooming white flowers. It grows 2-3 feet tall and wide, in a rounded mound shape, but needs to be pruned by removing ⅓ of canes annually to avoid looking unkempt. (Berkshire)

PRUNUS Species *Rosaceae*

A very large genus, *Prunus* includes stone fruits like almond, cherry, nectarine, peach, and plum, as well as florals like choke cherry, blackthorn, and cherry laurel. Most shrubs in the genus are alternate-leaved and deciduous. Flowers can be pink, white, red, or greenish, and are usually borne in clusters.

A true multi-season plant, *Pyracantha* is enjoyed by birds, that often build their nests in it to be nearer the profusion of berries, as much as by humans.

BEST CONDITIONS Deciduous species need full sun (though cherry laurel requires shade); evergreens will tolerate some shade. Soil should be well drained, with a neutral pH; mix in lime if the soil is too acid.

PLANTING Plant in early spring or fall.

FERTILIZER Shrubs in the genus require fertilizer, but too much will leave them increasingly susceptible to disease. Try to strike a balance.

PESTS/DISEASES Watch out for aphids, beetles, fruit worms, borers, and scale, as well as twig blight, powdery mildew, and fungus leaf spots.

PRUNING In the early years, prune to shape. Some varieties need regular pruning to avoid overcrowding; removing large branches will help to discourage rot. Prune carefully, avoiding unnecessary cuts and leaving branch collars intact.

PROPAGATION Sow seeds outdoors or in a cold frame, or take cuttings.

USE Fruiting varieties are grown for their edible bounty as well as their showy spring blossoms. Ornamentals generally have dramatic blooms as well and are often grown as specimens or in eye-catching groups.

SPECIES *P. besseyi* is a low-growing (about 2 feet tall), many-branched shrub native to sandy or rocky prairies of the northern Great Plains. It is very hardy and drought-tolerant. It produces flowers in April and fruit in July.

P. laurocerasus 'Otto Luyken', cherry laurel, is an evergreen shrub with dense foliage and creamy-white flowers. Growing to 25 feet, it is often used in southern gardens as a formal hedge or screen. Susceptible to scale and fungal leaf spot. Hardy to Zone 6. 'Schiptaensis', a compact cherry laurel, is hardy to New York City and Boston.

P. lusitanica, Portugal laurel, is evergreen, with white flowers and purple fruit.

P. glandulosa 'Rosea', Chinese bush cherry, is grown largely for its pretty pink or white flowers. Easy to propagate; hardy to Zone 4 and above, but it does not perform well at Chicago Botanic Garden.

P. maritima, beach plum, is a spiny shrub native to coastal areas from Maine to Virginia. Tolerant of salt spray, it adorns seaside gardens with clusters of white flowers. Grows 3-6 feet.

P. triloba, flowering almond, is covered with large double pink flowers in early spring.

Above: The intense pink flowers of *Raphiolepsis indica* 'Ballerina' contrast beautifully with its glossy bright green foliage.

PYRACANTHA Species FIRETHORN *Rosaceae*

This thorny broadleaf evergreen is a valuable three-season shrub, with showy white flowers in spring and spectacular red-orange fruit in fall. Irregular in form, it is often a nesting plant for the birds that favor its fruits.

BEST CONDITIONS *Pyracantha* will grow in full sun or partial shade in any well-drained garden soil that is neither too wet nor too dry. It is used extensively at the Desert Botanical Garden because it tolerates the heat, low water, and alkaline soil of the region. It sometimes suffers from root rot problems if watered too heavily in clay soils.

PLANTING In spring; best if planted as a containerized plant. Pick a permanent site if possible, as *Pyracantha* is difficult ot move after it becomes established.

RHODODENDRONS IN HIGH-PH REGIONS

Galen Gates of the Chicago Botanic Garden suggests two extensive soil amendments for people who very much want to grow long-term rhododendrons in areas where both soil and water are of high pH.

1. 40 percent medium to large bark pieces, 25 percent sand, 20 percent peat, 15 percent soil.

2. A 50-50 mix of peat moss and medium-to-small bark chips. Ideally, existing soil should be removed as much as possible, and amendment should be made 15 inches deep (or 9 inches deep with plants 6 inches above grade). With the second option, greater watering is necessary for the first year, until the plant is established.

PESTS/DISEASES *Pyracantha* is prone to fireblight: Avoid lingering moisture on foliage and cut out affected areas. Pest problems include scale, aphids, spider mites, apple scab, and lace bugs.

PRUNING Its thorns make it difficult to prune, so allow it room to spread. If espaliering, prune shortly after flowering.

PROPAGATION Take cuttings in late summer; root in a cold frame or greenhouse.

USE *Pyracantha* is often espaliered, especially on west-facing walls. It also makes a fine hedge, specimen, or foundation shrub.

SPECIES AND VARIETIES 'Mohave' boasts beautiful, abundant fruit and is scab-resistant. *P. coccinea* 'Lalandei' is hardy to Zone 6. 'Rutgers' produces superior foliage and fruit and is disease-resistant; grows to 3 feet tall and 10 feet wide. 'Rogers' is strongly vertical.

RAPHIOLEPSIS INDICA INDIAN HAWTHORN *Rosaceae*

Hawthorn is a favorite of southern gardeners, with its lustrous, leathery foliage, showy clusters of white or pink spring flowers, and blue-black to purple-black berries.

BEST CONDITIONS Though hawthorn prefers a fertile loam, it tolerates a wide spectrum of soils and will thrive in either full sun or partial shade.

PLANTING Plant container-grown specimens in spring or fall.

PESTS/DISEASES Nematodes, leaf spot, scales, and twig blights.

PRUNING Prune after flowering, if necessary, to shape and keep in bounds.

PROPAGATION Sow seeds, or propagate hardwood cuttings under glass.

USE This Southern belle is as versatile as it is attractive, planted singly as a striking specimen, massed in a mixed-shrub border or foundation planting, or used as a formal or informal hedge. It can also be planted in containers to dress up a patio or balcony.

CULTIVAR 'Ballerina' is more compact, growing only to 3-4 feet, and its flowers are an intense rosy-pink.

RHODODENDRON Species *Ericaceae*

The genus *Rhododendron* encompasses a wide variety of broadleaf evergreen shrubs (a rare few are deciduous), grown as often for their foliage as for their showy spring flower trusses. These include the shrubs commonly known as azaleas, though most gardeners—and therefore the authors of this book—treat them as a separate group entirely. Offering a dazzling selection of cultivars in virtually every size and hue, rhododendrons are the quintessential shrub for shady gardens to many a northern gardener. Look for bushy plants with at least four main branches at the base.

BEST CONDITIONS Rhododendrons grow best in partial shade—light in the North and heavier in the South—in a light, well-drained, humus-rich soil with an acid pH (4.5-5.5). Avoid poor drainage, clay, alkaline, or salty soil.

PLANTING In the North, choose a site offering protection from winter wind and, especially, sun; in general, larger-leaved rhododendrons require more shelter than the small-leaved types. Dig the hole deep and wide, adding coarse peat

RAPHIOLEPSIS INDICA 'BALLERINA' (HAWTHORN) Mature size: 3-4 feet tall. Lustrous, leathery foliage, showy clusters of pink flowers in spring, dark berries. Full sun or partial shade, loamy soil. Zones 7-10.

RHODODENDRON CAROLINIANUM (CAROLINA RHODODENDRON) Mature size: 6 feet tall. Small-leaved, rounded shrub with white, pale, yellow, rose, or lilac-rose flowers. Partial shade, heavier shade in South; light well-drained, humus-rich, acid soil. Zones 5-8.

RHODODENDRON CATAWBIENSE (CATAWBA RHODODENDRON) Mature size: 8-18 feet tall. Large-leaved evergreen with large magenta-lilac flowers in mid-late spring. Partial shade, heavier shade in South; light, well-drained, humus-rich, acid soil. Zones 4-7.

RHODODENDRON MUCRONULATUM (KOREAN RHODODENDRON) Mature size: 8 feet tall. Deciduous variety with upright to rounded habit, purple or rosy pink flowers in early spring. Partial shade, heavier shade in South; light, well-drained, humus-rich, acid soil. Zones 4-7.

RHODODENDRON 'BOULE DE NEIGE' Mature size: 6 feet tall. Large-leaved shrub with compact, rounded habit and white flowers. Partial shade, heavier shade in South; light, well-drained, humus-rich, acid soil. Zones 5-8.

RHODODENDRON 'BRAVO' Mature size: 6 feet tall. Large-leaved shrub with compact, rounded habit and magenta flowers. Partial shade, heavier shade in South; light, well-drained, humus-rich, acid soil. Zones 5-8.

RHODODENDRON 'HOLDEN' Mature size: 6 feet tall. Large-leaved shrub with sprawling habit and magenta flowers. Partial shade, heavier shade in South; light, well-drained, humus-rich, acid soil. Zones 5-8.

RHODODENDRON 'NEPAL' Mature size: 6 feet tall. Large-leaved shrub with compact, rounded habit and white flowers. Partial shade, heavier shade in South; light, well-drained, humus-rich, acid soil. Zones 5-8.

moss or other composted organic matter to increase the humus content. If drainage is poor, construct a raised bed. Rhododendrons can be planted in fall or spring, but those planted in fall require an application of thick mulch over the soil. If containerized plants are root bound, make vertical slits through the circling roots and tease them out with your fingers before planting.

WATER During establishment and periods of drought.

FERTILIZER Apply nitrogen in early spring.

WEEDING Protect rhododendron's shallow root system by hand-pulling weeds; do not cultivate the surrounding soil.

PESTS/DISEASES Stressed rhododendrons are troubled by a host of pests, but proper culture will greatly reduce the incidence of insect and disease damage.

PRUNING Deadhead spent blossoms in spring and pinch out terminal leaf buds in fall.

PROPAGATION Cuttings taken in mid August will root in 2-4 months. Rhododendrons can also be propagated by layering.

USE One of the most popular shrubs for foundation plantings and shrub borders, rhododendrons are also impressive when massed in open woodland glades, and the more vigorous cultivars make effective screens and informal hedges. The best companies are other members of the heath family, as well as oaks, pines, magnolias, white birches, conifers, and hollies.

SPECIES *R. catawbiense,* Catawba rhododendron, is a large-leaved evergreen with 5- to 6-inch lilac-magenta flower trusses. Mature size: 8-18 feet tall. Cultivars: 'America' is highly floriferous, with trusses of a brilliant deep red. Hardy Zones 5-6. Mature size: 8-18 feet tall. 'Cunningham's White' is low and compact with white flowers. Hardy in Zone 5. Mature size: 4 feet tall. 'Nova Zembla' is a tall shrub with red flowers. Hardy in Zone 5 and above. Mature size: 8-18 feet tall. 'Roseum Elegans' offers heat tolerance, uniform habit, and lavender-pink blooms. Hardy in Zone 5. Mature size: 8-18 feet tall. *R.* 'Boule de Neige' is a large-leaved shrub with a compact, rounded habit and white flowers. Hardy in Zone 5 and above. Mature size: 6 feet tall. *R. carolinianum,* Carolina rhododendron, is small-leaved, evergreen, and rounded; floral color can be white, pale yellow, rose, or lilac-rose. Hardy Zones 5-8. Mature size: 4-6 feet tall and wide.

R. mucronulatum, Korean rhododendron, is a deciduous variety with an upright or rounded outline. In early spring (late March in Philadelphia) it produces flowers of purple or rosy pink. Hardy Zones 4-7. Mature size: 4-8 feet tall and wide. 'Cornell Pink' has bright pink flowers. 'Pink Peignoir' has soft pink flowers.

R. yakusimanum, Yak rhododendron, is a slow grower that forms a dense, low, evergreen mound. Flowers are pink in bud, fading to white as they open. Hardy Zones 6-7. Mature size: 3-5 feet tall. 'Mist Maiden' is a robust grower with attractive white indumentum on young stems and under leaves. Semievergreen, it retains its leaves for four years.

R. fortunei, Fortune rhododendron, has handsome foliage and fragrant, blush-pink flowers that fade to white as they open. Flowers are up to 4 inches

Above: Rhododendrons growing with ferns, a good combination.

RHODODENDRON 'NOVA ZEMBLA' Mature size: 8-18 feet tall. Tall shrub with red flowers. Partial shade, heavier shade in South; light, well-drained, humus-rich, acid soil. Zones 5-8.

RHODODENDRON 'ROSEUM ELEGANS' Mature size: 8-18 feet tall. Uniform habit, lavender-pink blooms. Partial shade, heavier in South, light, well-drained, humus-rich, acid soil. Heat-tolerant. Zones 5-9.

RHODODENDRON 'YAKU KING' Mature size: 3 feet tall, 4 feet wide. Compact, dense shrub with dark green leaves, large trusses of flowers. Partial shade, heavier in South, light, well-drained, humus-rich, acid soil. Zones 5-7.

RHODODENDRON 'YAKU QUEEN' Mature size: 3 feet tall, 4 feet wide. Compact, dense shrub with dark green leaves, large trusses of flowers. Partial shade, heavier in South, light, well-drained, humus-rich, acid soil. Zones 5-7.

across, 8-9 per truss, and loosely arranged. Hardy Zones 6-8. Mature size: 15 feet tall.

R. maximum, rosebay rhododendron, is a large-leaved woodland shrub. Its pink to white (rarely, red) early July flowers are unspectacular. Hardy Zones 5-6. Mature size: 15 feet tall.

Dexter rhododendron cultivars include 'Ben Moseley'which has light purple to pink flowers with a dark central blotch. Hardy Zones 6-7. Mature size: 6 feet tall. 'Parker's Pink' has bright, deep pink fragrant flowers heavily spotted with dark red, fading to white in the throat. Hardy Zones 5-7. Mature size: 6 feet tall. 'Scintillation' bears pastel pink flowers with amber throats in large trusses. Leaves are deep green and glossy, and habit is spreading. Hardy Zones 6-8. Mature size: 6 feet tall. 'Wyandanch Pink' has bright pink, lightly spotted flowers and large, glossy leaves. Hardy Zones 6-7. Mature size: 6 feet tall. Leach rhododendron 'Anna H. Hall' is compact and dense, with new growth conspicuously indumented. Flowers are pink in bud and open to white. Hardy Zones 5-7. Mature size: 4 feet tall. 'Bravo' grows up 12 feet in height.

Try to buy rhododendron plants in flower, so you are sure of their flower color and can plan color schemes.

AZALEAS

Azaleas are among the most popular and commonly-used shrubs in home gardens, and with good reason: given the proper site, they are long-lived, easy to care for, and present a stunning display of color every year. All azaleas are all rhododendron. The differences between azaleas and other rhododendron are not clear-cut, but most rhododendron are evergreen and have 10 or more stamens; most azaleas are deciduous and have 5 stamens.

BEST CONDITIONS Azaleas can be grown in a wide range of well-drained soils, providing they have been enriched with an abundance of humus or decomposed organic matter. These acid-loving plants prefer a pH of 5.0-6.0; if the soil is too alkaline, add sulfur or a mixture of 3 parts sulfur and 1 part iron sulfate, using 1 pound per square foot to lower the pH 1 point; water in thoroughly. Do not use aluminum sulfate. Azaleas have fine, shallow roots and require artificial drainage in heavy clay soils that drain poorly. An alternative is to grow them in raised beds (12-18 inches high), using a mix of 3 parts pine bark (¼-½ inch pieces), 1 part peat, and 1 part perlite.

Azaleas can be grown in full sun in the cooler parts of the country. In the Southeast, a location in semishade is desirable, particularly for late-flowering plants, which benefit from light midday shade.

Gardeners on much of the continent west of the Mississippi have little success with azaleas; they do not thrive in the alkaline soil that is prevalent in that region. They are, however, a staple in gardens around Houston and other areas on the Gulf coast. Research is being done on many fronts to find selections that will succeed in the West; the "Northern Lights" series developed in Minnesota is one example. Gardeners who love azaleas and live in areas where azaleas do not thrive are advised to try with potted plants, or with raised beds made with amended soil.

PLANTING Although azaleas in containers can be planted year-round, the ideal times to plant are early fall and early spring. The planting hole should be shallow—less than 12 inches deep for a 2- to 3-gallon plant—and 2-3 times as wide as deep; plant at soil level or slightly higher. On slopes, build a mound on the lower side, providing a basin to hold moisture. Plant on a firm base to avoid settling, and firm (but don't tamp or pack) the back-filled soil; water thoroughly to moisten the plant and the surrounding soil.

Spacing depends on the species or cultivar; do not overplant or disregard the plant's ultimate size and growth habit. A minimum distance for most azaleas is not less than 3-4 feet apart. Large-growing cultivars (reaching 6 feet or more) should be spaced not less than 5 feet apart and often require 6-8 feet; dwarf azaleas can be spaced at intervals of 18-24 inches (keep in mind, however, that some plants advertised as dwarfs develop into green giants). If you do make an error, azaleas are easily transplanted.

FERTILIZER Fertilizer is not a cure-all, but healthly plants do respond to a moderate application. Use a slow-release fertilizer such as 12-6-6 or a special azalea fertilizer, applying ½-1 pound per 100 square feet (for plants 12 inches or smaller, a teaspoon is ample; use a handful for moderate to large individual

Opposite: Just a few of the thousands of varieties of azaleas, showing the range of color, size, and flower forms.

RHODODENDRON AUSTRINUM (FLORIDA FLAME AZALEA) Mature size: 10 feet. Yellow and orange funnelform flowers. Full sun, partial shade in South; well-drained soil, rich in organic matter. Zones 6-9.

RHODODENDRON PRINOPHYLLUM (EARLY AZALEA) Mature size: 8 feet. Rosy or deep pink funnelform flowers. Full sun, partial shade in South; well-drained soil, rich in organic matter. Zones 4-8.

RHODODENDRON SCHLIPPENBACHII (ROYAL AZALEA) Mature size: 8 feet tall and wide. Deciduous plant with large leaves and large fragrant pink flowers. Full sun, partial shade in South; well-drained soil, rich in organic matter. Zones 5-9.

RHODODENDRON VASEYI (PINKSHELL AZALEA) Mature size: 8 feet tall, 6 feet wide. Deciduous shrub with light pink flowers, narrow leaves. Full sun, partial shade in South; well-drained soil, rich in organic matter. Zones 5-8.

plants). One application in early spring can be followed by a lighter application in early July. Do not fertilize later than this to allow plants to harden off in fall, and protect them from an early freeze.

PESTS/DISEASES Azaleas are relatively free of diseases and insect pests. The most common disease, petal blight, usually shows up in late spring on mid-season azaleas in hot, humid weather; infected flowers first develop water spots and then collapse, often remaining on the stem. Systemic fungicidal sprays are available to treat this unsightly but not lethal affliction. Another common disease, stem wilt, is soil-borne. Remove any diseased stems and use a fungicidal soil drench. Leaf gall, a fleshy, pale-green or whitish fungal growth, is easily controlled by hand-picking and destroying the galls. Lacewings—usually an affliction of azaleas growing in full sun—feed on the underside of the leaves, which turn spotted and yellowish and develop small black excretions. Spray the backs of the leaves with insecticidal soap every 7-10 days.

PRUNING Azaleas often require a light to moderate pruning to remove dead wood and to help them conform to the natural shape of the particular cultivar. Pruning into green globes or other unnatural shapes should generally be avoided, since nature has provided the azalea with an enviably graceful habit. Young plants, however, need to be well pruned to help them develop into compact shrubs, and tall, leggy plants can be sculpture-pruned into tree forms to emphasize trunk and branching habits.

Azaleas can be pruned either after flowering or before the new flower buds have begun to form in mid summer. Light pruning, however, can be done anytime. To rejuvenate an old, leggy, or misshapen plant, cut it back to ½ its size, or even more severely, to 6-12 inches from the ground. New vegetative shoots will develop from adventitious buds on the bare stems. Follow up with light pruning on the vigorous stems to develop lateral branching.

PROPAGATION Evergreen azaleas can be propagated from 3- to 5-inch cuttings of firm but not hardened wood. This can be done any season of the year, but the ideal time is mid to late spring after the new growth has firmed up. Remove ⅓-½ of the lower leaves and use a knife or fingernail to make a light, ½-inch basal wound. In a rooting box or enclosed plastic tent, stick cutting halfway down in a rooting medium and water them. Evergreen cuttings will normally root in 4-6 weeks, at which time they can be transplanted to pots. To avoid this first transplanting, root them in individual 2- to 3-inch pots.

Deciduous azaleas are more difficult to root from cuttings. If you want to try, take them from firm, soft wood in late spring, and root in individual small containers. The young, rooted cuttings can be lightly fertilized the same season to help boost active vegetative growth and/or develop flower buds; if this growth doesn't occur, the cutting will fail to come out the following spring. Recently, propagators have had greater success with deciduous cuttings that were moved into a greenhouse in winter with additional light.

SPECIES Deciduous azaleas include *R. calendulaceum* (yellow-orange to scarlet flowers); *R. austrinum* (yellow; fragrant); *R. alabamense* (white with yellow blotches; fragrant); *R. arborescens* (white, late in season; fragrant); *R. prunifoli-*

Above: R. calendulaceum (Flame azalea) keeps its vivid color, even in strong sun. Many modern selections are hybrids of this native American species.

VIEWPOINTS

NATIVE RHODODENDRONS

I understand why some gardeners use hybrid rhododendron–their vivid colors and compact habits are never found in the natives. But growing native plants gives a regional feeling to a garden, blending the natural history of the area into your site, and helps keep the gene pool diverse.
ETHAN JOHNSON, THE HOLDEN ARBORETUM, OHIO

There are many reasons to grow native azaleas. Many have a more graceful form than the Far Eastern hybrids, as well as more fragrance. Too, they bloom later than the hybrids–*R. prunifolium* lasts well into the summer.
CLAIRE SAWYERS, THE SCOTT ARBORETUM, PENNSYLVANIA

In our climate, with our soil, we can't use natives. The only selections that work here are those in the "Northern Lights" series, developed specifically for our region.
RICHARD ISAACSON, MINNESOTA LANDSCAPE ARBORETUM

My preference for natives is based on aesthetics–I prefer their softer colors and more natural growth habit. Although some of the southern natives do not do well in our region, many of them are quite hardy here.
DORTHE HVIID, BERKSHIRE BOTANICAL GARDEN, MASSACHUSETTS

I love native azaleas–but in our alkaline soil it is not possible to grow them. True azalea fanatics can grow them in pots, or replace all the soil in their gardens–but we usually recommend trying some of the great desert shrubs.
MARY IRISH, DESERT BOTANICAL GARDEN, ARIZONA

um (orange-red, late in season). *R. viscosum* (swamp azalea) has white flowers with a clovelike fragrance. It blooms in May and tolerates wet conditions; Zones 4-8. *R. vaseyi* (pinkshell azalea) grows 6-9 feet tall with an irregular, erect habit; rose-colored flowers emerge in early May. Zones 5-9. *R. periclymenoides {nudiflorum}* (pinxterbloom azalea) bears fragrant pink to white flowers in late April. It is native to dry, rocky soil. Zones 4-9.

Many hybrid deciduous azaleas were developed from two English hybrid groups, Knap Hill and Exbury; hybrid groups include Occidentalis, Girard, Carlson, and Windsor. These are medium to large shrubs, 4-10 feet tall, 4-6 feet wide at maturity. In addition to a wide range of floral color in spring–from white, yellow, and orange to pink and red–they offer attractive fall foliage and are hardy Zones 5-7. Among the many named cultivars available are 'Gibraltar' (vivid orange); 'Hotspur' (reddish orange); 'Homebush' (purplish red, semidouble); 'Cecile' (vivid red); 'Strawberry Ice' (yellowish pink); and 'Exbury White' (white, with yellow blotch).

The "Northern Lights" series of azaleas was developed for bud hardiness in Minnesota and so can tolerate rough winters; depending on the particular cultivar, they are hardy from -35° to -45° F. in Zones 4-8. Most are crosses between North American species and Mollis, Exbury, and other hybrids. Many are fragrant. Named cultivars include 'Pink Lights', 'Rosy Light', 'White Lights', 'Orchid Lights', 'Spicy Lights', and 'Northern Hi-lights'.

Evergreen azaleas include the Kurume group. These azaleas, originally from Japan, are large shrubs with a habit ranging from 4-6 feet and taller. The flowers can be either single or hose-in-hose, 1-1½ inches wide, and their colors encompass white, pink, red, and purple. Major cultivars include 'Hinode Girl' (red); 'Christmas Cheer' (strong red, hose-in-hose); 'Snow' (white, hose-in-hose); 'Appleblossom' (white, tinged with pink); 'Peach Glow' (yellowish pink); 'Coral Bells' (strong pink, hose-in-hose); 'Pink Pearl' (pink); 'Sherwood Red' (vivid red).

Kaempferi azaleas were hybridized in the United States and Europe from Japanese species, including *R. kaempferi, R. yedoense,* and *R. poukhanense.* They can reach a mature height of 4-10 feet or more and produce 1- to 2½-inch flowers with leaves that are periodically persistent. Among the many hybrid groups are Girard, Linwood, Shammorello, Greenwood, and Schroeder. Two outstanding cultivars are 'Delaware Valley White' and 'Ruth May' (light pink).

Belgian Indian hybrids are large-flowered azaleas (2-3 inches in diameter and larger) originally developed in Belgium as greenhouse plants. Flowers are single or double, in white, pink, red, or purple. Hybrids 'Nuccios', 'Kerrigan', and 'Mossholder' are usually hardy in Zones 8-9 (California and Florida), while others, including 'Red Wing' (red) and 'Easter Parade' (light pink), are more cold-hardy and can ususally survive in Zone 7.

Southern Indian azaleas are selections of Belgian hybrids. They were tested in South Carolina and proved hardy in Zone 8; some are hardy in Zone 7. Cultivars include 'Formosa' (deep purplish red); 'Mucronatum' {Indian Alba}

RHODODENDRON 'HOTSPUR' (EXBURY HYBRID AZALEA) Mature size: 4-10 feet wide, 4-6 feet tall. Deciduous plant produces reddish orange flowers and attractive foliage. Full sun, partial shade in South; well-drained soil, rich in organic matter. Zones 5-7.

RHODODENDRON 'BEN MORRISON' (GLENN DALE HYBRID AZALEA) Mature size: 8-10 feet. Very showy pink and white blossoms. Full sun, partial shade in South; well-drained soil, rich in organic matter. Zones 5-8.

RHODODENDRON 'GEORGE LINDSEY TABOR' (SOUTHERN INDIAN HYBRID AZALEA) Mature size: 6-10 feet tall. Evergreen plant produces white flowers laced with pink or lavender. Full sun, partial shade in South; well-drained soil, rich in organic matter. Zones 7-10.

RHODODENDRON 'GLORY' (KURUME HYBRID AZALEA) Mature size: 4-6 feet tall. Evergreen plant produces profuse pink blossom. Full sun, partial shade in South; well-drained soil, rich in organic matter. Zones 6-9.

RHODODENDRON 'GUMPO' (SATSUKI HYBRID AZALEA) Mature size: 4-6 feet tall. Evergreen plant produces pink and white flowers. Partial shade in afternoon, particularly in South; well-drained soil, rich in organic matter. Zones 7-9.

RHODODENDRON KAEMPFERI 'OTHELLO' (KAEMPFERI HYBRID AZALEA) Mature size: 4-10 feet tall. Evergreen plant produces 1- to 2½-inch flowers. Full sun, partial shade in South; well-drained soil, rich in organic matter. Zones 5-8.

RHODODENDRON 'BLUE TIP' (ROBIN HILL HYBRID AZALEA) Matures size: 4-8 feet. Full sun, partial shade in South; well-drained soil, rich in organic matter. Zones 5-8.

RHODOTYPOS SCANDENS (JETBEAD) Mature size: 4-6 feet tall. Single white flowers, shiny black berries. Full sun or shade, any garden soil. Zones 5-8.

(white); 'Daphne Salmon' (salmon); 'Criterion' (strong pink); 'Mrs. G.G. Gerbing' (white); 'President Clay's' (strong red); 'George Lindsey Tabor' (white laced with pink); 'Gulf Pride' (light purple); 'Mardi Gras' (white striped with purple); and 'Delaware Valley White' (white, a Mucronatum hybrid).

Satsuki hybrids bloom relatively late in the season (usually May and June). Usually compact, low to medium-sized shrubs, they require partial shade from noon to midafternoon. The flowers are usually single and can be striped or bordered and come in white, pink, purple, or red. Hardy Zones 7-9, the Satsuki hybrids originated in Japan and feature more than 500 cultivars, including 'Gumpo' (white, pink); 'Benigasa' (vivid red); 'Bunka' (light pink with a white center); 'Keisetsu' (light pink with a red center and blotches, variegated foliage); and 'Wakabisu' (yellowish pink, hose-in-hose).

Glenn Dale hybrids, encompassing more than 400 named cultivars, were developed in the United States. Medium to large shrubs, they offer a variety of bloom seasons (early, mid, and late), flower selection (single, double, and hose-in-hose), and color (white, pink, red, and purple); they are hardy Zones 6-9. Cultivars include 'Allure' (light pink, early); 'Day Spring' (light pink with a white center, early); 'Glacier' (white) ; 'Fashion' (salmon pink); 'Festive' (white flushed with pink); 'Refrain' (light pink); 'Treasure' (white, mid season); 'Ben Morrison' (pink with irregular white margins); and 'Sagittarius' (pink, late season).

Other recommended hybrid groups are Back Acre, Robin Hill, Greenwood, North Tisbury, Carlson, and Harris azaleas.

RHODOTYPOS SCANDENS JETBEAD, WHITE KERRIA *Rosaceae*

This adaptable shrub sports four-petaled white flowers in spring and shiny black fruits, carried in clusters of four, that persist throughout the winter.

BEST CONDITIONS Jetbead generally thrives in any garden soil, in full sun or shade, and is highly tolerant of urban pollution.

PLANTING Plant in spring or fall.

PESTS/DISEASES None serious.

PRUNING Prune to shape, if necessary, in early spring.

PROPAGATION Soft- and hardwood cuttings root easily. Seeds can also be sown.

USE Though no one would classify the homely jetbead as showy, it makes a serviceable addition to the mixed-shrub border. Modest size and pollution tolerance make it a natural for small urban gardens.

RHUS Species SUMAC *Anacardiaceae*

The genus *Rhus* encompasses a large group of shrubs and small trees, many of them desirable for their blazing fall foliage and brilliant fruit (and some of them—including poison sumac, poison ivy, and poison oak—entirely undesirable). These are not the most ornamental of shrubs year-round, but if fall color is an important consideration, the sumacs are simply unbeatable.

BEST CONDITIONS Sumacs are highly tolerant of dry soils and can be planted

Above: Rhus typhina 'Laciniata' is the most ornamental of the sumacs, with elegantly cut leaves that keep their rich color well into fall; shown above with *Pennisetum.*

SHRUBS FROM THE WILD

There is too much damage being done to wild populations of plants. If someone really wants to grow a plant that is not available commercially, he or she should collect seeds; that will not harm the native population and will perpetrate genetic diversity.
GALEN GATES,
CHICAGO BOTANIC GARDEN

I discourage people from taking wild plants; in most cases, the plant will not survive when taken from its natural habitat and put into an artificial landscape. Furthermore, I advise gardeners to make sure that they buy plants only from nurseries that propagate them; look for nurseries that advertise "nursery-propagated" plants rather than "nursery-grown" ones. "Nursery-grown" plants may have been taken from the wild and replanted in the nursery.
ROBERT BOWDEN, ATLANTA

I believe plants should never be taken from the wild; it depletes the amount of desirable plants available for everyone's enjoyment and destroys natural habitats.
DORTHE HVIID, BERKSHIRE BOTANICAL GARDEN

The only time I'd suggest that a plant be taken from a wild area is if you are getting there just before the bulldozer. If the plant is going to be destroyed anyway, you may as well take a chance at saving it. Otherwise, there is no good reason for taking a plant from the wild.
CHRIS GRAHAM,
ROYAL BOTANICAL GARDEN

where few other shrubs will grow, including exposed banks and rocky slopes. Any garden soil will suffice, along with either full sun or partial shade.
PLANTING Easily transplantable, sumacs can be planted in either spring or fall.
PESTS/DISEASES None serious.
PRUNING Sumacs can be rejuvenated with ease; to keep them vigorous, prune back judiciously every 1-2 years.
PROPAGATION Propagate by seeds, divisions, or root cuttings.
USE With the exception of *R. typhina* 'Laciniata', most sumacs make poor specimens, but work well in masses, especially where their extraordinary fall show can be appreciated.
SPECIES *R. aromatica*, fragrant sumac, is a sprawling, dense, vigorous shrub with aromatic foliage and small, red late-summer fruit. Excellent for dry, exposed banks, it boasts vivid yellow and scarlet fall color. Hardy Zones 3-8; grows to 6 feet high and 10 feet wide. The cultivar 'Gro-Low', developed in the Chicago area rarely exceeds 3 feet in height, but can spread as far as 8 feet in width; it is quite useful as a foundation plant and along walkways where people can brush against its fragrant stems and foliage.
R. copallina, shining sumac, derives its name from its eye-catching glossy foliage, which turns a bright scarlet in fall. With its crimson fruit, it is one of the few sumacs showy enough to stand on its own as a garden specimen. The young plant has a compact habit, but as it matures it becomes more loose and picturesque. Hardy Zones 5-9; grows to 30 feet high.
R. typhina, staghorn sumac, has velvety branches reminiscent of the antlers of a young stag. Its yellow-green flowers are showier than most of the sumacs' flowers, but its greatest assets are its small crimson fruits borne in pyramidal clusters and its red fall color. Very tolerant of dry soils. Hardy Zones 3-8; grows to 20 feet high. The cultivar 'Laciniata', noted for its elegantly cut leaves and spreading habit, is far and away the most ornamental of the sumacs.

RIBES ODORATUM CLOVE CURRANT, GOLDEN CURRANT, BUFFALO CURRANT *Saxifragaceae*

It's easy to see why this old-fashioned shrub, native to much of the Great Plains, was beloved of many a turn-of-the-century gardener. With its profusion of delightfully fragrant yellow flowers, its edible black fruit, and yellow fall color, it continues to be a highly useful plant for all seasons. Flowers and foliage appear together, in mid May, followed in summer by fruit. A caveat: Because the clove currant is a host for white pine blister rust—a highly destructive disease of five-needled pines—its cultivation is either forbidden or severely limited by the U. S. Department of Agriculture. (Since white pines are rarely grown in the Great Plains—the area where clove currant has its greatest utility as a landscape plant—this isn't as serious a problem as it may sound.)
BEST CONDITIONS Clove currant will do well in any good garden soil, particularly if it is somewhat dry and well drained. Though it tolerates full sun, it does best in a partially shaded site. It should be grown in areas of the Midwest

RHUS AROMATICA (SUMAC) Mature size: 6 feet tall, 10 feet wide. Sprawling, dense shrub with aromatic foliage that turns vivd yellow and scarlet in fall. Full sun or partial shade; any garden soil, tolerant of dry soil. Zones 3-8.

RIBES ODORATUM (CLOVE CURRANT) Mature 6 feet tall. Fragrant yellow flowers, edible fruit. Best in partial shade, tolerates full sun; any good garden soil, dry, well-drained soil is best. Zones 3-7.

ROSA X BORBONIANA 'ZEPHERINE DROUHIN' (BOURBON ROSE) Mature size: 10-12 foot canes. Profuse double pink flowers, repeat blooming in warm climates. At least 6 hours of sun per day; rich, well-drained soil. Zones 5-9.

ROSA 'BETTY PRIOR' (FLORIBUNDA ROSE) Mature size: 6-8 feet tall and wide. Vigorous hardy rose with clusters of medium-pink single flowers. At least 6 hours of sun per day; rich, well-drained soil. Zones 5-8.

where there is low atmospheric moisture; it does not perform well in the Chicago area, and often develops severe leaf fungal problems.

PLANTING Plant bare-root stock in early spring; containerized shrubs can be planted in spring or fall. Space 3-4 feet apart.

PESTS/DISEASES See the caveat above.

PRUNING Trim out some of the oldest wood after flowering. Prune anytime to shape or keep in bounds.

PROPAGATION Softwood cuttings can be taken in June and July, or propagate by division or suckers in early spring.

USE A welcome addition to the informal shrub border, this is an especially valuable plant for difficult very dry and shady areas. Indeed, its preference for shade makes it useful as a facer for taller shrubs or trees. By all means, plant it where its delightful clovelike fragrance can be enjoyed—and consider using the fruit in preserves. (Dyck Arboretum)

VARIETY *R. odoratum* 'Crandall' is valued for its large fruit.

ROSA Species ROSE *Rosacea*

Roses exert a unique appeal among flora—in literature, in the etiquette of romantic love, and in the garden itself. Beloved of contemporary gardeners, they claim a long and complex history, medicinal, metaphorical, and ornamental. Not surprisingly, tracing the ancestry of the genus has proved a daunting horticultural task. However, most authorities agree that the majority of our modern garden roses have been derived from only 7 or 8 of the 150 or so wild species native to the temperate to subtropical regions of Asia, Europe, and North America. Extensive hybridization—particularly during the 19th century—has resulted in considerable diversity despite a rather limited gene pool. But the greatest contribution to *Rosa* as we know the genus today came in the late 18th century with the introduction to Europe of the Asian species, most notably the China rose (*Rosa chinensis*). These exotic beauties not only added new flower colors to the gene pool, but also introduced the desirable capability of repeat bloom.

The botanical classification of roses has befuddled many an experienced gardener. No other botanical genus has been examined in such detail, as attested by the International Registration Authority for Roses, which currently recognizes 44 distinct classes. For the lay gardener, however, roses need only be grouped according to their basic characteristics and use in the garden.

Species roses: These are the only roses that occur and reproduce naturally in the wild. While only a few are commonly cultivated, this group represents the gene pool for future hybridization.

Shrub roses: Botanically speaking, virtually all roses fall into this category, but for the purpose of the home gardener, the group is more limited, including the hybrid rugosa, hybrid spinosissima, eglantine, hybrid musk, polyantha, and shrub rose types. Growth habits are diverse, ranging from prostrate ground covers to vigorous tall shrubs, but all are versatile and easy to grow. Most are hardy without winter protection and require only occasional prun-

Below: Antique roses sprawl charmingly around stone benches.

ing. Many of the newer hybrids have excellent flowers and are remontant (reblooming) and extremely disease-resistant. Shrub roses are normally used as specimen or background plants in borders and foundation plantings.

Antique garden roses: Now enjoying a renaissance, these were the dominant bedding roses of the 19th century, though in modern landscapes they seem better suited to less formal settings. Many are fragrant, remontant, and hardy without winter protection. Included in this group are the classes alba, Bourbon, centifolia, China, damask, gallica, hybird perpetual, hybrid sempervirens, moss, noisette, Portland, and tea.

Modern hybrid roses: Including the classes for floribunda, grandiflora, hybrid tea, and miniature, these are complex hybrids primarily distinguished by their floral characteristics. Floribundas are generally bushy plants that produce clusters of small flowers; hybrid teas typically bear solitary flowers of a larger size on strong stems. Most of the grandifloras are tall plants that throw off the large blooms of the hybrid teas in floribunda-like clusters. Collectively, these three classes make up the main bedding roses used in modern gardens and are normally displayed in group plantings, both to simplify their culture and to maximize their visual impact. Miniature roses produce small flowers on primarily dwarf plants and are particularly well-suited to growing in containers. All require, or benefit from, winter protection from Zone 6 northward.

Above: Modern roses at The Royal Botanical Garden, Hamilton, Ontario.

BEST CONDITIONS Roses need at least 6 hours of full sun daily; a site with good air circulation will help combat the spread of disease. Soil should be well-drained, neutral to slightly acidic, and rich in organic matter. Incorporating generous amounts of well-rotted manure, compost, or peat to a depth of 18-24 inches will improve the site. Adjust the pH as necessary, by adding sulfur (to lower pH) or agricultural lime (to raise it). At Chicago Botanic Garden, almost 200 kinds of roses grow beautifully in soil with a pH of 7.2-7.6.

PLANTING Fall or spring is preferable for bare-root plants, though container-grown stock can be carefully planted at any time. In cold regions, plant by mid-September if planting in fall, so that plants will be established before frost. For budded plants in areas where winter protection is required, make sure that the bud union is 1½-2 inches below grade.

PESTS/DISEASES Roses are prone to attack by a wide variety of insect and disease pests, though the specific type of problem and the severity of infestation can vary greatly depending on location and cultivar. Some of the new hardy shrub roses display good disease resistance and may require very little spraying. Most of the modern hybrids, however, require a regular program of spraying to control common rose problems like blackspot, powdery mildew, aphids, and spider mites.

PRUNING Species, shrub, and most antique garden roses require only occasional pruning. Young plants will probably need only a light tidying in early spring to remove dead or damaged branches. To maintain vigor in older plants, periodically remove a few of the oldest canes immediately following the first flush of bloom. Modern hybrid roses and hybrid perpetuals require a different pruning regime. After winter protection has been removed, cut back winter-dam-

ROSA 'QUEEN ELIZABETH' (GRANDIFLORA ROSE) Mature size: 4-8 feet tall. Large, double fragrant flowers, repeat bloom. At least 6 hours of sun per day; rich, well-drained soil. Zones 5-8.

ROSA 'PEACE' (HYBRID TEA ROSE) Mature size: 4-6 feet tall. Glossy dark foliage, creamy yellow flowers tinged with pink. At least 6 hours of sun per day; rich, well-drained soil. Zones 4-8.

ROSA 'CAREFREE BEAUTY' (SHRUB ROSE) Mature size: 3-6 feet tall. Profusely flowers, vigorous grower. At least 6 hours of sun per day; rich, well-drained soil. Zones 4-8.

SALIX GRACILISTYLA (ROSEGOLD PUSSY WILLOW) Mature size: 6-10 feet. Narrow, blue-green leaves, pinkish-red catkins. Any ordinary garden soil, moist soil is best. Zones 6-10.

aged canes to healthy wood (which will have white pith, or center). The resulting plant height will vary, but is typically 12-15 inches in the North and 18-24 inches in the South. Remove entirely any dead, weak, or crossing canes. Ideally, the pruned plant will have 3-5 strong canes, each with a healthy, outward-facing bud at the top. To encourage repeat bloom in modern hybrid roses, especially hybrid teas and grandifloras, spent flowers must be removed. This deadheading process simply involves pruning the spent flower stem just above the first or second set of 5-leaflet leaves. In late autumn, cut the plants back to about 24 inches, just prior to protecting for winter.

WINTER PROTECTION Most hybrid roses will require some winter protection north of Zone 5. The simplest method is to mound 12-15 inches of soil over each plant. You can use plastic, metal, or cardboard collars to help contain the soil. This "hilling" should be done in late autumn, after the plants have defoliated, and should be left in place until the soil has thawed in the spring. At the Chicago Botanic Garden, mounding is not done until temperature has dropped to 18° F., to ensure that plant is dormant; a mix of leaves, soil and compost is used; this mixture "breathes" and does not suffocate the plants.

CULTIVARS 'The Fairy' is a surprisingly hardy rose with a low, spreading habit-that grows without winter protection even in Minneapolis. It blooms freely over the summer season and is not troubled by the usual pests and diseases. 'Carefree Beauty' is a superior garden rose for both its hardiness and disease resistance. 'Peace' has been the most popular hybrid tea rose since its 1945 introduction. A vigorous upright grower with glossy dark green leaves, it blooms all season and makes a fine cut flower. 'Betty Prior' is a vigorous, hardy, and disease-resistant floribunda, with medium-pink single flowers borne in clusters of up to 10. 'Queen Elizabeth' is one of the best grandifloras, with excellent repeat bloom and large fully double fragrant flowers.

SALIX Species WILLOW *Salicaceae*

The genus *Salix* includes a large number of vigorous plants, from low-growing shrubs—the most familiar of which is that harbinger of spring, the common pussy willow—to very large trees. All, however, sport alternate, usually slender leaves, and when they flower produce catkins that appear before the leaves in spring. Because many of the plants are brittle-wooded, they are susceptible to damage from both pests and the elements.

BEST CONDITIONS Willows do best in soil that is fairly moist, but most will be nearly as vigorous in any ordinary garden soil.

PLANTING Most of the dwarf willows are extremely easy to transplant and can be planted out in either spring or fall; indeed, in some cases, unrooted cuttings can simply be placed directly in the soil where they are to grow, ideally in early spring prior to leaf emergence (if the soil is kept uniformly moist).

PESTS/DISEASES As a genus, *Salix* is susceptible to a wide variety of pests and diseases, among them twig and leaf blights, leaf spots, many cankers, powdery mildew, rust, aphids, willow lace bug, willow flea weevil, and willow scurfy scale.

Observe this dew-drenched rose
   of Tyrian gardens
A rose today.
But you will ask in vain
Tomorrow what it is;
and yesterday
It was the dust, the sunshine,
   and the rain.
LUCRETIUS

PRUNING Prune anytime to shape or keep in bounds.
PROPAGATION Softwood cuttings taken in late spring or early summer root easily.
USE Shrub willows have an affinity for naturalistic and woodland settings; they are simply out of place in more formal gardens.
SPECIES *S. gracilistyla*, rosegold pussy willow, is recommended for its long, narrow blue-green leaves and its pinkish-red catkins with orange anthers. Hardy Zones 6-10; grows 4-10 feet tall.
S. repens var argentea has dense, woolly foliage that is nearly white.
S. r. var rosmarinifolia is an upright shrub with narrow deep green leathery leaves with silver undersides, highly attractive when blown by the wind.
S. sachalinensis 'Sekko', Japanese fantail willow, is often grown as a small tree; flower arrangers prize it for the sculptural quality of its twisted branches. Hardy Zones 5 -9; grows to 10-15 feet tall.
S. purpurea 'Nana', dwarf arctic willow, is a coarse-textured shrub that grows 3-4 feet tall and can be used as a ground cover or hedge in the North. Foliage has a bluish cast. It is easily grown and disease free.

SPIRAEA Species SPIREA *Rosaceae*

A favorite of many gardeners, spirea is among the most widely planted shrubs in the landscape. There are many species and cultivars ranging in size from only a few inches tall to 8 feet or more. Spireas are found natively throughout the United States and Asia. The large clusters of flowers in early spring and summer that are a trademark of this plant provide immense enjoyment for those gardeners who prefer carefree plants.
BEST CONDITIONS Most spireas can be grown happily in partial shade or full sun, in any well-drained garden soil.
PLANTING This easy-to-establish shrub can be planted anytime from containers.
PESTS/DISEASES None serious.
PRUNING See individual varieties.
PROPAGATION Softwood cuttings, taken in early summer, root easily.
USE Spirea adds a note of interest to foundation plantings and shrub borders.
SPECIES *S. japonica* 'Shibori', which bears flowers of white, pink, and deep rose all on the same plant, is considered by many to be the best of the Japanese spireas. It begins to bloom in early summer and continues until frost, over the years forming a tidy 2- to 3-foot mound. Plant in full sun. Removal of spent flower heads helps promote continuous bloom. If propagating from softwood cuttings, note that flower color may vary depending on from which section of the stock plant cuttings were collected.
S. japonica 'Snowmound' is quite popular because of its blue-green foliage and arching sprays of flowers. Hardy to Zone 4.
S. x Bumalda 'Goldflame' is usually grown for its handsome foliage. New growth emerges with flaming streaks of orange and red, fading to a greenish yellow as it matures. Flowering is intermittent during the summer, with peak bloom generally in early July. The pink flowers develop on new growth and are borne in 2- to 4-inch flat-topped terminal clusters. In quantity, this is a useful plant for low massing or soil retention on sunny slopes. Pruning back

Below: Golden spirea with gold-twigged dogwood

SPIRAEA ALBIFLORA (JAPANESE SPIREA) Mature size: 2 feet tall. Dense compact shrub with white flowers in rounded clusters. Full sun or partial shade, any well-drained soil. Zones 4-8.

SPIRAEA X BUMALDA (BUMALDA SPIREA) Mature size: 3 feet tall and wide. Handsome foliage, pink flowers throughout summer, peak in early summer. Full sun or partial shade, any well-drained soil. Zones 4-8.

SPIRAEA JAPONICA 'SNOWMOUND' (NIPPON SPIREA) Mature size: 8 feet tall. Blue-green foliage, clusters of white flowers. Full sun or partial shade, any well-drained soil. Zones 4-8.

SPIRAEA VANHOUTTEI (VANHOUTTE SPIREA) Mature size: 8 feet tall and wide. Large, vigorous shrub, arching branches, profuse clusters of small white flowers in early spring. Full sun or partial shade, any well-drained soil. Zones 3-7.

Above: Stewartia pseudocamellia has a flaking bark similar to Stewartia ovata grandiflora, and camellia-type white flowers. Its leaves turn deep maroon in fall.

to 1 foot in early spring will promote colorful foliage and won't inhibit bloom. *S.* x *cinerea* 'Grefsheim', one of the most beautiful and elegant early-spring-flowering shrubs, bears clusters of fragrant small white flowers that completely cover its gracefully arching branches and turns warm gold or yellow in the fall. It makes a fine hedge and, for smaller gardens, is superior in every way to the larger-growing Vanhoutte spirea, which it resembles. Removal of a few of the oldest stems each year after blooming will help maintain vigor. Zones 4-7. *S.* x *vanhouttei,* the Vanhoutte spirea, a very vigorous shrub that forms a tall vase-shaped mound, bears profuse clusters of small white flowers in early spring. While beautiful in bloom, it is too large and coarse for many of today's small residential gardens. Space permitting, however, it makes an effective screen, background plant, or informal hedge. Aphids can be a nuisance. Cut back up to ⅓ of the oldest stems to the ground annually after flowering to maintain shape and vigor.

STEPHANANDRA INCISA CUTLEAF STEPHANANDRA *Rosaceae*

Dense yet graceful, cutleaf stephanandra derives its botanical and common names from its deeply cut, bright-green foliage. As the plant matures, its long, arching stems tend to root where they touch the ground, forming a nearly impenetrable mound. Small yellow-white flowers–pleasing but not spectacular–are borne in loose terminal panicles in June.

BEST CONDITIONS This adaptable shrub will grow happily in sun and shade, though it prefers a good garden soil of neutral pH.

PLANTING Plant anytime.

PESTS/DISEASES None serious.

PRUNING Because the branches form such an entanglement, it is virtually impossible to prune in the conventional manner. It may be necessary, therefore, to cut back hard every 5-6 years.

PROPAGATION Softwood cuttings, taken in early summer, root easily. The shrub's tendency to self-layer makes gathering new plants from a mature specimen quite easy.

USE This site-adaptable plant can be used for facing a foundation planting or shrub border, or for massing in larger landscapes. Particularly useful for draping over walls or rocks, it can also be close-clipped as a small formal hedge.

CULTIVAR 'Crispa' is a the most desirable cultivar.

STEWARTIA OVATA GRANDIFLORA SHOWY STEWARTIA *Theaceae*

Showy stewartia has several valuable attributes: pretty white flowers that appear in summer; foliage that turns orange or red in autumn; and a variegated flaking bark that adds interest to the winter garden.

BEST CONDITIONS This shrub grows best in rich, moist soil and in partial shade. It will tolerate full sun if kept moist. Good drainage is important.

PESTS/DISEASES None serious.

PROPAGATION From seeds or cuttings.

USE Showy stewartia is an excellent specimen plant that can be enjoyed through most of the year.

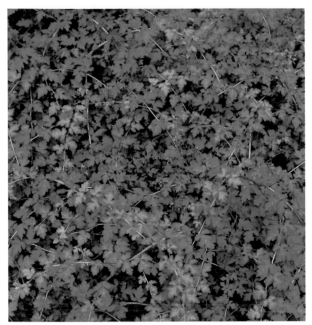

STEPHANANDRA INCISA 'CRISPA' (CUTLEAF STEPHANANDRA)
Mature size: 3 feet tall, 4 feet wide. Long arching stems reach the ground and form a mound; small yellow-white flowers in late spring. Sun or shade, good garden soil. Zones 4-7.

STEWARTIA OVATA GRANDIFLORA (SHOWY STEWARTIA) Mature size: 15 feet. Large white blossoms with purple stamens, foliage turns red or orange in fall, flaking bark. Full sun, moist soil. Zones 6-10.

SYMPHORICARPOS X CHENAULTII 'HANCOCK' (CORALBERRY)
Mature size: 2½ feet tall, 8 feet wide. Small blue-green leaves, small pink flowers, followed by deep coral berries. Any garden soil, full sun to heavy shade; needs protection in coldest climates. Zones 4-7.

SYMPLOCOS PANICULATA (SAPPHIREBERRY) Mature size: 10-20 feet tall and wide. Small white flowers in late spring, spectacular blue fruit in fall. Full sun, any well-drained garden soil. Zones 5-8.

SYRINGA X HYACINTHIFLORA (EARLY LILAC) Mature size: 8-14 feet tall, 7-12 feet wide. Similar to common lilac, but blooms one week earlier. Full sun, tolerates many soil types. Zones 3-7.

SYRINGA VULGARIS (COMMON LILAC) Mature size: 8-14 feet tall, 7-12 feet wide. Large-growing deciduous shrub with spectacular flowers in late May. Full sun, tolerates many soil types. Zones 3-7.

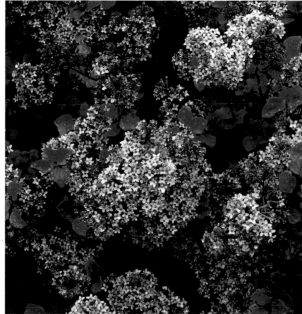

SYRINGA X PRESTONIAE (PRESTON LILAC) Mature size: 8-12 feet tall and wide. Fuller foliage than other lilac species, large flowers in upright or slightly pendulous terminal panicles. Full sun, tolerates many soil types. Zones 2-7.

SYRINGA MEYERI 'PALABIN' (MEYER LILAC), Mature size: 5-6 feet tall, 7 feet wide. Small shrub with broadly rounded outline, smaller leaves than most lilacs. Light pink flowers in 4-inch panicles. Full sun, tolerates many soil types. Zones 3-7.

SYMPHORICARPOS X CHENAULTII CORALBERRY *Caprifoliaceae*

The arching branches of this low-growing, spreading shrub tend to root where they touch the ground. The small blue-green leaves contrast effectively with the red of new stem growth, which supports small pink bell-like flowers in summer. Flowers are followed in September by deep-coral berries that persist into winter.

BEST CONDITIONS Adaptable to any garden soil with pH below 7.0, coralberry does well in almost any light, from full sun to quite heavy shade.

PLANTING Transplants easily.

PESTS/DISEASES Though other members of the genus are plagued by powdery mildew, this one seems to be immune.

PRUNING Any minor pruning to shape the plant should be done in early spring.

PROPAGATION Softwood cuttings, taken in early summer, root easily; where small numbers of new plants are required, simply remove several self-layers from the mother plant.

USE Shade tolerance, site adaptability, and a low-growing habit make this a very versatile plant for the modern garden. It is equally successful as a ground cover or a facer plant for the border.

CULTIVAR 'Hancock' is the best cultivar.

SYMPLOCOS PANICULATA SAPPHIREBERRY *Symplocaceae*

This slow-growing shrub can also be pruned to form a low-branched tree. In June fragrant white flowers are borne in 3-inch panicles. But it is the fruit of the sapphireberry that is truly spectacular: ⅓-inch berries (actually single-seeded drupes) of vibrant sapphire and cobalt blue, produced in September and October. Because fruit production can vary, select heavily fruiting forms and propagate vegetatively.

BEST CONDITIONS Sapphireberry thrives in full sun in any well-drained garden soil, but may also tolerate partial shade.

PLANTING Spring planting is best.

PESTS/DISEASES None serious.

PRUNING Pruning is required only to shape the plant. To encourage a tree-form plant, allow several branches to develop and select the best. Remove others the following season. The reason for this is to allow the foliage of other stems to provide support for the root system.

PROPAGATION Cuttings taken in summer root easily, but subsequent establishment can be difficult. Rooted cuttings should be left in the rooting containers and protected for the first winter; plant out when buds begin to break the following spring. Many plants self-sow.

USE Sapphireberry can be used as a small specimen tree or as a backdrop in the border. The fruit is an absolute beacon for attracting birds to the garden. The fruit is seldom retained for more than a few days once it begins to ripen.

SYRINGA Species LILAC *Oleaceae*

Among the most familiar shrubs, particularly in older gardens, lilacs are rarely grown for their habit or foliage but for their graceful nodding blooms and

At the Katie Osborne Lilac Dell at Royal Botanical Gardens, Hamilton Ontario, hundreds of varieties of lilac create a stunning vista.

'Krasavitsa Moskvy'

'Monge'

'Maiden's Blush'

'Dwight D. Eisenhower'

'Nadezhda'

'Agincourt Beauty'

'Sensation'

'Firmament'

'Flora'

heavy fragrance. In the species, the flowers are purple, single, and borne in 4- to 8-inch terminal panicles. Beyond the species, there are over 1,600 cultivars, of which a few are commercially grown for garden use. Flowers come in a range of colors, encompassing white, violet, blue, lilac, pink, magenta, and purple, and can be either single or double in form. Royal Botanical Gardens, Hamilton, is the registrar for the genus and has the world's largest documented collection of lilacs, currently numbering over 780 different taxa. Lilacs are well-adapted to much of the Great Plains area and are sometimes found growing untended in old cemeteries.

BEST CONDITIONS Lilacs require full sun to bloom effectively, but are very adaptable as to soil, tolerating reasonably (but not extremely) heavy clay soils and high pH.

PLANTING Bare-root plants can be set out in spring or fall; container specimens can be planted anytime.

PESTS/DISEASES Lilac borers, oyster shell scale, and powdery mildew are potential problems. Powdery mildew is not as much a problem in western areas, where humidity is lower and winds higher.

PRUNING Any required pruning should be done immediately after flowering. To maintain shape and vigor of mature plants, remove a few of the oldest stems to ground level.

PROPAGATION Common and early lilacs are difficult to propagate from softwood cuttings without special facilities; otherwise, take softwood cuttings in early summer. If plants are on their own roots, suckers may be severed from the parent plant in early spring and replanted. (This will not be effective for grafted plants.)

USE Some critics have denigrated lilacs as coarse, old-fashioned shrubs, too large for today's small residential gardens—a pity, since their beauty and fragrance are unrivaled in mid spring. Through careful cultivar selection, and with a bit of judicious pruning, lilacs can be accommodated in any landscape.

SPECIES *Syringa vulgaris*, common lilac, is a large-growing deciduous shrub with spectacular fragrant flowers borne in late mid spring.

Syringa meyeri 'Palibin', Meyer or dwarf lilac, is a small shrub with a broadly rounded outline. In mid spring, deep rose-pink buds open to light pink flowers borne in 4-inch panicles. Though not as heavily perfumed as common lilac, they are softly fragrant, and even young plants are very floriferous. The leaves, which have a purplish cast as they emerge, are slightly less than half the size of those of the common lilac and seem unaffected by late-season powdery mildew. Dwarf lilac is well suited to the smaller garden and can be employed as a medium-height hedge; displaying it against an evergreen background or wall will enhance the effect of its blooms.

Syringa x *prestoniae*, Preston lilac, is significantly different from its common or French hybrid relatives. Extremely hardy, it boasts larger and more luxuriant foliage. The flowers, which open a week or two after those of the French hybrids, are produced in large upright or slightly pendulous terminal panicles. Flowers range in color from light pink to deep wine and have a distinctive fra-

TAMARIX RAMOSISSIMA 'ROSEA' (TAMARISK) Mature size: 15 feet tall. Graceful shrub with slender feathery branches, small pink or white flowers. Full sun, good drainage. Zones 4-9

VACCINIUM CORYMBOSUM (HIGHBUSH BLUEBERRY) Mature size: 6-12 feet tall. Blue-black berries, orange-scarlet foliage in autumn. Full sun, well-drained acid soil. Zones 3-8.

VIBURNUM DILATATUM 'ERIE' (ERIE VIBURNUM) Mature size: 7 feet tall, 10 feet wide. Deciduous bushy shrub with many creamy white flowers in flat clusters; foliage turns red, orange, and yellow in fall. Full sun or partial shade, rich moist soil. Zones 5-7.

VIBURNUM LANTANA 'MOHICAN' (WAYFARING TREE) Mature size: 15 feet. Clusters of flat white flowers, foliage turns red in autumn. Full sun or partial shade. Tolerates dry soil. Zones 3-8.

grance. While Preston lilac can stand alone as a lawn specimen, it is more commonly incorporated into shrub borders or used as a background or screening plant.

Syringa x hyacinthiflora, early lilac, is quite similar to the common lilac in terms of flower color and form, though it blooms a week or two earlier.

TAMARIX Species TAMARISK *Tamaricaceae*

This graceful shrub has slender, feathery branches, tiny scalelike leaves, and small pink or white flowers borne in narrow racemes that bloom in mid to late summer. Avoid balled-and-burlapped plants if possible, since root systems can be weak.

BEST CONDITIONS *Tamarix* has only two demands: full sun and good drainage. Otherwise, it will tolerate both an acid, neutral, or high pH (up to 7.8) and will thrive in salty, sandy, or dry soils. In fact, the soil need not be fertile; *Tamarix* often performs best in poor ground.

PLANTING Set bare-root plants out in early spring; container-grown can be planted anytime. A word of caution when choosing a site: because of its sparse roots, *Tamarix* doesn't take well to transplanting.

WATER Occasional watering may be necessary in very dry climates or during periods of prolonged drought.

PESTS/DISEASES None serious.

PRUNING Prune in late winter or early spring, removing old growth and spindly shoots. To renovate, cut the plant back to 2-3 inches from the ground. Prune annually or every 2-3 years, depending on desired effect.

PROPAGATION Propagate from seed in pots of sandy soil. Or take 8-inch cuttings from the shoots and plant them with only their tips protruding from the soil.

USE *Tamarix* makes a delicate contrast to more massive plants. It is good for use at the seaside.

CULTIVAR *T. ramosissima* 'Rosea' is hardy in Zones 4-9 and is an especially valuable plant for the seacoast and in the arid Southwest. In milder areas, however, or in rich soil, it can be invasive. A word of warning: This plant has naturalized along stream banks in the southwestern U.S. and taken over the habitat of many native Southwest species. In the North, this has not been a problem, but this should be considered when planting in warmer parts of the U.S.

VACCINIUM Species BLUEBERRY *Ericaceae*

The genus *Vaccinium* includes many edible-berry bushes; they have creeping, trailing, or upright habits. All produce small flowers, some of which are quite attractive, several weeks before the berries, which ripen in mid summer. In addition to their deservedly popular fruit, blueberries are grown for spring flowers, crimson fall foliage, and ornamental winter twigs. The shrubs are so effective at attracting birds that they may require special protection from their feathered admirers, who can strip a bush of its fruit in an astonishingly short time; netting is usually a good deterrent. Look for 2-year-old potted plants.

BEST CONDITIONS All do well in full sun, and a few will tolerate shade as well.

Ah, nature. The very look of the woods is heroical and stimulating. This afternoon in a very thick grove where Henry Thoreau showed me the bush of mountain laurel, the first I have seen in Concord, the stems of pine and hemlock and oak gleamed like steel upon the excited eye.
From Journals, Ralph Waldo Emerson

plant selector

I don't understand why *Actinidia kolomikta* (hardy kiwi) is not used more. The effect of silver and pink variegated foliage is striking wherever its put, and it grows beautifully in most areas with very little care.
ROBERT BOWDEN, ATLANTA

Enkianthus perlatus (White enkianthus) merits more attention. It produces white flowers in spring, fine-textured foliage, and brilliant red color in fall; and it remains under 6 feet tall.
ETHAN JOHNSON,
THE HOLDEN ARBORETUM

All the viburnums should be used more in the Great Plains. They are quite hardy here, even in difficult situations, and provide flowers, fruit, and colorful fall foliage.
JAMES LOCKLEAR,
DYCK ARBORETUM OF THE PLAINS

Dalea greggii–and other members of the *dalea* family–should be used more in desert gardens. They are beautiful plants, usually covered with purple blooms. They are easy to care for, and benefit our environment in many ways.
MARY IRISH,
DESERT BOTANICAL GARDEN

Caryopteris x clandonensis is a very useful plant that is often overlooked. It presents blue flowers late in the season, which is unusual for a shrub. And it also has a nice fragrance.
CHRIS GRAHAM,
ROYAL BOTANICAL GARDENS

Spirea x *cinerea* 'Grefsheim' has many attractive qualities. It flowers in early May, when most perennials are small and beds look bare. In fall, its foliage turns a warm golden yellow to bronze. And in winter it adds dramatic structure. It can be used as a hedge in small spaces, remaining attractive and dense with minimum effort. It has a sweet fragrance, and is easy to grow.
GALEN GATES,
CHICAGO BOTANIC GARDEN

Blueberries thrive in a well-drained acid soil, rich in organic matter. (Any pH from 4.2 through 5.8 is acceptable; 4.8-5.0 is ideal.)

PLANTING Blueberries transplant easily, though their fine and shallow root systems require the protection of an organic mulch–either peat moss, leaf mold, or manure–applied in spring. For a hedge, space 4-6 feet apart.

FERTILIZER For maximum growth and fruit production in the highbush blueberry, fertilize when growth begins in the spring, again–lightly–during flowering, and once more 5-6 weeks later. If soil pH is too high, apply iron sulfate or powdered sulfur. (This may lead you to believe that blueberries require pampering; quite the opposite–these are amazingly hardy shrubs that naturalize readily even when given minimal care.)

PESTS/DISEASES None serious.

PRUNING Though pruning will increase yield, it isn't necessary except to remove deadwood. If you want to encourage the highbush blueberry to fruit more heavily, prune when the plant is dormant in early spring, retaining no more than 10 stems per plant and removing any wood 5 years or older as well as low branches. Then thin out and shorten those branches that remain.

PROPAGATION In the spring, sow ripe seeds in peaty, sandy soil, or divide old bushes. In the summer, propagate by leafy cuttings.

USE Blueberries combine well with rhododendrons, azaleas, heaths, and heathers, adding life to the winter landscape with their appealing bare twigs, which are sometimes reddish. If growing for fruit, plant more than one cultivar in groups to encourage cross-pollination. Cultivars are classified by their season of bloom and fruit; be sure to select varieties that bloom the same time when buying companion cultivars.

RECOMMENDED VARIETIES *V. angustifolium,* a lowbush blueberry, provides much of the edible fruit found in America's markets. With its red fall foliage and tendency to naturalize, it makes a fine ground cover for larger areas. Hardy Zones 3-7 (cultivars 'Wells Delight' and 'Bloodstone' are hardy from Zone 5). *V. corymbosum* (highbush blueberry) produces a blue-black berry ⅓ inch in diameter and is also grown for its orange-scarlet fall foliage and red twigs. For the deep South, choose 'Becky Blue', 'Bluegem', 'Choice', 'Bonita Blue', or 'Climax'. *V.* 'Jersey' is a late bearer of small-to-medium-sized fruit with a mild flavor. *V.* 'Top Hat', a highbush hybrid, is a lowbush blueberry growing no more than 3 feet in height.

For Northern garden, half-high blueberries (crosses between *V. angustifolium* and *V. corymbosum)* are grown as ornamentals. Cultivars include Northblue', 'St. Cloud', 'Northland', 'Bluecrop' and 'Toro'.

VIBURNUM Species VIBURNUM *Caprifoliaceae*

Viburnum is an important group of shrubs, providing three seasons of pleasure: flowers in summer, fruit in fall, vividly-colored foliage that sometimes lasts into winter. Although they are favorites of many horticulturists, some home gardeners are not aware of them.

BEST CONDITIONS Most viburnum prefers a deep, rich, moist but well-drained

VIBURNUM OPULUS 'ROSEUM' (SNOWBALL) Mature size: 6-12 feet tall, 7-10 feet wide. Clusters of sterile white flowers in spring, 3-4 inches wide. Full or partial shade. Zones 3-8.

VIBURNUM PLICATUM VAR. TOMENTOSUM (DOUBLEFILE VIBURNUM) Mature size: 12 feet tall and wide. Flat clusters of white flowers in mid to late spring, followed by showy red fruit and orange foliage in fall. Full or partial shade. Zones 5-8.

VIBURNUM PLICATUM 'MARIESII' (DOUBLEFILE VIBURNUM) Mature size: 9-12 feet tall, 6 feet wide. Twin clusters of white flowers with red stalks in mid spring, followed by showy red fruit. Full sun or partial shade. Zones 5-8.

VIBURNUM RHYTIDOPHYLLUM 'ALLEGHENY' Mature size: 9-14 feet tall, 8-10 feet wide. Clusters of showy white flowers in late spring; crinkled oblong leaves. Full sun or partial shade. Zones 6-8.

Viburnums have many useful qualities–graceful forms, showy flowers,
interesting foliage that often turns
vivid red, yellow, or orange in fall, and
large, bright red fruit that attracts
birds to the garden.

loam, in full sun or partial shade; see individual species for other requirements.

PLANTING Plant in spring.

PESTS/DISEASES Some leaf spotting and powdery mildew can be expected.

PRUNING Normally, only minor pruning is required to maintain the plant's
shape; prune after flowering.

PROPAGATION Usually from softwood cuttings; see individual species.

SPECIES *Viburnum carlesii* (Korean spice viburnum), an old-fashioned deciduous
shrub, is grown primarily for its highly fragrant spring flowers, which, alas,
are subject to winter damage in more northerly areas. In late April or early
May the clusters of flower buds, which are often a dark pink color, expand
and open to form pure white, highly fragrant, 3-inch hemispherical clusters.
The fragrance of this plant in the early spring landscape is absolutely intoxi-
cating. Otherwise, the plant is somewhat unprepossessing: upright-growing
with a rounded outline and leaves of a dull dark green that are hairy on both
surfaces. In some years Korean spice viburnum develops good wine-red
autumn color, but typically has little fall interest. Choose a protected site in
northern areas. This is one of the more difficult viburnums to root from cuttings. Those cuttings that do root greatly resist fall planting and should be
left undisturbed until spring. Many nurserymen propagate cultivars by grafting; if doing so, avoid rootstock suckers. This shrub does well in foundation
plantings and shrub borders, sited where its spring fragrance can be readily
appreciated. It is also an excellent shrub for naturalizing along a woodland
edge. Although it loses its shape, the plant blends well into the landscape.
'Aurora' has bright red buds that open to blush-pink flowers.

Viburnum cassinoides (witherod viburnum), a native deciduous shrub, is compact and rounded when young, becoming more upright and vase-shaped as it
matures. Unaccented creamy-white flowers appear in June, borne in 2- to 5-
inch flat-topped clusters. Fruit is extremely showy, passing through phases of
green, pink, red, and blue, and eventually ripening to black. Autumn interest
is further enhanced by the turning foliage, which varies from orange-red to
purple. Softwood cuttings, taken in early summer, root easily. A hardy plant,
it has lovely flowers and arresting autumn fruit and foliage. It can be massed,
naturalized, or incorporated into a shrub border and is unsurpassed for
attracting birds to the garden. 'Winterthur' is perhaps the only selection of
this species and is the one most widely available on the market.

Viburnum dilatatum 'Erie' (Erie viburnum), a deciduous, bushy shrub, is
clothed in mid to late spring in a profusion of unaccented creamy-white flowers borne in 4- to 6-inch flat clusters. The foliage is a clean, handsome medi-
um-green, which changes in autumn to rich shades of yellow, orange, and red.
Handsome enough to be used as a specimen, this can also stand at the back of
the border or, space permitting, in a foundation planting. The shrub's greatest
asset, however, is its fruit, which is highly ornamental and produced prolific-
ly, beginning in August as a bright red and gradually changing to coral. Frost
intensifies the color of the fruit, which persists, in a more subdued hue,

VIBURNUM LENTAGO (NANNYBERRY) Mature size: 30 feet. Flat clusters of white flowers in mid spring, black berries in fall and winter, good fall color. Full sun to partial shade. Zones 2-8.

WEIGELA (WEIGELA) Mature size: 6-9 feet. Profuse tubular flowers in spring on arching branches. Full sun to light shade; soil should not be too wet or too dry. Zones 5-9.

ABIES BALSAMEA 'NANA' (BALSAM FIR) Mature size: 3-6 feet. Short gray-green leaves, purple cones, mounded habit. Full sun or partial shade, well-drained soil. Zones 3-5.

CEDRUS DEODARA 'WHITE IMP' (DEODOR CEDAR) Mature size: 2-3 feet. Very diminutive, white foliage. Graceful form with dramatic branches. Full sun or partial shade, well-drained soil. Zones 7-9.

through mid winter in some areas. Softwood cuttings do not root easily.

Viburnum 'Eskimo' (Eskimo Viburnum) This fine cultivar possesses many of the best ornamental characteristics of its parents: it grows into a dense, compact, rounded plant with leathery, dark-green, lustrous leaves that may be evergreen in warm climates. In mid spring, pale-cream buds give way to 4-inch snowball inflorescences, each containing 80-175 unscented tubular flowers of a pure white. The rather unspectacular fruits that follow are dull-red to black. Viburnums are often judged too large for small residential gardens, but Eskimo's compact habit makes it just right. It is especially useful as an accent plant in the shrub border or foundation planting. Young plants may be shy to branch and develop a full crown, but the gardener's patience will be well rewarded. At the northern limit of its range, choose a sheltered spot to protect the naked flower buds from winter damage; both 'Eskimo' and its breeding-program stable mate, *V.* 'Chesapeake' have performed admirably at Royal Botanical Gardens in Hamilton, Ontario.

Viburnum lantana (wayfaring tree) is one of the few viburnum species that tolerates dry conditions.

Viburnum lentago (nannyberry) is a vigorous native with shiny green leaves that turn purplish red in autumn, flat clusters of white flowers in spring. Old branches often arch over to the ground and take root.

Viburnum opulus (European cranberrybush) produces flat clusters of sterile white flowers, bright red fruit, and green foliage that turns red-orange in the fall. 'Roseum' (snowball) has been grown in American gardens since colonial times. It produces very round flowerheads, up to 3 inches in diameter. Although it is one of the showiest of the viburnum, it is often attacked by plant lice.

Viburnum plicatum var. *tomentosum* (doublefile viburnum) Among the most distinctive and elegant of flowering shrubs, the doublefile viburnums are large, upright-growing plants with strongly horizontal, tiered branches. One of the few plants that can add strong horizontal lines to the garden, the doublefile viburnum makes an excellent specimen if given sufficient space to mature. Its size also makes it useful for screening. Dark green leaves are arranged in pairs along the stems and hang in a nearly vertical position, accentuating the plant's horizontality; fall color is a rich reddish-purple. Appearing in May, each flat-topped inflorescence is comprised of a halo of pure-white sterile flowers that surround a less showy, fertile bloom. These clusters are held above the foliage in rows on either side of the branches (hence the name "doublefile"), and the overall effect is dramatic.

Doublefile viburnums prefer full sun, and a deep, rich, well-drained soil. Doublefile viburnum grows extremely well in partial shade at the Royal Botanical Garden in Hamilton, Ontario, and needs more shade the father south it is grown; in Philadelphia, it does far better in partial shade than in full sun. They are not hardy at Chicago Botanic Garden.

Spring planting will yield the most satisfactory results, especially in the North, but bare roots can be planted in the early spring, and containers can be planted almost anytime. Doublefile viburnum cannot tolerate severe drought and suffers severe stem dieback when placed under stress. Pruning is seldom necessary; leave the pruners in the shed and allow the plant to develop naturally.

'Mariesii' is one of the better-flowering forms. 'Pink Beauty' is slightly smaller in stature than most of the doublefile viburnums, and the flowers, white as they emerge, turn a deep pink as they mature. 'Shasta' is one of the best doublefile viburnums for the modern home landscape. It stays compact and refined and does not spread out like other species. This introduction made by the late Donald Egolf at the U.S. National Arboretum is truly a superior clone. Mature size is 8 feet by 10 feet.

Viburnum sargentii 'Susquehanna' (Susquehanna viburnum). This large, deciduous shrub has an upright habit, stout branches, and a corky trunk, with large, leathery 3-lobed leaves of a bold dark green. In late May whorls of creamy-white infertile flowers combine with inner, less showy fertile blooms in large flat-topped clusters. The berrylike fruit ripens to a glossy dark red in early fall and persists to mid winter, though after a few hard freezes it tends to discolor.

Very easy to transplant and establish, 'Susquehanna' can be planted anytime from containers, and in either spring or fall if bare-root. It is intolerant of intense heat, preferring climates with cool summers. Occasional removal of the oldest stems to ground level will help maintain the vigor of mature plants.

Maturing to an impressive height and girth, 'Susquehanna' must be carefully sited in the landscape. Squeezing it into too small a space will result in a perpetual battle with pruning shears and saw. Where space does permit, however, this makes a handsome and impressive screen or background plant. For the average garden, consider the similar but gentler *V. sargentii* 'Onandaga' and *V. trilobum* 'Compactum'.

Viburnum x *burkwoodii* 'Mohawk' (Mohawk viburnum). Compact habit, superior flowering, and disease resistance make this one of the most desirable viburnums. In early spring dark red flower buds begin to develop at the ends of the previous seasons' growth, slowly opening to 3-inch-round clusters of waxy white flowers with a spicy fragrance. The dark green lustrous leaves turn a brilliant orange-red in autumn. Mohawk viburnums growing at the Royal Botanical Garden in Hamilton, Ontario, have shown a bit of tenderness when young, but have proven to be quite hardy over time. Gardeners at the Dyck Arboretum have reported some winter dieback on these viburnums. Mohawk viburnum is resistant to bacteria leafspot and powdery mildew.

Softwood cuttings, taken in summer, root with relative ease. In northern areas, leave the rooted cuttings in rooting flats for the first winter, protecting them from extreme cold; plant out the following spring.

Viburnum x *rhytidophylloides* 'Willowwood' (willowwood viburnum) has attractive foliage that persists well into the winter. Well-adapted to full-sun conditions at the Dyck Arboretum.

Viburnum rhytidophyllum (leatherleaf viburnum) has attractive crinkled leaves and outstanding red or black berries in the fall. It needs protection from wind.

Above: Viburnum growing with lilac.

Above: A sheared juniper, behind a 'Crimson Pygmy' barberry, adds a vertical note to a perennial border.

wind or other extreme conditions.

Viburnum rafidulum (rusty blackhaw viburnum) grows up to 9 feet tall, with an attractive, blocky bark pattern and dense covering of reddish-brown hairs on buds and young twigs. This native tolerates dry, rocky soils in the western portions of its range.

Viburnum trilobum (Cranberrybush Viburnum) grows 8-12 feet tall, making it an excellent plant for screening. It has deep red foliage color in fall and is a heavy-fruiting form.

WEIGELA WEIGELA *Caprifoliaceae*

Though their bloom is short-lived, weigelas are unsurpassed for an exuberant burst of spring color, peaking late in the season. The abundant flowers are tubular and wide-mouthed, each over an inch across, borne on graceful arching branches. Old-fashioned varieties are pink, but modern hybrids are a dark pink-red. The plant itself is bushy in form, with opposite leaves.

BEST CONDITIONS Weigelas do well in full sun to light shade in almost any soil and thrive in an urban setting. Avoid excessively dry or wet conditions.

PLANTING Set bare-roots out very early in the spring; containers can be planted anytime from the spring to early fall.

PESTS/DISEASES None serious; weigela is very pest- and disease-resistant.

PRUNING Pruning is necessary to maintain the shrub's shape; after flowers have faded, remove old stems and shorten leggy ones. The plant may die back a little; when this occurs, prune back severely to maintain shape.

PROPAGATION Seeds do not reproduce to type; instead, plant summer cuttings of firm shoots in a greenhouse or cold frame.

USE With their full shape and dazzling spring show, weigelas are an excellent choice for the shrub border.

SPECIES *W. florida* 'Pink Princess' bears rose-pink flowers.

CONIFEROUS SHRUBS

In cultivation since antiquity, conifers have been a mainstay of the American garden for most of the 20th century. With their evergreen foliage, handsome coloration, and striking, often architectural form, they remain among the most useful of shrubs. For the purposes of this book—and of most home gardeners—the conifers can be described as a group of evergreen, resinous plants, either shrubs or trees, with branched stems, central trunks, and short branches, their seeds usually (though not always) carried in cones and their leaves generally either scalelike (as in the cypresses), needlelike (pines), or flat and linear (yews). The listing of recommended varieties, below, represents by necessity only a small percentage of the conifers presently in cultivation, but encompasses some of the very best in the group, whether for hardiness, versatility in the landscape, or spectacular visual effect.

BEST CONDITIONS Most conifers are highly adaptable, thriving in full sun or partial shade, in a wide variety of soils (though good drainage is a must). In general, soil pH should be neutral to slightly acidic, though some conifers will

CEPHALOTAXUS HARRINGTONIA VAR. DRUPACEA (PLUM YEW)
Wide-spreading shrub with long, shiny needles. Full sun or partial shade; well-drained soil. Zones 6-9.

CHAMAECYPARIS OBTUSA 'NANA GRACILIS' (HINOKI CYPRESS)
Mature size: 4 feet tall, 2-3 feet wide. Horizontal branches with lustrous dark green foliage. Full sun or partial shade, tolerates heat better than most conifers. Zones 5-8.

PICEA GLAUCA 'CONICA' (DWARF WHITE SPRUCE) Mature size: 15 feet. Pyramidal form, bright green needlelike foliage. Full sun or partial shade; well drained soil. Zones 2-6.

PINUS MUGO MUGO (MUGHO PINE) Mature size: 9 feet tall, up to 18 feet wide. Dark green twisted needles, rounded cones. Full sun, well-drained soil. Zones 3-6.

Conifers have more to offer than dull background screening; they can supply shape and color to any garden. *Above:* The gold foliage of a false cypress contrasts with vivid red lilies and bright yellow yarrow.

tolerate high alkaline conditions.

PLANTING Established conifers need surprisingly little care if the site was well prepared at planting time. In addition to providing good drainage, take care to keep the roots moist while transplanting. Though conifers can be planted out anytime (dig earlier in the year for mid-summer planting) the best time to transplant is late summer and early autumn. For hedges, dig a generous trench and place plants 4-6 feet apart, depending on mature size.

FERTILIZER If conifers have been well sited and well planted, they require little or no fertilizer.

PESTS/DISEASES As a group, the conifers are relatively pest- and disease-free, though rodents and deer can be significant problems in certain areas; for other exceptions, see individual varieties.

PRUNING Conifers with a pyramidal habit require very little pruning, except to remove competing leaders. Other, less regular conifers should be pruned according to growing season. Firs, pines, and spruces, for example, do most of their growing in early spring; they should be pruned, if desired, in spring, by removing a portion of each "candle"–the new budlike shoot sending out young, soft needles. This will result in moderate new growth this season and more abundant growth the following year. (Complete removal of the candle will stimulate dense, compact growth.) For conifers whose growing season is virtually the entire summer (yews and junipers, for example), remove a small amount of branch, near the tip, at any time from late spring through mid summer (pruning too late in the season can cause a spurt of new growth that won't have enough time to harden off before winter). Always follow the shrub's natural shape when pruning; don't try to torture a plant into a shape nature never intended. The exception, of course, is a formal hedge, which should be pruned to shape, allowing the bottom of the hedge to be slightly wider than the top.

PROPAGATION In general, conifers can be propagated most easily by seed or by cuttings. To collect seeds, remove the cones just when they begin to open. Dry them in a cool place until fully open, shake them to remove the seeds, then tumble the seeds to remove the wings. (Note that the seeds of some conifers–notably the berry-bearing junipers and yews–will take 2 seasons to germinate.) The smaller conifers lend themselves relatively well to propagation by cuttings, taken after growth has slowed (anytime from late summer to early winter) and rooted in sand.

USE To imagine the American garden without conifers is nearly unthinkable; among the most versatile of shrubs, they serve as the evergreen backbone of home landscapes from Maine to California. Larger, pyramidal forms such as white spruce and deodar cedar make spectacular specimens; procumbent varieties like savin and shore juniper are wonderful as ground covers (and a refreshing alternative to the ubiquitous pachysandra and English ivy). Because of their evergreen foliage and dense habit, most of the yews make virtually impenetrable year-round hedges. And dwarf conifers–try *Abies balsamea* 'Nana' or *Pinus parviflora* 'Adcock's Dwarf'–add structure and year-round

PINUS PARVIFLORA 'ADCOCK'S DWARF' (JAPANESE WHITE PINE)
Mature size: 8-10 feet tall. Irregular pyramidal form, bluish-green needles. Full sun or partial shade, well-drained soil. Zones 5-8.

SCIADOPITYS VERTICILLATA (JAPANESE UMBRELLA PINE) Mature size: 40 feet. Slow-growing conifer with whorls of lustrous bright green needles. Full sun, well-drained soil. Zones 5-8.

TAXUS X MEDIA 'DENSIFOLIA' (ANGLO-JAPANESE YEW) Mature size: Up to 40 feet. Dark green needlelike leaves, fleshy red berries, broadly pyramidal form. Full sun, well-drained soil. Zones 5-7.

TSUGA CANADENSIS 'PENDULA' (CANADA HEMLOCK) Small needlelike leaves, small cones. Full sun or partial shade, well-drained soil. Zones 5-7.

This collection of conifers and broadleaf evergreens makes use of their different shapes, textures, and colors. It includes *Picea glauca, Berberis* 'Crimson Pygmy', *and Tsuga occidentalis.*

The rate of growth and "mature size" of ornamental conifers depends mainly on soil drainage and fertility. "Dwarf" conifers are genetic mutations that do not always grow at a uniform rate; they sometimes have branches that revert to more typical growth rates (these should be pruned off). Even plants that don't revert are not always typical; cuttings taken from a side branch of a dwarf Hinoki cypress, for example, tend to grow wider than tall, and those taken from the top will be taller than wide. It is often difficult to assign a sizes; many listings do not specify the age at which the conifer will reach a given size. The chart on the opposite page lists sizes for some of the conifers pictured in this book at 10 and 20 years; captions under the illustrations show mature heights at 40, 60, or 80 years.

appeal to the rock garden. For more on use, see the individual varieties listed below.

SPECIES *Abies balsamea,* balsam fir, bears short, roundish gray-green leaves and violet-purple cones roughly 2-3 inches in length. It needs cool summers to thrive. 'Nana' is a slow-growing dwarf with a mounded habit, well suited to smaller rock gardens.

Cedrus deodara, Deodar cedar, has a graceful form and dramatically declined branches. 'White Imp' is a very diminutive cultivar with white foliage, developed in British Columbia. Zones 5-8.

Cephalotaxus harringtonia var. *Drupacea,* plum yew, resembles the prostrate-growing species, but with its graceful shiny needles, it is a welcome alternative to the overused *Taxus.* Much underutilized in the home garden, plum yew is at its best when planted in masses. Look for deep-green container-grown specimens with a spreading habit. 'Duke Gardens' is the most highly refined plum yew, with arching branches and a uniform, mounded habit.

Chamaecyparis obtusa, Hinoki cypress, is characterized by horizontal branches bearing smaller, pendulous branchlets with scalelike leaves of a dark, shiny green. 'Nana Gracilis' is a lovely dwarf with dense, dark green foliage. Hardy Zones 5-8; grows to 4 feet tall and 2-3 feet wide.

Chamaecyparis pisifera, Sawara false cypress, has a pyramidal form, reddish bark, and flat, slightly pendant branchlets. Leaves are dark green and glossy. 'Golden Mop' is a slow grower with dense yellow foliage. Hardy Zones 5-8; grows to 3 feet tall.

Juniperus conferta, shore juniper, is a low, spreading shrub with tapering needlelike leaves and black fruit. As its common name implies, it is very much at home in sandy, seaside plantings, where other junipers may fail to thrive. 'Pacific Blue' has striking blue-green needles–bluer than the species–and a dramatically procumbent habit.

Juniperus sabina, Savin juniper, is a spreading conifer with slender branches and dark green needles. 'Blue Danube', in cultivation for centuries, has a low, spreading habit that makes it a natural ground cover.

Picea glauca 'Conica', dwarf white spruce, is a longtime favorite among the conifers, characterized by a compact, pyramidal "Christmas-tree" form and needlelike foliage whose new growth is an eyecatching bright green. Often grown as a small tree, it dislikes hot summers and is highly prone to infestation by spider mites. Hardy Zones 2-6; grows to 15 feet high.

Pinus mugo mugo, Mugho pine, has dark-green twisted needles and rounded cones about an inch in diameter. Slow growing, it is a favorite for hedges and foundation plantings, but is highly susceptible to scale and absolutely requires a well-drained soil. Choose vegetatively propagated plants to ensure dwarf proportions. Mugho pine can be very effective, especially when used with other evergreens. (Minnesota Landscape Arboretum)

Pinus parviflora, Japanese white pine, has an irregular to pyramidal habit, reddish-brown bark, and bluish-green needles that form small "brushes" at the end of the branchlets. This denizen of the seashore is highly tolerant of sandy soil and salt spray. A natural for the rock garden, 'Adcock's Dwarf' is characterized by slow growth and a compact form.

Pinus pungens, table mountain pine or hickory pine, is an often flat-topped shrub with twisted dark green needles that are quite sharp and heavy cones that can persist for many years.

Sciadopitys verticillata, Japanese umbrella pine, bears its lustrous bright-green needles in whorls. Mature trees produce 3- to 5-inch cones. Though it tolerates partial shade, it grows most vigorously in full sun, especially when given good drainage and some protection from wind. Hardy Zones 5-8; grows to 40 feet, at a modest rate of about 6 inches a year.

Taxus baccata 'Repandens', spreading English yew, is a low, flat-topped shrub with widely spreading branches, dark green leaves, and fleshy red fall berries. Hardy in Zones 5-7; grows to 6 feet high and 12 feet wide.

Taxus cuspidata 'Nana', dwarf Japanese yew, is one of the country's most popular landscape conifers. Low and spreading, with a compact, shrublike habit, it bears short leaves and produces an abundance of fleshy red fall berries. Hardy Zones 4-7; grows to 10 feet high and 20 feet wide.

Taxus x *media* cultivars. These hardy hybrids of *T. baccata* and *T. cuspidata* have handsome dark green (often olive-hued) needlelike leaves, fleshy red fall berries, and a broadly pyramidal form. Hardy Zones 5-7. 'Amherst' is dense, compact, and slow growing, maturing to 6 feet tall and 9 feet wide. 'Brown' is rounded, compact, and slow growing, maturing to 4-8 feet high and wide, often used for hedging. 'Hatfeldii', an old-fashioned favorite, has wide-spreading leaves, upright branches, a compact form, and a conical outline. Matures to 12 feet high and 10 feet wide. 'Hicksii' is a hardy form with a columnar silhouette, growing wider as it matures. 'Kelsey' bears its fruit earlier than most of the other cultivars, maturing to 12 feet high and 9 feet wide. 'Sentinalis' derives its name from its columnar form; matures to 8 feet high and 2 feet wide. 'Stoveken' is a columnar yew, slightly more stout than 'Sentinalis', growing to 12 feet high and 6 feet wide. 'Vermeulen' is a slow grower with a rounded form, maturing to 8 feet high and 9 feet wide. 'Wardii', a dense, spreading yew, grows slowly to 6 feet high and 19 feet wide.

Tsuga canadensis, Canada hemlock, is a large timber tree often attaining a height of 100 feet or more. There are, however, a number of desirable dwarf forms; all require cool summers and moist, well-drained soil. Leaves are small and needlelike, borne on a flat plane, and cones are small as well, rarely exceeding ¾ inch. A caveat: In many parts of the country, hemlocks have fallen prey to the woolly adelgid, a Japanese aphid that eventually kills the entire tree if left unchecked (dormant oils, assiduously applied, can sometimes keep the pests in check); contact your local coop extension to see if this is a problem in your area. Hardy Zones 4-8. 'Pendula', weeping or Sargent hemlock, is a low form with weeping branches that grows quickly into a dense, pleasingly rounded shrub. 'Cole's Prostrate' is the lowest growing of the hemlocks and makes a fine addition to the rock garden.

Above: Tsuga canadensis (top) and *Taxus* 'Repandens'.

Name	10 years ht/width (in feet)	20 years ht/width
Abies balsamea		
'Nana'	2/3	3/4½
Cedrus deodara		
'White Imp'	5/7	10/14
Cephalotaxus harringtonia 'Duke Gardens'	2/3½	4/8
Chamaecyparis obtusa		
'Nana Gracilis'	3/2½	6/6
Chamaecyparis pisifera		
'Golden Mop'	2½/3½	5/8
Juniperus conferta		
Pacific Blue	1/6	1½/12
Juniperus sabina		
'Blue Danube'	3½/6	7/14
Picea glauca 'Conica'	5/3	10/6
Pinus mugo mugo	3/5	6/10
Pinus parviflora		
'Adcock's Dwarf'	2/2½	4/5
Pinus pungens	8/8	16/16
Sciadopitys verticillata	5/4	12/8
Taxus baccata		
'Repandens'	3/6	6/12
Tsuga canadensis		
'Pendula'	3/6	6/12
Tsuga canadensis		
'Cole's Prostrate'	6"/4	10"/8

Vines have developed a range of methods for climbing. Some (such as *Euonymus fortunei, Hedera helix,* and *Parthenocissus tricuspidata*) send out rootlets that cling to support (below). Some (including *Passiflora,* and *Vitis*) produce clinging tendrils (center) that wrap around stems and wires. Others (including *Actinidia, Aristolachia, Clematis,* and *Ipomoea*) twine around their supports (bottom).

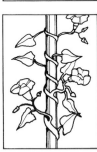

VINES

ACTINIDIA Species ACTINIDIA *Actinidiaceae*

Actinidia species are twining vines grown for their faintly fragrant flowers, edible kiwi fruit, or appealing colored foliage, which is unsurpassed in its ability to brighten shady spots in the garden. For ideal fruit production, plant both male and female varieties to ensure good pollination.

BEST CONDITIONS For best foliage color, grow actinidia in a site that receives morning sunlight and afternoon shade, perhaps on the north side of a fence or building. Actinidia is tolerant of heavier soils with a pH up to 7.3.

PESTS/DISEASES None.

PRUNING See individual varieties.

PROPAGATION By cuttings, but not easily done.

USE Because actinidias are fast-growing with a wild habit, they are best suited to less formal gardens where they can cover arbors, scramble up large trees, or clamber over fences. To make the most of their faint fragrance, grow these plants near benches and patios, or let them screen a wooden gazebo.

SPECIES *A. polygama* has silvery foliage, and flowers abundantly in spring. Because it flowers on the current season's wood, it can be hard-pruned in either late winter or early spring to keep it in bounds.

A. kolomikta (hardy kiwi) shares a blooming period with *A. polygama* (which benefits fruit set). It is grown primarily for its foliage, which is an arresting mixture of pink and silver. It blooms on old wood, so should be pruned immediately after flowering.

A. arguta 'Issai' is self-pollinating, which recommends it for smaller spaces (since 1 vine can be used rather than 2), but its real appeal is its edible fruit.

AKEBIA QUINATA FIVELEAF AKEBIA *Lardizabalaceae*

Handsome semievergreen foliage and vigorous growth make akebia one of the best twining vines for shade or sun. In mid May clusters of small purple night-blooming flowers release their intense fragrance into the evening air, followed–if conditions for pollination are right–by large purple fruit pods later in the season.

BEST CONDITIONS Grow in any well-drained soil, in full sun or partial shade.

PLANTING Plant in spring or fall. As the plant grows, tie it at intervals to its support; if training against a wall, provide wire for support.

PESTS/DISEASES None serious.

PRUNING Prune when needed to check too-vigorous growth; fiveleaf akebia is an excellent candidate for renovation pruning.

PROPAGATION Propagate by seeds, cuttings, or root divisions.

USE Fiveleaf akebia is unsurpassed at masking unsightly downspouts and will effectively cloak a wall, given the right support. This is a fine plant for shady spots.

ACTINIDIA KOLOMIKTA (HARDY KIWI) Mature size: up to 30 feet. Green, pink, and silver foliage. Morning sun, afternoon shade; tolerates heavier soils with high pH. Zones 4-10.

AKEBIA QUINATA (FIVELEAF AKEBIA) Mature size: 15 feet. Handsome glaucose green foliage, clusters of small night-blooming purple flowers in spring. Full sun or partial shade, any well-drained soil. Zones 4-9, evergreen from Zone 7 and warmer.

ARISTOLOCHIA DURIOR (DUTCHMAN'S PIPE, PIPE VINE) Mature size: usually 15-20 feet. Large heart-shaped leaves, 3-inch yellow-green tubular flowers in early summer. Full sun or partial shade, any soil. Zones 4-8.

BOUGAINVILLEA GLABRA 'SCARLETT O'HARA' (BOUGAINVILLEA) Mature size: 20-30 feet. Insignificant flowers, spectacular bracts in vivid colors. Full sun (partial shade in warm areas), loamy soil. Zone 10.

PLANTING VINES AGAINST TREES

To plant against a tree (which is best practiced with woody vines that don't die back: *Actinidia, Aristolochia, Clematis, Euonymus, Hedera, Hydrangea, Parthenocissus, Vitis,* and *Wisteria*), dig the hole at least 18 inches away and train a strong cane along a stake set diagonally against the trunk. About 18 inches above the ground, provide additional support in the form of an open-mesh plastic or wire screen. (Be sure this doesn't strangle the tree over time–it is necessary only for a year or two and then should be cut away.) To grow a vine through a shrub, dig the hole at least 2 feet away from the shrub's main trunk (to minimize competition for water and nutrients) and train a strong cane along a stake so that the vine will begin twining along the shrub's main framework. See page 203 for illustration.

ARISTOLOCHIA DURIOR DUTCHMAN'S PIPE, PIPE VINE

Aristolochiaceae

This vigorous grower with a twining habit boasts dramatic heart-shaped leaves up to 12 inches in length, which gives the plant a distinctly tropical appearance. Both of its common names are derived from the 3-inch, yellow-green tubular flowers that appear in early summer. The fruits are 2- to 3-inch-long tubular capsules.

BEST CONDITIONS Easy to grow, *Aristolochia* will tolerate adverse soil conditions and is adaptable to full sun or partial shade.

PRUNING Light pruning of individual leaves helps to expose the flowers, which otherwise are somewhat hidden by the dense foliage. To restrict its size, prune back hard in early winter or early spring. This, however, is rarely necessary, since it usually does not grow more than 15-20 feet in height (though it may reach 30 feet under optimal conditions).

PROPAGATION Propagate by division or cuttings taken in early summer or from seed planted in the fall.

USE *Aristolochia* provides a quick cover for porches, buildings, and other structures. Because of its hint of the tropics, it is often grown in colder climates as a substitute for the figs that are a staple of traditional English gardens. These large-leaved plants provide a welcome relief and contrast to the many smaller-leaved plants seen in most American gardens.

SPECIES *A. manshuriensis* is similar in habit to *A. durior*, with slightly larger leaves and longer fruit growing to 4½ inches.

A. grandiflora produces 6- to 7-inch flowers, beautifully striped in purple and yellow with a lemon-yellow throat. To attract pollinators, the flowers emit a somewhat unpleasant odor for about a day as they first open.

BOUGAINVILLEA BOUGAINVILLEA *Nyctaginaceae*

Few vines are as evocative of the tropics as bougainvillea; screening a patio or clambering over a pergola, it clothes itself nearly year-round with large, colorful blooms in shades that range from crimson, salmon, yellow, and orange to mauve, deep purple, cream, and true white. In fact, the floral show is provided not by the flowers, which are insignificant, but by the surrounding bracts. Though it climbs via hooked thorns, its twining stems require some additional support to keep the plant securely in place and to ensure a tidy appearance.

BEST CONDITIONS A loamy soil well enriched with composted organic matter is optimum, but bougainvillea will perform well in any well-drained soil, given full sun (or partial shade in extremely hot areas).

PLANTING Though bougainvillea can be planted anytime, its roots are delicate and should be protected during transplanting.

FERTILIZER Fertilize in spring with a general-purpose fertilizer and again in summer if growth is unsatisfactory.

PESTS/DISEASES Aphids, scales, and mealybugs.

PRUNING Prune after flowering to shape, keep in bounds, and remove dead wood. Suckers can be removed at any time.

PROPAGATION Stem cuttings, taken in late spring or early summer, root best in moist sand.

USE Striking enough to use as a specimen or accent, bougainvillea also makes a fine dense screen and can rapidly clothe a porch, pergola, or arbor.

CAMPSIS RADICANS TRUMPET VINE *Bignoniaceae*

This vigorous vine, native to the Southeast, will grow in tough sites and reward the gardener with clusters of bright orange flowers throughout much of the summer; the compound leaves are also attractive.

BEST CONDITIONS A tough plant, trumpet vine will grow generously in a variety of soils, though it does best in full sun.

PLANTING Until the aerial rootlets appear, young vines should be firmly tied to their intended support.

PESTS/DISEASES None serious.

PRUNING Prune to control spread. Trumpet vine sends out suckers from underground roots, which can become a nuisance; to control, cut the roots with a sharp spade.

PROPAGATION Take softwood cuttings, or sow seeds.

USE With its lush, vigorous growth, trumpet vine will quickly clothe and transform an unsightly building, stump, trellis, or fence.

CLEMATIS Species CLEMATIS *Ranunculaceae*

Among the most popular of vines, clematis offers a breathtaking range of colors, stunning blooms that can be as large as 6-10 inches in diameter, and clean, attractive foliage. These twining vines require support or a structure to climb.

BEST CONDITIONS In general, clematis need a deeply worked, well-drained soil enriched with composted organic matter. Most flourish with their tops in full sun and their roots shaded (either with mulch or low-growing plants).

PLANTING In fall or early spring, dig an 18 x 18-inch hole, filling the bottom with 2-3 inches of well-composted organic matter; to aid moisture retention in well-drained soils, add a mixture of loam, peat, or organic matter to the newly dug soil. Make sure that the top of the plant's rootball is at least 2 inches below soil level in well-drained soils or at ground level in moist soils. To plant clematis against a wall, dig the hole at least a foot away and train the plant along a stake set diagonally against the wall.

WATER To establish clematis in extremely well-drained soils, sink a pot into the soil about 6 inches away from the base of the vine. This acts as a reservoir —it's like having an inch space above the soil in a potted houseplant. You can water and walk away with this method, rather than giving it a little moisture and waiting for it to soak in. A very effective method to establish newly planted clematis is to create a dam above the outer edge of the root system, which provides the same effect.

PESTS/DISEASES In particular, clematis are prone to wilt and chlorosis. Wilt is a fungus that first appears as a drooping of leaves and shoot tips and then pro-

Clematis is a twining vine; like all vines, it needs support to climb. A mesh screen or invisible wire behind it will help it grow.

PRUNING CLEMATIS

Clematis fall within three pruning categories. For category A, spring bloomers, cut out all the shoots that have flowered immediately after blooming, and certainly no later than mid to late July. Category B, blooming in early summer (before mid-June), should be trimmed back to a pair of plump flower buds in February or March; prune off dead growth. Vines in category C are summer (late June) and early fall bloomers and require cutting back 1-2 inches from the ground in February or March to keep them from displaying bare legs. Often, a hard pruning every 2-3 years is sufficient.

gresses to the entire stem. Within a week the stems and leaves are black. Wilt must be treated or controlled; it's best to consult a local expert for the best method. Be sure not to damage stems or, if you have problems already, plant in a site with good light and air circulation (without high humidity, as near a pond). It also helps to place the plants slightly below ground level so if a stem dies you can cut it off at ground level, and it may resprout in several weeks to a month or a year. Any affected plant parts should be removed (not composted) and burned if possible. Avoid chlorosis by growing plants in soils with a pH of 6.5-7.2.

USE Clematis have a multitude of uses in the garden. They can be trained to climb a wall, trellis, fence, arbor, or lamppost; they can clamber over shrubs, or twine gently around other vines; and if allowed to sprawl, species like *C. maximowicziana* and *C. viticella* make a lovely ground cover.

SPECIES AND CULTIVARS *C.* x *Jackmanii,* probably the best-known of the clematis, was the first of the genus to combine large flower size with purple coloration. This lavish bloomer flowers in midsummer and again, lightly, in early fall. 'Perle d'Azur' boasts flowers of a clear, light, true blue that individually last up to 8 days. The plant continues to display flowers from late June through the end of September. Its vigorous habit and slightly pendulous flowers make it a top candidate for a wall, fence, shrub, or tree, where its lavish blooms can be easily admired from below. Mature size: 12-15 feet. Pruning category C.

'Marie Boisselot' is purest white and largest-flowered of all the clematis, bearing huge flowers of up to 8 inches in diameter, each one lasting up to an astonishing 17 days, from late June to early July. The spectacular blooms, which may open with a subtle blush of lilac-pink, sport 8 sepals so wide that each reaches the center of the adjacent one. The overall flower is recurved, giving it the appearance of an inverted saucer; this makes a dramatic statement against the large heart-shaped leaves. Because the blooms are often positioned in a horizontal plane, this is a vine best displayed close to eye level. 'Marie Boisselot' needs less sun than many other clematis; it will do quite well in 4 or 5 hours of shade. Mature size: 8-12 feet. Pruning category B or C.

'Nelly Moser' is an early bloomer (beginning in May or June), deservedly popular for the last hundred years for its striking bicolored flowers. These are distinguished by pale pink petals, each adorned with a bar of deep carmine, and reddish anthers. 'Nelly Moser' is best placed on an east- or north-facing wall, where afternoon shade helps boost its dramatic coloration. Mature size: 8-12 feet. Pruning category B (needs little or no pruning).

'Bill Mckenzie' is a clematis with three-season interest: the glossy bright yellow, bell-like flowers measure 3 inches across and bloom from midsummer to autumn, eventually forming silvery "spinning" seedheads that can last the entire winter in warmer climates (mid-winter in colder climates). Leaves are 9 inches long and somewhat coarse in appearance; for this reason, it is best sited where it can be admired from afar. Quite vigorous, it provides the perfect mask for an unsightly chainlink fence or can be trained to reach into the top of an evergreen. Mature size: 25 feet. Pruning category C.

CAMPSIS RADICANS (TRUMPET VINE) Mature size: 30-40 feet. Vigorous vine with bright orange or red flowers and compound leaves. Full sun, any soil. Zones 4-9.

CLEMATIS 'MISS BATEMAN' (CLEMATIS) Mature size: 12-20 feet. Large white flowers with dark stamens in mid spring. Full sun or partial shade; rich, moist soil. Zones 5-9.

CLEMATIS 'PICADILLY' (CLEMATIS) Mature size 8-12 feet. Large pink and white flowers, bright green foliage. Full sun or partial shade. Rich, moist soil. Zones 5-9.

CLEMATIS MACROPETALA (BIG PETAL CLEMATIS) Mature size: 8-12 feet. Profuse blue semidouble flowers in very early spring. Tolerates both sun and shade; rich, moist, well-drained soil. Zones 5-9.

'The President' is a vigorous and prolific clematis whose large purple-blue flowers sport 8 cupped and pointed sepals; stamens are striking as well, with white filaments and reddish-purple anthers. This repeat bloomer begins to throw flowers in June and continues through September. Its modest habit makes it perfect for a small fence or gazebo, or the corner of a single-story house. It also makes a fine addition to a small ornamental tree. Mature size: 10 feet. Pruning category B.

C. maximowicziana has been charming American gardeners since 1860 with its delightfully sweet fragrance; in late summer its diminutive cruciform flowers of pure white give it the appearance, and aroma, of a scented cloud. It is extremely tolerant of alkaline soils (up to 7.7 or 7.8), and its fine, threadlike roots make it easier to move than the large-flowered clematis. Grow it with a companion vine, through shrubs, or over an arbor, where its handsome leaves, dark green on both sides and sporting 3-5 leaflets, display themselves to best effect. In the North it exhibits the remarkable characteristic of being able to maintain attractive, green foliage after temperatures go down to 14° F. In some areas it has naturalized and can be aggressive. Mature size: 25 feet. Pruning category C.

C. macropetala has blue flowers that appear in profusion in April and May, complemented by neatly unfurling foliage. Technically, the 3-inch blooms are semidouble, but the inner bluish-white staminoids—up to 20 per blossom give them a fully double appearance. Tolerant of both sun and shade, *C. macropetala* combines well with shrubs. An excellent choice for a vine with very early spring color. Mature size: 8-12 feet. Pruning category A.

C. pitcheri (Pitcher's clematis) is an herbaceous, somewhat woody native perennial vine with beautiful leathery, grayish-purple, urn-shaped flowers in midsummer followed by attractive clusters of seeds. (Dyck Arboretum)

EUONYMUS FORTUNEI BIGLEAF WINTERCREEPER *Celastraceae*

The virtues of the humble *Euonymus* are many: shade-tolerant and highly adaptable, it can be grown as a free-standing shrub 4-5 feet high or as a vine that will climb 40 feet or more. Its 1- to 2-inch evergreen leaves are glossy green, set off by small greenish-white flowers that develop pea-sized, berrylike fruits of a pale pink. Later in the season, these fruits burst open to reveal attractive orange seeds that persist well into the winter months. A true clinging vine, *Euonymus* needs no support to clamber, attaching itself easily to wood or brick.

BEST CONDITIONS *Euonymus* does best on an eastern or northern exposure, or in any naturally shady site. It is tolerant of acid and alkaline soils but does not like wet soils.

PLANTING *Euonymus* is easy to transplant from containers in the spring or early fall.

WATER When newly transplanted, soak the root system every 1-2 weeks for the first growing season, then water during dry periods. To establish on a wall, an occasional moistening of the surface during the summer months will keep

Few plants rival clematis for sheer drama; when they are in bloom, they invariably steal the show. *Opposite: Clematis* 'General Sikorski'.

Above: Clematis 'Betty Corning' is a favorite of many gardeners; its blossoms are not as large as some others, but they are profuse.

temperatures down and help the branches to cling.

PESTS/DISEASES *Euonymus* scale and crown gall can be serious threats; also possible are anthracnose; leaf spot, powdery mildew, and thrips.

PRUNING Prune only in narrow beds, to allow people to pass, or for formal presentation.

USE Evergreen leaves and winter fruit make *Euonymus* an excellent choice for the front of the house, where it can be seen and admired on a daily basis. Grow it either as a vine, or as a shrub in foundation plantings. To create additional interest, combine *Euonymus* with another vine, such as clematis 'Bill Mckenzie'.

CULTIVAR 'Colorata' is a vigorous climber whose foliage turns a very attractive maroon color in fall and winter. It has been used successfully as a ground cover in the Chicago Botanic Garden, where its neat, close-cropped appearance is maintained by the use of a lawnmower with a bag attachment.

HEDERA HELIX ENGLISH IVY *Araliaceae*

The attractive evergreen leaves of *Hedera helix* make it a useful all-around climber, for it anchors itself with whiskerlike holdfasts. It also works well as a quick-spreading (if not rampant in some climates) ground cover.

BEST CONDITIONS PH-adaptable and reasonably drought-tolerant, *Hedera helix* is easy to grow in any good garden soil. In colder climates it prefers growing on north- and east-facing walls where it is protected from both winter sun and summer heat; in milder climates, it is grown in full sun, and even along street medians, but it thrives in shady locations where it is best used as an evergreen under or up into trees.

PLANTING Because it takes several years for *Hedera helix* to become fully established, plant it as early in spring as possible. The American Ivy Society suggests planting the crown 2 inches below the soil surface, then adding an inch of native soil and an inch of mulch, will help the plant overwinter in northern climates.

PESTS/DISEASES None except perhaps leaf spots and mites.

PRUNING Rarely needs pruning except when grown in restricted areas, such as along a sidewalk or in a narrow plot, and in such cases it should be pruned to keep it within the area it's intended to cover.

PROPAGATION Cuttings can be taken at any time of the year and rooted with rooting hormone.

USE *Hedera helix* will cling to virtually any vertical surface; it is especially stunning when grown on the chimneys of larger houses. In colder areas, it tends to work best as a ground cover, protected from winter's desiccating winds and kept warm by radiant heat. Additional protection can be provided during the dormant season with evergreen boughs.

CULTIVAR 'Treetop' is a dense, shrubby plant whose leaves open bright green and darken as they mature. This is a mature form that does not have the common lobed leaves.

CLEMATIS 'NELLY MOSER' (CLEMATIS) Mature size: 8-12 feet. Pale pink petals, striped with deeper pink or red, red anthers. Afternoon shade; rich, moist soil. Zones 5-9.

CLEMATIS 'MARIE BOISSELOT' (CLEMATIS) Mature size: 8-12 feet. Large white flowers with white stamens, up to 8 inches in diameter, lasting over 2 weeks from late June to July. Tolerates 4-5 hours of shade per day. Zones 3-9.

CLEMATIS X JACKMANII (JACKMANII CLEMATIS) Mature size: 12-15 feet. Profuse large purple flowers in mid summer, lighter rebloom in early fall. Full sun or partial shade, rich, moist soil. Zones 5-9.

EUONYMUS FORTUNEI (BIGLEAF WINTERCREEPER) Mature size: 4-5 feet as a shrub, up to 40 feet as a vine. Glossy evergreen leaves, small flowers and fruit. Acid or alkaline soil, not too wet; shade. Zones 5-9.

HEDERA HELIX (ENGLISH IVY) Mature size: 30-40 feet. Attractive evergreen leaves. Any good garden soil; shade is best, but tolerates sun. Zones 5-10.

HYDRANGEA ANOMALA SSP. PETIOLARIS (CLIMBING HYDRANGEA) Mature size: up to 60 feet. Glossy oval leaves, flat-topped clusters of large, fragrant flowers. Partial to full shade. Rich, well-drained soil. Zones 4-9.

JASMINUM NITIDUM (STAR JASMINE, CONFEDERATE JASMINE) Mature size: 10-20 feet. Shiny dark green leaves, purple flower buds opening to white flowers. Full sun to partial shade; light, rich, well-drained soil. Zones 9-10.

LONICERA HECKROTTII (EVERBLOOMING HONEYSUCKLE) Mature size: to 30 feet. Red and yellow flowers (flowerbuds are shown in photograph), lasting over a long period, attractive stems and foliage. Rich, well-drained soil, full sun or partial shade. Zones 5-9.

HYDRANGEA ANOMALA SSP. PETIOLARIS CLIMBING
HYDRANGEA *Saxifragaceae*

For sheer drama and beauty, few vines can surpass climbing hydrangea. In mid-June it sports flat-topped clusters of subtly fragrant white flowers, 6-10 inches across, comprised of 1- to 1½-inch sterile florets that can be effective for as long as 2 months. (In fact, these can remain on the plant until spring, adding winter interest.) The glossy oval leaves are 2-4 inches in diameter, with finely toothed margins. The growth habit forms plates of foliage that extend 1-3 feet from the wall it is covering, giving the plant a pleasant three-dimensional effect; this, of course, lends itself to dramatic effects, livening up walls and trees. Though the foliage boasts little in the way of dependable fall color, the vine has beautiful cinnamon-hued exfoliating bark, a boon during the dormant season. Climbing hydrangea is a truly aristocratic plant. It takes roughly 5 years to become established and grow into a vigorously flowering plant, but once established it rewards its owner with years of pleasure. A mature, flowering plant is a sign of a garden that has been faithfully tended for several years—and is ample reward for the gardener's efforts.

BEST CONDITIONS Climbing hydrangea does well in shade or semishade, on the east or north side of a structure. Grow in a rich, well-drained soil with a pH of up to 7.2.

PLANTING Climbing hydrangea is best planted as a container plant in spring or fall. Since fruits and foliage can extend out as much as 3 feet, the vine should be sited where it can grow freely.

PESTS/DISEASES Disease and insects are rarely a problem, though a soil pH of more than 7.2 can cause chlorosis, a yellowing of the leaves.

PRUNING Prune only as necessary to control direction or size.

PROPAGATION Difficult to propagate from cuttings; the home gardener can take stems and layer them to produce new plants.

USE Because it attaches itself with rootlike holdfasts, this vine can go vertical readily on any surface except metal, which retains too much heat in the summer. (Wood and brick, however, should be monitored, since the holdfasts can cause structural damage over time.) For best results, train climbing hydrangea into a tree, along a fence, or over aluminum siding—be sure to keep it cool. (Daily moistening of the surface with a garden hose is beneficial.)

Above: The striking and unusual blossom on *Lonicera sempervirens,* which is hardier than *Lonicera heckrottii.*.

JASMINUM OFFICINALE POET'S JESSAMINE, JASMINE *Oleaceae*

This semievergreen vine, popular for its vigorous growth and profuse, deliciously fragrant flowers, has been grown in English gardens for 400 years. Appearing from June to October, the blossoms are ¾-1 inch in length and width; leaves are dark green, pinnate, and composed of 5-7 leaflets. The glossy black fruits are not particularly ornamental, but nor are they a nuisance.

BEST CONDITIONS Full sun or partial shade.

PLANTING Can be planted throughout the growing season from a container; before fall if there is a limited root system.

MANDEVILLA 'ALICE DU PONT' (CHILEAN JASMINE) Mature size: 20 feet. White or pink trumpet-shaped flowers, narrow heart-shaped leaves. Full sun or partial shade, any rich, well-drained soil. Zones 9-10.

MINA LOBATA (CRIMSON STARGLORY) Mature size: 20 feet. Deeply lobed leaves, long stalks of red flowers that turn yellow and orange. Full sun or light shade, light, well-drained soil. Zones 8-10.

PARTHENOCISSUS HENRYANA (SILVERVEIN CREEPER) Mature size: 20 feet. Striking variegated foliage, rich green with silver-white and pink veining, turns red in fall. Full shade, rich, well-drained soil. Zones 7-10.

PASSIFLORA CAERULEA (BLUE PASSIONFLOWER) Mature size: 12 feet. Spectacular blue and white flowers in summer, large fruit. Full sun or light shade, well-drained rich soil. Zones 7-10.

PRUNING Pruning is not necessary unless you want a tidy appearance.
USE Can be grown over an arbor or used as a shrub, in which case it is best
near living space outdoors or a window for the wonderfully fragrant flowers.
SPECIES *Jasminum nitidum* (star jasmine, Confederate jasmine) grows 10-20 feet
long and produces purple flower buds that open into white flowers.

LONICERA HECKROTTII EVERBLOOMING HONEYSUCKLE
Caprifoliaceae

One of the most attractive of the honeysuckles, everblooming honeysuckle is a
rambling vine of twining habit, less invasive than the infamous *japonica* but
also fragrant. Literally covered with flowers in May, it continues to bloom
through October as new growth is produced. The arresting blossoms are
carmine in bud, exposing a yellow interior as they open and turning pink on
the outside within a day or two. Stems are an attractive pink, and leaves are
green with glaucous undersides. Maintaining its attractive foliage down to 16°
F., this vine can be considered semievergreen.
BEST CONDITIONS Flowering best in a rich, well-drained soil, *Lonicera heckrottii*
will flourish in a site that receives full sun as well as half a day's shade.
PESTS/DISEASES None serious.
PRUNING Prune only if grown as a shrub or to keep it in a tight mound.
USE Because of its appealing fragrance, this vine is best placed near a sitting
area or pathway. At the Chicago Botanic Garden it has been allowed to clam-
ber over a rock wall just upwind from a bench.
SPECIES *Lonicera* x *brownii* 'Dropmore Scarlet', developed by Dr. Frank Skinner
in Dropmore, Manitoba, is the hardiest vining honeysuckle for the North,
blooming from June until frost. (Minnesota Landscape Arboretum).

MANDEVILLA SUAVEOLENS CHILEAN JASMINE *Apocynaceae*

This woody twining vine produces abundant pink or white trumpet-shaped
flowers in early summer, with a second blooming in early fall. It is hardy only
in the warmest parts of North America (Zones 9-10) but can be grown
indoors, or as an annual in other parts of the continent.
BEST CONDITIONS *Mandevilla* will grow in any rich, well-drained soil in full sun or
partial shade.
PLANTING Plant from seed in spring; water generously during first growth, then
reduce watering.
PRUNING Prune to maintain shape; deadhead to promote blooming. If grown as
a perennial, thin in spring.
PROPAGATION From stem cuttings, rooted in vermiculite.
USE *Mandevillas* can be trained on arches or pergolas in warm climates; else-
where, they look lovely in hanging baskets.

MINA LOBATA CRIMSON STARGLORY *Convolvulaceae*

This little-used vine has deeply lobed leaves and delicate flowers that turn
from red to yellow and orange; they add an unusual, delicate touch to a trellis

Above: Parthenocissus quinquefolia,
growing in its native habitat on a limestone cliff, photographed in autumn.
The texture and color of this natural
stone sets off the deep red fall foliage
of the vine.

POLYGONUM AUBERTII (SILVER FLEECE VINE, SILVER LACE VINE)
Mature size: 15-30 feet. Bears slender panicles of white and
pale pink flowers and leaves that emerge as red or bronze-
red and turn green. Full sun or partial shade; light, soil.
Zones 4-9.

ROSA 'TAUSENSCHOEN' (CLIMBING ROSE) Mature size: to 20 feet.
Profuse deep pink blooms. Rich, well-drained soil, at least
6 hours of sunlight per day. Zones 4-9.

**SCHIZOPHRAGMA HYDRANGEOIDES (JAPANESE CLIMBING
HYDRANGEA)** Mature size: 12 feet. Large flat-topped clusters
of pure white flowers, foliage turns warm yellow in fall.
Rich soil with even moisture; best in shade, tolerates sun.
Zones 5-9.

VITIS LABRUSCA 'SHERIDAN' (EDIBLE GRAPE) Mature size: 60 feet
or more. Luxuriant foliage, red fruit upon maturity. Full
sun, rich soil, good air circulation. Zones 5-9.

or wall. Although this vigorous twining vine is winter-hardy only in Zone 8 or warmer, it can be grown as an annual in colder regions.

BEST CONDITIONS Crimson starglory needs light, well-drained soil. It thrives in full sun and partial shade, but not in dense shade.

PLANTING Plant in spring from seeds started indoors about 6 weeks before date of last frost; mulch to keep soil moist.

PRUNING None required.

USE Crimson starglory adds interest to a fence or trellis.

PARTHENOCISSUS HENRYANA SILVERVEIN CREEPER *Vitaceae*

This vine is most often grown for its striking variegated leaves. Composed of 3-5 leaflets, these emerge scarlet and unfurl to a rich, velvety green. The tops are filigreed with silver-white and pink veining, and the undersides are a deep purple. In the fall, the foliage turns a rich crimson. The vine's blue grapelike fruits are not showy but are nevertheless much appreciated by birds.

BEST CONDITIONS For best variegation, plant in nearly full shade.

PESTS/DISEASES No serious problems, but leaf spot is occasionally encountered.

PRUNING No pruning should be required.

USE Silvervein creeper grows well on arbors or trellises and makes a good ground cover; its unique variegation and stunning color make it good as a specimen plant as well. At the Chicago Botanic Garden, where it is marginally hardy, it is used as a small-scale ground cover.

SPECIES *P. quinquefolia* (Virginia creeper), a commonly used vine, has a loose, open growth habit. It performs well when allowed to cover stone walls or other large areas and turns bright red in autumn.

P. tricuspidata (Boston ivy) clings to stonework with small holdfasts and tolerates city pollution. A vigorous grower, it has large, lustrous leaves that turn scarlet in autumn. Several smaller-leaved cultivars do not grow as quickly as the species, but work well in smaller areas.

PASSIFLORA PASSIONFLOWER *Passifloraceae*

Passiflora is a large genus or tendril-climbing vines; some species are grown for their spectacular flowers, others for their luscious, edible fruit. Although most passionflower vines are hardy only in the southern part of North America, they can be grown indoors or as annuals elsewhere.

BEST CONDITIONS Passionflowers grow best in well-drained soil that is rich in organic matter and in full sun or light shade. They benefit from the protection of a sheltering wall or other structure.

PLANTING Plant from seeds in spring; cuttings can be taken in summer.

PRUNING Prune heavily in spring or fall to remove dead wood.

PESTS/DISEASES Passionflowers are sometimes damaged by nematodes.

USE The exotic bloom of the passionflower adds drama wherever they are planted.

SPECIES *P. caerulea* bears large, beautiful blue or pure white flowers in early summer through early fall. It is hardy in Zones 7-8. *P. incarnata* (maypop) is a

Above: Foliage and blossoms of *Passiflora* 'Sunburst'.

Above: Wisteria floribunda, trained to a tree.

native plant that bears white flowers and edible fruit. *P.* 'Incense' is a cold-tolerant passionflower, hardy to Zone 5.

POLYGONUM AUBERTII SILVER FLEECE VINE, SILVER LACE VINE

Polygonaceae

Recommended for its fine-textured, natural habit and late-summer flowers, this vigorous rambler blooms in mid to late summer through early fall. The white and pale pink flowers, borne in numerous slender panicles throughout the top of the plant, are mildly fragrant, and the leaves, which emerge red or bronze-red, mature to a bright green.

BEST CONDITIONS Easy to establish, this vine grows in full sun or half-day shade. It tolerates dry soil and may languish in heavy soils; to grow well and produce flowers its first season, it needs a well-drained, oxygenated growing medium.

PLANTING This vine can be planted as a containerized plant at any time during the spring, summer, or early fall.

PESTS/DISEASES None except Japanese beetle (in areas where present).

PRUNING In those areas where stems do not die back, this requires hard pruning to keep it in bounds if you desire something under 25-35 feet in spread. In the Chicago area, it grows to about 12-15 feet.

PROPAGATION Easily propagated from stem cuttings, seed, or division.

USE Sometimes referred to as "mile-a-minute vine," *Polygonum aubertii* offers ease of care and rapid growth in difficult sites. At the Chicago Botanic Garden it was used to quickly cover a variety of structures in the English Walled Garden before the garden's formal dedication.

ROSA Species CLIMBING ROSE *Rosaceae*

Rambler roses are not true vines in that they do not twine or attach themselves; they always need to be tied to their support. Many species of rose will climb or grow if properly trained. They require quite a bit of care, including frequent pruning, spraying, fertilizing, and mulching. The results are spectacular, however, and the sight of roses growing on an arbor, fence, or pergola is many gardeners' favorite.

BEST CONDITIONS Roses need rich, well-drained soil and at least 6 hours of sunlight daily.

PLANTING Plant as for other roses; see page 120.

PESTS/DISEASES See page 120.

PRUNING/TRAINING Immediately after flowering, choose a strong, flexible cane and tie in place with soft twine. As the plant grows over the next few seasons, prune out all dead wood, removing about ⅓ of the canes, and continue to tie canes in position loosely.

CULTIVARS Climbing roses can be broken into 2 groups, climbers and ramblers; climbers have stiffer canes, ramblers have smaller leaves and very flexible canes. Most climbing roses are hybrids of *R. wichuraiana, R. setigera,* or *R. multiflora.* Among the best rambler cultivars are 'Dorothy Perkins' and 'Excelsa'; 'New Dawn' and 'Blaze' are excellent climber cultivars.

SCHIZOPHRAGMA HYDRANGEOIDES JAPANESE CLIMBING HYDRANGEA *Saxifragaceae*

Why this lovely and versatile vine isn't more widely cultivated remains a mystery. All summer long its intricate tracery of branches is covered with large, flat-topped floral clusters, often as large as 10 inches in width, of the purest white. Fall foliage is an arresting yellow, and in winter the reddish-brown young stems make for an eye-catching display. Climbing via adhesive roots, it grows flat against any surface, a habit that serves to emphasize the cascading effect of its blossoms.

BEST CONDITIONS Though this vine performs best in shade, it tolerates sun admirably, preferring a rich organic soil of even moisture.

PLANTING Plant in spring, placing transplants close to their support and cutting them back to 6 inches or so to encourage new shoots.

Above: An underused but valuable vine: *Schizophragma hydrangeoides* (with *Cotinus coggygria* in the background).

WISTERIA FLORIBUNDA (JAPANESE WISTERIA) Mature size: to 50 feet. Strong, vigorous climber with long, dense racemes of fragrant flowers. Full sun, best in moderately fertile, deeply worked soil. Zones 3-9 for foliage, zones 5-6 for flowers.

WISTERIA MACROSTACHYA (KENTUCKY WISTERIA) Mature size: to 50 feet. Foot-long racemes of lilac-purple flowers. Full sun, best in moderately fertile, deeply worked soil. Zones 4-9 for foliage and flowers, sometimes flowers in Zone 3.

DOLICHOS LABLAB (HYACINTH BEAN) Mature size: 15-30 feet. Large dark green leaves, white to purple flowers, purple seedpods. Full sun, any good soil. Annual.

IPOMOEA PURPUREA 'HEAVENLY BLUE' AND 'MORNING CALL' (MORNING GLORY) Mature size: 15 feet. Heart-shaped, deep green leaves, vividly colored trumpet-shaped flowers. Full sun, poor soil (fertile soil promotes foliage growth at expense of flowers). Annual.

PRUNING To keep in bounds, prune in late winter or early spring.

PROPAGATION Softwood or semihardwood cuttings, taken at any time during the growing season, root reasonably well, though layering may be the most efficient means of propagation.

USE Its vigorous vining habit makes this a good candidate to cover a large rock, stump, or stone wall (but never wood, which can be seriously damaged by the clinging aerial roots). Or consider allowing it to clamber up the trunk of a large tree, where its oversize blossoms are never in danger of fading into the background.

CULTIVAR *S. hydrangeiodes* 'Moonlight' is prized as much for its foliage—silvery blue-green leaves whose veins are outlined in dark green—as for its foamy white flowers. Even in shade, where it thrives, the foliage is a stand-out. (Morris Arboretum)

VITIS LABRUSCA EDIBLE GRAPE *Vitaceae*

With their luxuriant foliage and glistening clusters of edible fruit, grapes are beloved worldwide as a classic covering for arbors and a delicious crop for the home gardener. In their growing season, grapes provide shade and soften architectural details. Best of all, gardeners can choose from among dozens of varieties, depending on their intended use—for eating, for juice- and winemaking, for drying, or for processing.

BEST CONDITIONS Cultivated grapes are best grown in a south-facing site that receives full sun and allows good air circulation. Soil can be acid to alkaline.

PLANTING Plant in the spring at soil level, where the roots originate. Because grapevines can become quite heavy, they require a strong structure such as a large fence or canopy to ramble over. It is advisable to plant two different types of vines to ensure good pollination and fruit set.

PESTS/DISEASES Grape phylloxera (an insect that feeds on the roots and leaves of grapes) can present serious difficulties. To avoid problems with phylloxera, make sure the vines you buy are not on the European understock of *Vitis vinifera* but on *V. labrusca*.

PRUNING Grapes require a fair amount of pruning. If your goal is a bountiful harvest, cut the vines back hard in winter to a pair of leaf buds, leaving short renewal spurs—short woody stems that will elongate the following year into main stems—for future production. Less severe pruning will result in a denser screen but fewer grapes.

USE These highly attractive vines should ideally be sited where they can be viewed at leisure and where their fruit is easily accessible for harvesting and yet not where they may create a mess—such as over a doorway or heavily traveled path. Grapes are ideal for shading a pergola.

SPECIES *Vitis labrusca* is a native of the eastern U.S. and one of the parents of most of the American grapes now in cultivation; it is the rootstock of choice for resistance to phylloxera. Its sweet, musky flavor and black fruit have earned it the common name of fox grape. Leaves are dark green with white undersides, 3½-6 inches wide.

Morning glory cultivars encompass a wide range of colors, including whimsical stripes.

IPOMOEA BATATAS 'BLACKIE' (SWEET POTATO VINE) Mature size: 6-10 feet. Deeply lobed 8-inch leaves, dark purple to near black in color; cascading habit. Full sun, susceptible to frost, any garden soil. Annual.

THUNBERGIA ALATA (BLACK-EYED SUSAN VINE) Mature size: 6-8 feet. Vigorous vine with bright orange or yellow flowers with black centers, triangular green leaves. Full sun or partial shade; rich, moist soil. Annual.

TROPAEOLUM PEREGRINUM (CANARY CREEPER, CANARY BIRD-FLOWER) Mature size: 8-12 feet. Large, deeply lobed leaves, canary-yellow flowers. Acid or alkaline soils, full sun, cool areas. Annual.

TROPAEOLUM SPECIOSUM (SCOTTISH FLAME THROWER) Shown against *Taxus* hedge. Mature size: 8-12 feet. Green foliage, ornamental blue fruit, bright red flowers. Acid or alkaline soil, cool areas. Annual.

V. coignetiae (gloryvine, crimson glory) is one of the fastest-growing species, with large leaves that turn bright red in autumn. Its ability to cover up to 1,000 feet of trellis in just a few years has made it a staple in large gardens; it needs constant pruning if it is to be kept small. Zones 5-9.

WISTERIA FLORIBUNDA JAPANESE WISTERIA *Fabaceae*

This strong and vigorous climber is spectacular in spring when the long, dense racemes of sweetly fragrant flowers burst forth. Always buy cutting-grown or grafted plants, which flower in 2-3 years, as opposed to those grown from seed, which can take 7-10 years to bloom.

BEST CONDITIONS Although wisterias tolerate a variety of soils, they perform best in a deeply worked soil of moderate fertility, in full sun.

PLANTING Wisterias should be planted during their growing season. Wisterias require a strong, long-lasting support at soil level, either galvanized pipe, which won't rust, or 4 x 4- or 6 x 6-inch posts and beams of a decay-resistant wood like redwood or cedar. (Treated lumber is also acceptable if the posts are not in contact with vegetables or herbs intended for consumption.) Arbors should be 8-10 feet tall for best viewing.

FERTILIZER It is best not to push this plant with too much fertilizer, which can impede flowering. A moderate application of high-phosphorus fertilizer (such as 5-10-5) in early spring will boost flower growth.

PESTS/DISEASES Powdery mildew can be a problem in areas of poor air circulation, but this is usually only an aesthetic issue and does not affect the health of the plant.

PRUNING For floral impact, 2-4 weeks after flowering, prune back lateral growth just off the main trunk to 3-5 of the larger flower buds. A second pruning later in the season, when plump flower buds are more in evidence, is useful. This plant can become quite large and deadly if allowed to wrap around smaller plants or itself. Consequently, it is best to keep the main stems from wrapping around themselves.

PROPAGATION By grafting.

USE Best suited to large gardens, wisterias provide a magnificent cover for pillars, arbors, walls, and even trees, as long as they can tolerate the vine's often substantial weight. Ideally, grow wisterias where their magnificent show can be admired from a variety of vantage points. For smaller spaces, the vine can be trained to tree form: Use a strong post for support to ensure that the branches don't encircle or choke off the main stem.

SPECIES *W. floribunda* boasts numerous cultivars, including white, rose-pink, blue, violet, and even double-flowered forms. 'Ivory Tower' is one of the most impressive, with exceptionally fragrant flowers of the purest white. Its foliage is hardy in Zones 3-9, it will flower in Zones 5 or 6 through 9. Blooms in April in the South, in May in the North.

W. macrostachya, Kentucky wisteria, is a boon to northern gardeners, since it is fully flower hardy from Zone 4, and may even flower in Zone 3. Blooming later, in mid to late June, it sends out foot-long racemes of lovely lilac-purple.

When the tendril, which sweeps a full circle in 67 minutes, finds a perch, within 20 seconds it starts to curve around the object, and within the hour has wound itself so firmly it is hard to tear away. The tendril then curls itself like a corkscrew and in so doing raises the vine to itself. . . . A climbing plant which needs a prop will creep toward the nearest support. Should this be shifted, the vine, within a few hours, will change its course into the new direction. Can the plant *see* the pole? Does it sense it in some unfathomed way? . . . Plants {says biologist France} are capable of *intent;* they can stretch toward or seek out what they want in ways as mysterious as the most fantastic creatures of romance.
FROM *THE SECRET LIFE OF PLANTS,* BY PETER TOMPKINS AND CHRISTOPHER BIRD

ANNUAL VINES

Annual vines are helpful when trying to soften a structure the first year, or when deciding whether or not you want to grow a vine permanently. They can help you determine if a vine is appropriate, if it is the right size and height. Annuals give you a sense of its textural effect–too large, heavy, or perhaps not dramatic enough.

ANNUAL VINES

DOLICHOS LABLAB HYACINTH BEAN, EGYPTIAN BEAN *Fabaceae*

Visually striking and easy to cultivate, hyacinth bean is a twining vine with large dark green, purple-veined trifoliate leaves and equally impressive flowers, white to purple in hue and 10-12 inches in diameter. The flowers, which continue to appear throughout the season, give way to flat purple seedpods, about 6 inches long. This is a perennial in warmer climates, where it benefits from some pruning to keep it attractive.

BEST CONDITIONS Hyacinth bean will grow vigorously in any good, reasonably fertile garden soil, in full sun.

PLANTING Start from seed, either directly in the garden after danger of frost has passed or inside in late winter or early spring. For upright growth, train onto wrought iron, wooden trelliswork, string, or fishing line.

USE This showy vine makes a dramatic focal point as well as an effective screen. In an adequate container that holds 1-2 cubic feet of soil, it can also be grown on a terrace or patio.

IPOMOEA Species MORNING GLORY *Convolvulaceae*

Morning glory (*I. purpurea*) and its cousin moonflower (*I. alba*) have heart-shaped leaves of a deep green and trumpetlike flowers up to 6 inches in diameter. Morning glory flowers are available in a wide range of colors. As the name suggests, moonflower's blossoms are pure white and open just before dusk, when they release their fragrance, lasting till noon of the next day.

BEST CONDITIONS Both moonflower and morning glory thrive in full sun and warm temperatures. If the soil is too rich or fertile, the vine will produce foliage in preference to flowers.

PLANTING Start from seeds outdoors after the danger of frost has passed, or indoors in March. These twining stems benefit from the support of an arbor, trellis, or well-branched tree.

FERTILIZER For optimum flower production, keep fertilizer to a minimum.

USE These vigorous vines provide almost instant foliage and spots of color. Moonflower was used to great effect as a quick screen in the Chicago Botanic Garden's newly established English Walled Garden. To take full advantage of its nocturnal perfume, place it outside a bedroom window. Moonflower and morning glory can be grown together to to complement each others blooming times.

SPECIES *I. purpurea* comes in many colors; among the best cultivars are 'Heavenly Blue' (dark sky blue); 'Scarlet O'Hara' (red); and 'Pearly Gates' (white). Flowers are effective from midsummer to frost. *I. alba* is also a good cut flower and has been known to attract night-flying moths.

I. batatas 'Blackie' (sweet potato) has deeply lobed 8-inch leaves, deep purple to near-black in coloration. With its cascading habit, it is the perfect container plant, especially when used in combination with brightly colored annuals; for a stunning effect try it with *Helichrysum petiolatum* or *Scaevola* or *Coleus*. Hardy to Zone 7 but susceptible to frost; don't set out too early in the season.

THUNBERGIA ALATA BLACK-EYED SUSAN VINE *Acanthaceae*

This fast-growing vine is accented by profuse bright yellow or orange flowers with dark, almost black centers, on triangular green leaves. It blooms throughout the summer and is usually grown as an annual.

BEST CONDITIONS Moist, rich, well-drained soil. Full sun or partial shade. It will not survive frost.

PLANTING Plant seeds in spring.

PROPAGATION From seeds or cuttings.

USE At The New York Botanical Garden, this plant has been used to screen out construction; it can also be grown in hanging baskets.

SPECIES *Thunbergia grandiflora* (sky vine, clock vine) is another outstanding species; it produces pendulous clusters of blue and white tubular flowers in midspring. Hardy to Zone 8.

TROPAEOLUM SPECIOSUM SCOTTISH FLAME FLOWER

Tropaeolaceae

Hardiest and most spectacular of all the *Tropaeolum, T. speciosum* has dainty, fresh-green foliage, ornamental blue fruit, and bright vermillion-scarlet flowers 1½ inches in diameter, with 2 wedge-shaped petals above and 3 larger, rounded petals below. Leaves are deeply divided into 6 (sometimes 5 or 7) ovate leaflets.

BEST CONDITIONS This tolerant vine will grow in either acid or alkaline soil, but performs best in cool areas and should be sited on the north side of a hedge or the east or northern section of a wall or fence.

PLANTING The frail stems die down to fleshy roots, which can be sliced up into 1½-inch sections and inserted either vertically or horizontally into a good growing medium and taken indoors as soon as the plant goes dormant in the fall; another means of propagation is to save the fruits and plant them in the spring. Seeds can also be sown directly in warm soil; for best results, start 1 month before the first frost-free date.

USE Like canary creeper, *T. speciosum* is at its best against a framework of evergreen shrubs, or intertwined with other vines; try English ivy or early flowering clematis.

SPECIES *T. peregrinum* (canary creeper, canarybird flower) sports canary-yellow flowers, whose erect upper petals resemble a delicate set of wings. The summer-blooming flowers also sport a short green hooked spur and a red spot at the bottom of each petal. Leaves are large—2-3 inches across—grayish, and deeply divided, like the palm of an open hand. Most effective when coiling up through other plants, canary creeper can be used as a scrambler through gray- and green-leaved shrubs, though it's most dramatic when allowed to festoon an evergreen hedge. Both the flowers and young leaves are edible, with a peppery flavor similar to that of nasturtium *(Tropaeolum majus)*.

Above: False cypress shrubs flank a brick entryway; these evergreen shrubs provide color throughout the year, and soften an otherwise stark wall.

Previous pages: An elaborate collection of shrubs (including hydrangeas, rhododendron, and conifers) adds to the air of luxury in this lush poolside setting.

Every gardener, whether starting from scratch on newly cleared ground, revamping an existing garden, or just incorporating a new specimen or two, eventually faces the question of design. Shrubs, because of their relatively large size and permanence in the landscape, dictate an especially careful approach to design. Perennials placed willy-nilly in the border can be dug out and moved with relative ease; annuals can simply live out their season to serve as lessons for next year; but an ill-placed shrub on its way to maturity is a great deal harder both to move and to ignore. This is where design comes in. Good garden design takes into account a multitude of factors: the overall type of garden, its color scheme, the mix of plants, their size and shape, the look of the landscape year-round, new or existing architectural elements, and the special uses required of individual plants. The best way to consider all these elements—and to avoid costly (or backbreaking) mistakes—is to plan first on paper: Measure twice, dig once might well be the garden designer's credo and caveat.

PLANNING ON PAPER Before drawing up your plan, choose a scale that fits the site. For small gardens, a scale in which ¼ inch equals one foot is suitable; for landscapes that exceed ⅓ acre, an inch to the foot. (Highly detailed plans, even in smaller areas, require the first, more generous scale.) Next, take an inventory of the site, including buildings, property lines, walkways, walls, fences, and existing vegetation; learn and write down soil pH, soil type, hours of sun, and drainage conditions. Armed with this information, you're ready to make a site analysis, which will consist of your opinion, both positive and negative, of existing elements. These could include problem views as well as panoramas, off-site noise, drainage problems, sunny exposed banks or highly shaded areas, and any other landscape blessings and blemishes. Keep in mind the general categories of plants that might solve your problems: a dense evergreen hedge to muffle noise, a group of moisture-loving shrubs to incorporate into a poorly drained area, a flowering vine to cloak an unappealing wall or tumbledown shed. Consider, too, your intent: finding a spot for a pool, planting a flower garden, camouflaging a drab foundation. Then begin your sketch, which can usually be done on a single sheet of paper (though more ambitious plans may necessitate the use of overlays). Once the site has been successfully mapped out, pace it off in the landscape to make sure it will translate from paper to topsoil; strategically placed stakes will help you visualize the intended effect.

CHOOSING A GARDEN TYPE Design preferences, existing architecture, and the natural environment will all help to dictate the type of garden being planned. What follows is a brief summary of the most popular garden types, including representative shrubs and vines for each.

Woodland gardens have a naturalistic look and therefore tend to include native species. By nature, they are shade gardens for most of the season, with the exception of spring, when flowering bulbs and blooming understory shrubs and vines produce welcome color in the still-available spring sunlight. For evergreen shrubs, consider leucothoe and inkberry or any of the rhododendrons; for a deciduous shrub, try clethra and fothergilla. Though most vines work well in a woodland setting, honeysuckle is a special favorite.

Rock gardens incorporate plants associated with dry and rocky conditions, usually from alpine habits. Appropriate shrubs include the evergreen creeping junipers and cotoneaster adpressa, and the deciduous potentilla; Virginia creeper is one of several vines at home in larger rock gardens.

Low-lying, wet areas may necessitate the planting of a swamp garden, which would incorporate high-moisture shrubs like chokeberry and grounsel bush and vines that prefer wet soil like bittersweet. In addition, bog gardens often include some kind of water feature to serve as a design anchor or focal point.

In formal gardens the human hand is always evident—in structured walks, formal architectural elements, and a linear or geometric layout. For a formal landscape, choose slower-growing shrubs, whose habit is more easily controlled—evergreens like boxwood and yew, or deciduous shrubs like *Euonymus alatus* and *Ligustrum vulgaris* (privet). For an impressive formal vine, the classic wisteria is unparalleled. The use of a particular shrub can also make it a contender for inclusion in the classic garden: Viburnum, for example, is usually considered too blowsy for a classic scheme, but pruned into a neat hedge, it's right at home among the classic statuary and topiary.

Cottage gardens, on the other hand, have a deliberately haphazard look, derived from a liberal mix of colors, shapes, and plant types. Scotch broom, hydrangea, and lilac are all comfortable in the cottage garden, as are any of

The two gardens on this page represent successful examples of formal and natural styles. Achieving a woodland look can take just as much planning as creating a tightly-stylized garden.

Above: Acer palmatum 'Waterfall' turns a brilliant scarlet in fall. *Right:* This row of closely spaced rhododendron screens a busy highway on the other side of it.

the clematis species.

SPECIAL USES In addition to their aesthetic properties, shrubs and vines lend themselves to a number of very practical uses, some of which have been mentioned in the introduction. Vines like English ivy and bigleaf wintercreeper make superb ground covers; Boston ivy and Virginia creeper cloak unsightly walls; and grapes provide both shade and sustenance. Dense shrubs like red cedar and arbor vitae form natural windbreaks, barberry and privet make fine sound baffles, while clethra (summersweet) and lilac add a sensual note in the form of fragrance. Two of the most popular uses for shrubs are as hedges and edgings. Most of the shrubs used for hedging are evergreen, particularly if the hedge is a baffle or barrier; popular varieties include boxwood, inkberry, holly, and cotoneaster. Barrier hedges should be virtually impenetrable–thorny barberry, for example, will quickly transform itself into an impassable green wall–but any hedging shrub should grow into itself well. Forsythia, for example, has a looser habit than boxwood but still makes a fine informal hedge, as does weigela.

Any of the smaller evergreen shrubs can be used as edging; for an attractive continuous edge, try a dense shrub such as holly. Although vines are rarely used in edging, English ivy can serve in this capacity, though its rampant habit makes continual vigilance necessary. ("Seafoam" shrub rose makes a lovely border, and in the South, Confederate jasmine often serves this purpose.) On the other hand, vines make excellent ground covers, from the aforementioned English ivy to the ever-popular vinca to the lesser-known but eye-catching deciduous honeysuckle. Remember, however, that as soon as the vine gets next to a structure, it will do what it does best–climb.

Shrubs can also do duty as ground covers and offer an alternative to the overused ivy, vinca, and pachysandra. Choose from any of the smaller ever-

Left: Climbing hydrangea combines with pink and purple rhododendron to form a stunning screen.

green varieties (mature size should not exceed 1½ feet)—including cotoneaster, juniper, and potentilla.

COLOR Novice gardeners often ignore the notion of a color scheme, and though the result of such blissful ignorance can sometimes be felicitous, it is just as often an unappealing hodgepodge. Personal preference, and perhaps the surrounding architecture, will dictate whether your color scheme is hot, warm, or cold, monochromatic or mixed, as will the type of garden being planned (cottage gardens, for example, are intrinsically more colorful than formal gardens, which tend to be subdued or even monochromatic). For a hot color scheme in the spring garden, few shrubs can beat the vibrant azaleas, planted alongside forsythia, coral-red quince, and golden-yellow scotch broom; these can be succeeded in summer by red-pink *Spirea bumalda,* yellow potentilla, and *Berberis thumbergii,* with its striking, deep red foliage. Shrubs provide their most vibrant colors in the spring; hot colors are usually provided by flowers in the summer. For a cooler look in summer, you might mix blue-toned hydrangea, white and pink glossy abelia, and rose-of-sharon, whose blossoms can be white, light pink, lavender, or gentle blue. Hot-color vines include fiery red *Campsis,* annual nasturtium with its riotous mix of red, orange, and yellow, and hot-pink honeysuckle; among the cooler-toned vines are blue morning glory, white or lavender wisteria, and many of the species clematis.

Because shrubs—and, to a lesser degree, vines—tend to have three and even four seasons of use in the garden, the gardener needs to consider their range of colors year-round, from spring and summer flowers and foliage to fall foliage and berries, to winter bark.

GARDEN COMPLEMENTS In addition to color, a plant's size and shape will deter-

You need not rely on flowers for color in your garden; the foliage of many shrubs provides brilliant hues ranging from gold to deep purple. *Below:* Golden spirea and deep red barberry.

Above: **A group of shrubs blends into the cool colors of The New York Botanical Garden's perennial garden. Included above are** *Cotinus coggyria* **'Royal Purple' and** *Hydrangea macrophylla,* **all enclosed in a yew hedge.**

mine whether it fits harmoniously into the general scheme or stands out like an interloping weed. The majority of shrubs should be similar in leaf texture and density, even if the shades of green vary. Loose-leaved shrubs like rhododendron and weigela, for instance, make natural companions, as do the tight-leaved boxwood and yew. Another important consideration is the plant's habit, with shrubs generally falling into one of four categories: full, deciduous, and upright (e.g., viburnum, fothergilla, and the species lilacs); wide and mounding (weigela, quince, and forsythia); open and mounding (oakleaf hydrangea, buddleia); or dense and mounding (spirea, burning bush, barberry). Shrubs with distinctly different shapes can then be incorporated as occasional accents—the vertical English yew, for example, planted among a group of mounding shrubs like weigela, oakleaf hydrangea, and deutzia. Any one garden might contain shrubs of varying sizes, but a certain hierarchy ought to prevail, with larger shrubs serving as a backdrop.

Vines, too, can be grown to complement one another, but here great prudence—not to mention self-control—is called for: more than two, and you've got a confusing tangle. In addition, vines grown together should be of like habit. While some gardeners prefer to prolong the blooming season by interplanting late and early varieties, the most stunning effect is achieved when vines bloom at the same time.

MIXING PLANTS Though shrubs are frequently used alone—in shrub borders and foundation plantings, and as accents—they are more often mixed with other plants, and very successfully so. Keeping in mind the principles outlined above, you can create a harmonious combination of shrubs, vines, trees, annuals, perennials, grasses—even herbs and vegetables. Shrubs and vines represent one of the more interesting horticultural pairings. Galen Gates of the Chicago Botanic Garden has had great success combining early flowering shrubs with later-blooming vines—a clever way to extend the blooming season. Even more dramatic is the pairing of vines and shrubs that share a blooming season, though finding the right mix is a greater aesthetic challenge.

PLANNING FOR FOUR SEASONS Unlike the annuals and perennials that are the stars of the spring and summer garden, shrubs, and many vines, do year-round duty—a fact often overlooked by amateur designers. If a shrub has a real task to perform—screening out noise or the neighbors' bedroom window, for example—then it needs to be evergreen. But even deciduous shrubs can enhance the four-season garden. When making your choice, consider not just peak-season bloom and foliage, but early spring foliage and flower color, fall foliage and berries, and winter bark. In addition, deciduous shrubs and vines can add an architectural note when their branches are naked of leaf and blossom. Harry Lauder's walking stick, for example, is one of the few deciduous shrubs prized mainly for its winter aspect.

On the following pages you will find photographs of several successful gardens that make use of shrubs and vines.

Below: Deep magenta and lilac rhododendron mixed with other broadleaf evergreen shrubs, under a red Japanese maple.

Above: A far cry from the old-fashioned foundation plantings that con-
sisted of two scraggly conifers on
either side of the doorway, this imaginative design employs carefully
sheared evergreens softened by flowering azaleas and pieris bushes.

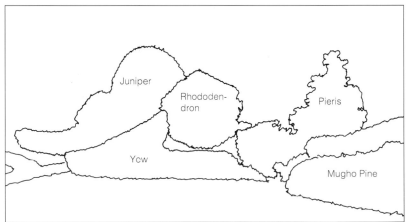

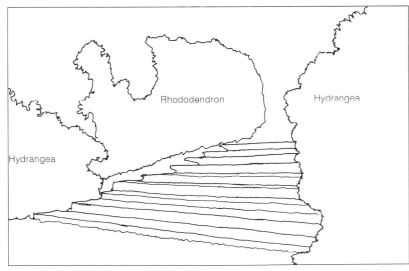

Above: A stone stairway is transformed by evergreen rhododendron and hydrangea. The rhododendron provide color in mid to late spring, and the hydrangea bloom later in the summer.

Above and opposite: Combining vines takes experience; the combinations on these pages–using *Vitis*, ivies, and flowering clematis–display a range of different textures, shapes, and colors without becoming overcomplicated.

This stunning display at England's justly famous Sissinghurst castle (above) combines *Clematis* 'Perle d'Azor', *Hedera helix,* and *Vitis* vines; the foliage and growth habits of these plants complement each other. The obviously healthy and vigorous plants are a main factor in the success of this vista; but the inanimate objects on view play a role as well.

It's easy to think of the garden as consisting exclusively of plants, but in fact virtually every garden incorporates inanimate objects as well–walkways and driveways, patios and porches, chairs and benches, and all manner of garden ornament from urns and birdbaths to statuary and sundials. Be respectful of anything with architectural significance: don't mask a decoratively bricked

wall with a dense vine, or hide a handsome facade with oversized foundation
plantings. On the other hand, nature seems to have designed shrubs and vines
specifically to disguise the unsightly, from rotting stumps to concrete walls.
Ideally, the plant should complement the structure by following its shape:
don't, for example, grow a squat vine on a tall trellis. If the structure is a new
element in the garden, consider its use: benches should be placed to take
advantage of a plant's fragrance or floral show; sundials really do require sun;
and birdfeeders belong where the birds are—under the trees or next to sheltering shrubs. In garden design as in all things architectural, form really does follow function.

CHOOSING AND IMPROVING THE SITE

Most of the shrubs and vines that you plant will stay where you plant them for a long time; unlike flowers or vegetables, which are easily moved, it is important to get them in the right place the first time. The following saying is old and corny, but it happens to be true: Provide a five-dollar hole for a fifty-cent plant. What this is means is that most plants know how to grow if placed in the proper setting. The gardener's first task is to find the right spot for each shrub or vine, the spot where it can use its own innate ability to thrive. It takes time, experience, and experimentation, but a gardener who wants to succeed must acquire an understanding of the site. Whether you are planting an elaborate shrub border, a clematis-covered arbor, or a single specimen plant, you should be aware of the following factors, their relationship to your site, and how they affect the plants you choose to grow.

SUN/SHADE When considering sites for your shrubs and vines, observe all possible areas over a period of time. Note how much sun each site receives and whether it is direct sunlight, sunlight that is filtered through trees and fences, or if the sunlight is totally blocked by buildings or dense tree foliage; note whether conditions change at different times of the day. The plant portraits in Chapter 2 discuss the type and amount of sunlight needed by particular shrubs and vines. In most cases, plants will not grow if not provided with the sunlight suggested.

SOIL Although you cannot change the type of sunlight your garden receives (without altering major structures), you can change the composition of your soil. Soil improvements can be made for the short run with the addition of chemical fertilizers; but serious gardeners are able to manage their soil to attain peak production over a long period of time.

There are three basic types of soil: clay, sand, and loam. Clay soil has very little space between its particles; clay soil is often very rich in nutrients, but water and nutrients have trouble traveling through clay soil to the roots of the plant. Sandy soil transports material easily, but it can't hold nutrients and water for very long. Clay and sand together, along with fibrous organic matter, or humus, comprise the ideal mix: loam, which is light but rich; this type of soil is often called "friable," which means it is easily pulverized.

To identify exactly what the soil in your garden needs requires a soil test. A small—but representative—amount of garden soil is analyzed for nutrient deficiencies and excesses. The acidity or alkalinity—pH—of the soil can be measured with a simple home kit. A full analysis can be done by a county extension service, an agricultural university, or perhaps even a local garden center. The analysis will generally be accompanied by recommendations for needed nutrients and their application rates.

There are many ways to maintain good soil; simply adding a lot of chemical fertilizer is not one of them. It takes experience to understand what your soil needs and to provide it. It is important to match the proper plant to the soil; the wrong plant will usually fail, and it may also damage the soil. Use organic matter generously for plants that need it. Adding compost and other fertilizers will keep your soil rich in organic matter. Use fertilizers that add missing ingredients, including trace elements, only when you have reason to suspect that they are necessary. If you manage your soil properly, it will increase in fertility after several years of cultivation and provide the best possible home for your plants.

SOIL PH Acidity and alkalinity of soil is measured on the pH scale; a measurement of under 7.0 indicates an acid soil, above 7.0 indicates alkaline soil, 7.0 is neutral. Many shrubs and vines, including many rhododendron and other members of the heath family, require acid soil. You can correct overly acid soil by adding limestone; this should be done several months before planting, and should be worked into the soil well. Overly alkaline soil can be corrected by adding organic matter and compost. However, these improvements will not last over time and must be done over a large area because the shrub's roots will spread. In most cases, amending the soil around a large shrub actually does it more harm than good, because it prevents the shrub from sending its roots past the immediate area of the "good" soil. Unless you are prepared to amend the soil heavily each year, it is advisable to choose a plant that can grow well in the existing soil, or to plant in raised beds or containers.

CLIMATE Wind, heavy rain, humidity, heat, and cold are damaging to many shrubs. If your area experiences extreme climate factors, take them into account when choosing shrubs and vines.

DRAINAGE Drainage is the ability of soil to move water so that the roots don't get too waterlogged and nutrients can percolate through the soil to the roots, where they are used. Most shrubs require well-drained soil. There are several ways to correct poor drainage:

    1. Add sand and organic matter to the soil. Sand plus clay results in cement; but sand, clay, and organic matter will give you friable soil.

    2. Use raised beds, which always provide better drainage and also allow you to mix better soil from elsewhere into your site.

    3. Insert a drainage pipe. These pipes, usually plastic, can be purchased at most garden supply or hardware stores and move water to a place where it will do less harm.

    4. Grade the area with terraces or retaining walls.

    5. If your problem is serious, or if you think it is worth the investment, talk to a professional landscaper about inserting a drainage system, such as tile, gravel beds, or more elaborate drainage ditches.

MICROCLIMATES No matter how small your site is, it probably encompasses several sets of conditions. The area near the protection of a wall or building is probably warmer than the open space in front. The strip that faces the street receives more pollution than the yard behind the house. The spot right in front of the house may be affected by limestone in the foundation.

SITE IMPROVEMENT Your plants will grow better if you take the time to improve the ground in which you put them. The first step in preparing a

Above: To determine whether your drainage is adequate, dig a hole large enough to hold a gallon pot. Fill the hole with water, and see how long it takes to drain. If water stands more than a few hours, drainage is probably a problem.

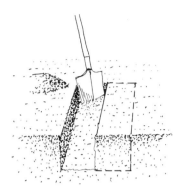

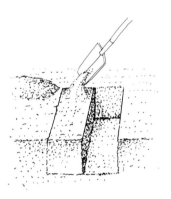

Above: Double digging creates a loose, well-tilled bed. Dig down one shovel deep. Break up all clods of earth. Then repeat the process by digging down a further shovel deep. Refill each trench you dig with soil from the previous trench.

garden site is a general cleanup, the removal of rocks, sticks, stumps, or other debris. Once the area is relatively clean, lay out the boundaries of your site using string, garden hose, or spray paint.

If the site is a grassy area, skin the turf off using a shovel or spade. Take the top 2 inches off—grass and roots—and knock the soil loose from the roots. Don't throw away the turf—use it to start a compost pile. If the area is covered with brush or weeds, mow first and then skin off the vegetation. Once you have bare ground, you're ready to begin improving the soil for a productive garden.

PREPARING THE SOIL Loosen the soil to a depth of 4-6 inches. If there is tender vegetation growing on the site, turn it into the top part of the soil. Pull out any woody stems. Wait at least 2 weeks after tilling to allow the tilled plants to decompose and again turn the soil under to a depth of 4-6 inches to ensure the breaking up of dead plants and to further loosen the soil.

After the second tilling, apply soil amendments such as fertilizer, lime, compost, or sand. Till once again, this time to a depth of 8-10 inches with a tiller, or 12-18 inches by hand with a spading fork.

Double digging is a process by which two spadesful of dirt are lifted and loosened to create a loose, well-tilled bed. It is time-consuming and back-breaking, but it is greatly beneficial to the future health of your shrubs. To be effective, it should be done in an area several square feet around the planting site. Although it seems complicated, the procedure simply requires digging down an extra shovel-depth. As you dig, place the soil you've removed alongside the trench; fill each trench with the soil from the trench before it. Break up all clods in the soil and amend as necessary. Very few people have the stamina to double dig a large area. If your site is very large, you might consider renting a tractor-tiller to prepare the soil.

BUYING SHRUBS When buying shrubs, you can usually choose between bare-root, containerized, and balled-and-burlapped specimens. Bare-root shrubs should be planted only during their dormant seasons. Containerized and balled-and-burlapped specimens can be planted at any time when conditions are not harsh—the newly planted shrub should not have to deal with mid winter cold or mid summer sun, especially in extreme climates. Buy plants from reputable nurseries, and make sure that they have healthy root systems before you put them in the ground. If you cannot plant your new shrubs immediately, store them in a cool place and water them regularly. If possible, dig a trench, lay each shrub into it, and cover it with soil up to the lowest branches.

PLANTING

Planting is a gardener's most rewarding task and also one of the most crucial. Without the right start, even the most carefully tended shrubs will languish. Whether the shrub is bought bare-root, containerized, or balled-and-burlapped, the roots need to be kept moist before planting. The maxim is simple, but apt: if they dry, they die. When digging the planting hole, make sure it's large enough to fit the roots without crowding. Prune

1. After the soil is prepared and the hole dug, break the rootball of the containerized shrub before planting. This plant is *Buxus* 'Empire Green'.

2. Container-grown plants often have matted roots on the outside of the ball. These roots should be teased outward with fingers before planting.

3. Ready for planting, this shrub will have a much easier time getting established now that its roots are no longer matted together in the shape of the container.

4. A boxwood on its way down into the planting hole. The plant at left has just had its roots cut with pruning shears in the process of breaking the rootball.

5. Set the shrub at the proper planting depth and firm the soil around the roots.

6. Water generously. A shallow depression can be made in the soil near the newly planted shrub to hold water.

After planting, smooth out the soil
along the newly planted hedge.

any crushed or damaged roots back to sound wood. Finally, be sure to plant at the proper depth; too deep is just as wrong as too shallow. The hole should be at least as wide as it is deep, and the sides should be roughed up so that the soil around the roots does not become solid. Rule-of-thumb is that the hole should be twice as wide, and twice as deep, as the rootball. Never dig when soil is very wet or very dry, as this will damage the soil structure.

To plant a bare-root shrub: Remove packing material, clods of earth, and broken or dead roots. Prune off dead or broken branches, and soak the plant for at least one, and not more than four hours. Mound soil in the bottom of the hole so that the center of the plant can be placed on the mound with the roots resting below it. Fill in half the soil; pack the soil firmly enough to avoid large air pockets, but not so firmly as to compact it.

To plant a containerized shrub: Remove the container (even if the manufacturer suggests leaving it on). It is important to break the rootball, which may have become potbound. Using a sharp knife or pruning shears, make cuts into the roots on all 4 sides of the rootball. Fluff out the roots with your fingers. Place the plant into the hole, and fill in soil. Create a rim above root level in the hole to hold water around the roots.

To plant a balled-and-burlapped shrub: Fill in half the hole and firm up the soil. The burlap need not be removed (unless it is synthetic), but all string, twine, and other packing material should be taken off. Place the plant in the hole and make sure it is at its proper depth by placing a rod across the hole; if the top of the rootball is not level with the rod, put in more soil, or dig deeper. Fill in remaining soil, and firm.

Perennial vines are planted in much the same way as shrubs. Annual vines are usually planted from seed and do not require as much care, since they are not permanent.

When the plant is in place, water well. During the first few months (and up to a year) after establishment, check frequently to make sure that plant is kept moist. Yellowing leaves or dry soil indicate that the plant needs more water. A shallow depression can be dug around the shrub to hold water. Mulch will also keep the soil around the plant moist.

Most shrubs do not need staking; staking can prevent the shrub from developing properly.

Sometimes, you will decide to move a shrub that is already growing. This is not always easily accomplished and requires quite a bit of preparation. For best results, root-prune the shrub one year before moving it; nurseries usually follow this practice. To root prune, dig a trench around the shrub, about 2 feet deep and 6 inches wide; the trench should be 3-4 feet distant from a small shrub, 5-8 feet distant from a larger one. Fill the trench with sphagnum moss. If this procedure is properly accomplished, the plant will form a compact root system and will be better able to withstand the move. Prune well several weeks before transplanting. Always move a shrub during its dormant season.

When you are ready to move the shrub, dig a trench in a circle

around the shrub, at least 12 inches from it. Dig down at least 2 feet, seg-
regating a ball of earth that includes the shrub's roots. Rock it gently until
it can be removed; you will have to cut some of the roots. Place the
removed shrub, with the ball of soil around its roots, on burlap, and
remove to a protected spot. Even small shrubs are heavy, and you may
need help with this procedure. For a large shrub, place a board under the
shrub to move it. Keep the shrub in its protected area for at least 2 weeks
before replanting, watering it gently and frequently.

PROPAGATION

To the avid gardener, nothing is as exciting as receiving a cutting of a long-
sought plant; and nothing is more frustrating than watching it fail, often in a
glass of water on the kitchen windowsill. With understanding and a little
planning, this kind of disappointment can be avoided with relative ease, but
you must keep in mind that no single method works for every plant all of the
time.

Plant propagation is the art and science of reproducing plants. Plants can
be propagated in several ways, including seeding, grafting, layering, division,
cutting, and tissue culture. The method selected is determined in large part
by the plant's genetic characteristics and growth habit, the available facilities,
the number of plants desired, and the skill and knowledge of the propagator.
For home gardeners looking to produce a few favorite shrubs without great
expense, cutting, layering, and division are generally the most appropriate
techniques.

SOFTWOOD CUTTINGS Many popular shrubs, including mock orange, azalea, forsythia, privet, spirea, and magnolia, can be propagated by softwood cuttings;
it is a good idea to try this method while you are gaining experience in propagation. The optimum time to take cuttings can vary somewhat among
species, and for certain plants, such as lilac, the period available may be limited. However, most shrubs will root well from cuttings taken in late spring
and early summer. At this time, the new growth is soft enough to root rapidly
but is sufficiently ripe to prevent premature wilting and deterioration. Ideally,
the cuttings should be collected in the cool early morning hours from vigorous, healthy, insect-and-disease-free plants. Using secateurs (pruning shears)
or a sharp knife, take cuttings from terminal or lateral shoots of the current-
season's growth. To prevent the possibility of spreading disease, clean cutting
tools with a solution of one part household bleach to six parts water before
moving to the next plant. Cuttings are usually 4-6 inches long and have several sets of leaves. Moisten the cuttings immediately, place them in a plastic
bag, and store them in a cool place out of direct sunlight. Refrigerated cuttings can last several days.

To prepare the cuttings, first remove flowers, buds, and seed heads; strip
all leaves and buds from the lower half of the cutting. Next, make a fresh cut
⅛-¼ inch below a node (where the leaf joins the stem—the site at which most
rooting activity takes place). Strip the leaves from the lower half of the cutting. Usually two or more sets of leaves will remain on the upper portion; if

1. Cuttings are usually 4-6 inches long and have several sets of leaves.

2. To prevent the spread of disease, clean and disinfect all surfaces before you start.

3. Propagation supplies: rooting hormone, soil mix, cuttings.

4. After stripping off leaves, dip cutting in rooting hormone.

5. Insert the cutting into rooting medium to a depth of ⅓-½ of its length.

6. After misting, place the entire cutting-filled container into a plastic bag and seal.

they are very large, reduce them by up to half to lessen water loss from the cutting and conserve space in the rooting container. The bottom inch of the cutting should then be dipped in a rooting-hormone/fungicide mixture. Several liquid and powdered formulations of varying strengths are available, each with its own merits; experience will suggest which is most effective for specific plants (or check a manual on plant propagation).

Almost anything can be used as a rooting container, provided it is well drained, clean, and appropriately used. For most shrub cuttings, a clay or plastic 6-inch bulb pan works well and will accommodate 6-10 cuttings. Recycled pots must be washed and rinsed with a bleach solution to ensure sterility.

Rooting media should be light and well drained. They may contain peat moss, vermiculite, perlite, coarse sands, or even polystyrene beads, alone or in combination. Experienced propagators alter the composition of the medium to suit the growing conditions and needs of specific plants, but a 50-50 mixture by volume of peat moss and perlite is a good general-purpose starting point. Before filling containers with the selected rooting medium, moisten the mixture to the consistency of a wrung-out sponge.

Insert the prepared cuttings to a depth of ⅓-½ their length and space about 2 inches apart: spacing will vary depending on the size of the cutting, but avoid the temptation to overcrowd. Mist the cuttings lightly and place the entire cutting-filled pot inside a clear plastic bag. Seal the bag and move to a shady location in the garden. Particularly soft cuttings may wilt initially but should soon recover. Check the cuttings once a week and remove any leaves that have dropped or cuttings that begin to rot. If the initial moisture content of the rooting medium was correct and the bag is properly sealed, no additional watering will be required throughout the rooting process. Depending on the type of plant being propagated, rooting can take 2-10 weeks.

When the cuttings are well rooted, remove the bag. At the first required watering, use a water-soluble transplanter (or "starter") fertilizer. Continue to grow the cuttings in the rooting container for 2-3 weeks, then transplant to a protected nursery site in the garden or cold frame where the plants can grow until they are large enough to be moved to a permanent location. Early autumn plantings will benefit from a protective mulch; late-fall plantings, especially in colder regions, should be avoided since the cuttings will not become established before winter. Alternatively, allow the cuttings to go dormant and store them in a cold frame or unheated but frost-free garage or cellar until spring.

HARDWOOD CUTTINGS Propagating deciduous shrubs from hardwood cuttings is a useful method for home gardeners since the cuttings are relatively nonperishable, easy to prepare, and require no special equipment or facilities for rooting. Unlike leafy softwood cuttings, which are prepared in spring or early summer when plants are actively growing, hardwood cuttings are made in late autumn, after defoliation but before severe winter weather has arrived.

Cutting wood is collected in the form of long, healthy, vigorous stems of the past-season's growth. These will vary in length depending on the species, and diameters will range from ¼-1 inch. In most cases, each stem will be sufficiently long to yield more than one cutting. To prepare the cuttings first remove and discard the thin terminal portion of the stem. The balance of the stem is then cut into 4- to 12-inch uniform lengths so that each cutting has at least two sets of buds. Where possible, make top cuts just above a bud and ½ inch below a bud at the base. Dust the lower inch of the cuttings with a rooting-hormone/fungicide mixture formulated for hardwood cuttings and secure with elastic bands in conveniently sized bundles.

Pack the base of the cuttings with damp sphagnum moss and place them in a plastic bag. Seal the bag with a twist-tie and attach a label that indicates the date, name of plant, and required treatment. Store the bag at temperatures of 55-65° F. for 14-21 days to promote callusing, and then place it in cold storage (the refrigerator will do) at 35-40° F. until spring.

Spring planting should be done as soon as the ground is workable. Select a particularly well drained area of the garden and plant the cuttings deeply so that only one or two buds are above the soil. The location and spacing of the cuttings must be adequate to allow the plants to grow undisturbed for a year.

In mild areas, the period of cold storage may be dispensed with and the cuttings planted out directly in the autumn. For colder regions, however, this is not advisable as repeated freeze and thaw cycles during the winter and early spring will heave the cuttings from the ground.

Not all deciduous shrubs will root from hardwood cuttings, but for those that will—including willow, privet, hydrangea, and dogwood—the method provides a simple, low-cost form of propagation.

DIVISION A number of shrubs, including bottlebrush buckeye, fragrant sumac, and bayberry, naturally spread and colonize by producing upright-growing shoots, known as suckers, from roots and underground stems. Division is simply the removal of these from the parent plant. For small plants it may be advantageous to dig the entire plant and sever the desired number of suckers with secateurs. For parent plants that are too large to dig, detach the suckers with a sharp spade. Do this in early spring before the period of active growth. Root systems of the suckers are usually not extensive, and pruning back the top by one half will help to compensate for the loss of roots.

LAYERING Some popular garden shrubs—rhododendron and Japanese maple are good examples—are difficult to root from cuttings without the aid of specialized, often costly equipment beyond the modest means and needs of most home gardeners. In such cases, a technique known as layering provides a viable alternative means of propagation. Layering is simply the development of roots on a stem while it is still attached to the parent plant. Once rooted, the layer is severed from the parent to become a new plant. A few garden plants, including cutleaf stephanandra, coralberry, and some types of cotoneaster, do this naturally. Gardeners may opt to use layering even for easy-to-root shrubs because of its simplicity.

There are several forms of layering, but simple layering is the technique most often used for shrubs. After growth has begun in the spring, select a long, low, supple branch. Sharply bend it to an upright position 6-12 inches from the tip. Often this is all that is required to begin the process, though in some cases a small notch is cut on the underside of the branch at the point of the bend. Dusting with rooting hormone will also aid in rooting. Next insert the bent portion into the soil and cover to a depth of 3-6 inches. Use a peg or wire over the bend to help hold it down and in place, and stake the upper part of the layer as it grows to keep it upright. The layer will be well rooted and developed by the following spring, when it may be detached from the parent plant.

Simple layering is a slow but nearly foolproof method of propagation; it can be applied to almost any shrub, through it is most easily accomplished on plants with long arching branches.

PRUNING

There are three basic reasons to prune a shrub: to keep the plant healthy, to promote flowering and fruiting, and to shape and maintain the shrub's size. Pruning for health entails the removal of dead, diseased, and weak wood; pruning for flowering and fruiting encompasses thinning, root pruning, dead-heading, and the removal of old wood; pruning for shape and size is essential-ly the selective removal of both old and new growth. Many gardeners view pruning as an arcane art, difficult to learn and taxing to practice. In fact, it is a relatively simple process, given a modicum of knowledge and the right tools, properly maintained.

To prune effectively and safely, you will need a few basic pieces of equip-ment: hand shears (which perform a clean cut that doesn't promote a way for disease to enter plant), hedge shears (electric or manual), lopping shears (wooden-handled or steel with ratchet), a hand saw (sheathed or folding), gloves, and eye protection. Store all tools out of the reach of children, and maintain them regularly.

Whatever your reason for pruning, a few general caveats apply. When removing branches, cut as close to the branch collar of the main stem as possi-ble, but do not cut into the branch collar. Leave just "enough to hang your hat on." Do not paint over the pruning wounds; this once-popular practice only promotes rot by providing a moist, sheltered environment for fungal organisms. Spring-blooming shrubs should be sheared directly after flowering, since next-season's flower buds will be formed on the new wood.

To maintain a shrub's optimum health, prune regularly to remove dead, diseased, and weak wood. Old multistemmed deciduous shrubs often profit from rejuvenation, the practice of cutting all the main stems back to within ½ inch of the ground during winter dormancy. Though it may take more than one season, rejuvenation produces spectacular results; in the year following rejuvenation, however, be attentive to mulching, fertilizing, watering, and weeding. Remember that conifers and most broad-leafed evergreens will die or be slow to recover if cut back this drastically. With most shrubs it's best to remove all main stems over a period of 3-4 years, cutting back the 2-3 oldest

Before: This winter-hazel, *Corylopsis veitchiana,* was planted 8 years ago and has never been pruned. Its branches are dense and tangled, with too many main stems converging. On the following pages, Ethan Johnson and David Allen of the Holden Arboretum will take us through the process of pruning it.

1. "Opening up the center by removing one of the weaker main branches. Those thin upright suckers arising from the ground will be removed too."

2. "Taking out a low branch."

3. "Out with one of the main branches. We chose the tallest, straightest one with the least interesting curves."

4. "There we go! Now there are still a lot of long branches and some overlapping and tangled branches yet to come."

5. "The suckers on the right side have been removed, and now there is room to get the pruning saw in to carefully cut off the stub of the big branch removed earlier."

6. "Most of the dead, weak, and tangled growth has been cut out, but two branches are still overlapping here."

7. "I'll cut the smaller one back to a side branch."

8. "There it goes—a nice close clean-angled cut."

9. "You have to look closely to notice that the cut has been made."

10. "Moving away from the base, I'll thin out some of the branches and remove dead twigs. Always make cuts back to a lateral branch. Don't leave long stubs."

11. "Let's not cut out this branch because it sticks up and out a bit. It has a graceful arch that will show up even when the shrub is in leaf."

12. "The pruning job is almost complete. There is just a bit more to do on the once-over to finish it up."

That's good! We have reduced the size, removed dead and weak wood, opened it up and yet maintained the natural grace and beauty of the shrub.

canes to the ground the first year, taking out another 2-3 of the old ones the year after, and so on.

Three techniques encourage heavy bloom. Root pruning is the practice of spading around the shrub or transplanting in early spring. Deadheading, the removal of spent flowers shortly after the blossoms fade, conserves the energy that would normally be spent on fruit production; it is commonly practiced on shrubs with profuse floral displays and nonornamental fruit, including rhododendrons, azaleas, and lilacs. Selective removal of old stems coupled with shortening and thinning of the remaining growth in early spring not only helps to maintain flowering shrubs, but is the key to better yield in fruiting shrubs.

Pruning to shape need not be daunting, especially if it is practiced regularly. To prune an ornamental shrub, begin directly after planting by cutting out all dead, diseased, and weak wood. Then evaluate the branching structure and consider removing branches that overlap and rub, and those that form V-crotches that are likely to split apart; branches that have a crotch angle of less than 45° F. should usually be removed. Retain branch collars and keep branch stubs short.

Shape formal hedges twice a year, informal hedges just once; in the North, July 4 is generally considered the cut-off date for shearing. Remove 1/3-2/3 of the new growth at each pruning until the hedge nears mature size, then prune more severely. Hedges should be narrower at the top than at the base, so that adequate sunlight can reach the lower leaves. Though personal aesthetics and garden style will dictate the shape of a hedge, avoid flat-topped shrubs to minimize snow- and ice-load damage.

To reduce a shrub's size without shearing, reach into the canopy and selectively prune branches back to a major limb, standing back from time to time to assess your progress. This method not only hides the cuts behind the remaining foliage, but gives the shrub a more open and natural appearance.

Don't hack back main branches in this manner, leaving long thick stubs. That sucker in the foreground that sticks straight up across Dave's right hand can go however.

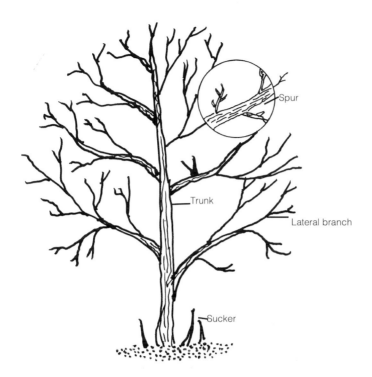

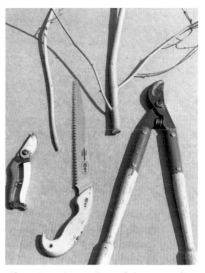

Above: Pruning tools, and the type of branch each is used used to cut: hand shears (which perform a clean cut that doesn't promote a way for disease to enter plant), a hand saw (sheathed or folding), lopping shears (wooden-handled or steel with ratchet). Always wear gloves and eye protection when pruning.

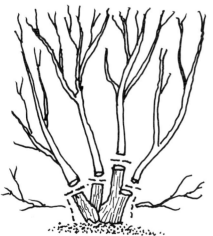

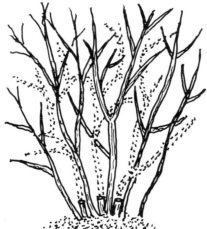

One way to prune shrubs is to cut back all canes almost to the ground; in cases, the shrub will not flower the first year, but will return the second year. This method is usually used on shrubs that have not been pruned in a long time.

For shrubs needing less work, a less drastic procedure is to prune about ⅓ of the weakest branches every year.

Above: Overview of a shrub.

Deadheading (removing old flower clusters) and disbudding (removing buds) promote flowering on shrubs and vines. *Above:* Save this rhododendron bud; remove the two smaller buds on the lower right.

ROUTINE CARE

WEEDING Rare is the gardener with an affection for weeds. Not only are they unsightly, but they compete with desired plants for available water and nutrients. By their very nature, weeds are prolific and tenacious; few gardens can be weed-free, but with a bit of knowledge and some assiduous elbow-bending, gardeners can maintain the upperhand. There are two approaches to weed control: chemical and manual. In home gardens, chemical controls are usually unnecessary, and often hazardous—not just to the environment, but to the health of the garden itself. Fortunately, most weeds can be controlled with a good hoe, a cultivator, and a little exertion. The trick is to cultivate regularly and eliminate the weeds when small. Large, established weeds require a great deal of effort to remove, and if allowed to go to seed provide an endless source of future aggravation. Mulching helps reduce the weeds.

Though rare, there are times when chemical controls are the only alternative. Perennial grasses with rampant root systems, for instance, can be particularly difficult to dislodge. Often the only practical method for ridding the garden of such stubborn interlopers is the application of a systemic nonselective herbicide containing glyphosate; these will kill anything that is green. Fortunately, these products are quickly degraded and have no residual effects.

WATERING Water is becoming an increasingly precious resource, and restrictions on its use are already in force in many areas. It is therefore sensible when designing a garden to select plants that are adapted to grow with the moisture that nature provides. Nevertheless, some watering to help establish new plants or compensate for unexpected droughts is inevitable. The key is to water only when necessary, but then to do so very thoroughly. Frequent light sprinkling, especially in the evening, is a waste of water and often does more harm than good by encouraging the growth of shallow root systems and creating ideal conditions for the spread of disease. The frequency and quantity of irrigation will be determined by a number of factors, including soil characteristics, exposure, and the type of plants being grown. However, most well-established shrubs growing in a good garden loam can easily tolerate a week or two without water.

Water may be applied in a variety of ways, from a simple watering can to a fully automated time-controlled system. Most home gardeners opt for driplines, soakers, or an ordinary garden hose fitted with an overhead sprinkler. Each method has its relative advantages and disadvantages with respect to convenience, maintenance, and cost. Whatever your method, however, you can conserve water by 1) watering only when necessary, 2) selecting plants that will thrive with the moisture nature provides, 3) using mulches over the soil, 4) watering in the early morning if possible, and avoiding midday, when evaporation is greatest, and 5) collecting rain water for future use.

MULCH The practice of mulching—covering the soil with protective and sometimes decorative materials—is as old as horticulture itself. Indeed, the first mulcher was Mother Nature, who wisely devised a way to spread leaves and other plant litter across the forest floor, thus creating an insulating, nutrient-rich, biologically active "duff" layer between bare soil and the elements.

Mulches help to conserve water, suppress weed growth, moderate soil temperature, reduce erosion, and, in the case of organic mulches, improve the soil structure and add nutrients as they decompose. The list of suitable mulches is virtually endless and includes such organic materials as wood chips, bark, and pine needles, as well as inorganic products like marble chips and pea gravel. Limestone gravels can raise soil pH, which can be detrimental to some species. Gardeners can also choose among several weed-barrier landscape fabrics; these are suitable as underlays for inorganic mulches but should be avoided if an organic mulch is being used, since they prevent much of the beneficial interaction that takes place between the decomposing mulch and the soil.

Just before applying the mulch, cultivate the surface of the soil to eliminate existing weeds and break up any hardpan that has built up. Two to 4 inches of mulch are usually adequate, but be careful not to pile the mulch too high around trunks or plant stems, which can lead to basal rotting. Mulches should remain light and porous; too heavy or compact a mulch can prevent water and air from reaching the plant's root system. Because organic mulches use nitrogen as they decompose, they can produce a temporary nitrogen deficiency in plants. You can avoid this problem by applying a light dressing of a 1-2-1 all-purpose garden fertilizer each spring.

FERTILIZER Like all living things, plants require a variety of nutrients, primarily nitrogen, phosphorus, and potassium, for healthy growth. These and other trace nutrients occur naturally in the soil, where they are absorbed by the plant's root system and metabolized for growth. Alas, not all soils are perfectly nutrient-rich; overworked soils, in particular, may be deficient in one or more elements, and this lack will manifest itself in stunted growth, poor flowering, or yellow leaves.

The only true way to determine which elements are lacking is to have the soil tested by a laboratory, which can also test for soil acidity. If you suspect serious deficiencies, have the soil tested once or twice a year.

Once you've determined the problem, you can amend the soil with the proper fertilizer. Fertilizers fall into one of two basic groups: organic and manufactured. Organic fertilizers include such naturally occurring materials as compost and well-rotted manure; they have the advantage of providing organic matter and microorganisms as well as nutrients, and because they tend to have low nutrient values, they can generally be applied without fear of damaging plants. Unprocessed organic fertilizers, however, may contain weed seeds, can harbor disease, and have unknown nutrient value. To avoid these problems, choose pasteurized and tested manures and composts, available bagged at many nurseries and garden centers.

Manufactured fertilizers can be granular or water-soluble. Their nutrient values are clearly stated on the label, with the percentages for nitrogen, phosphorus, and potassium listed in that order. A product marked 5-10-15, for example, contains 5 percent nitrogen, 10 percent phosphorus, and 15 percent potassium, with the remaining 70 percent nonnutrient filler. If trace elements like iron and sulfur are present, they will also be listed as percentages. Most manufactured fertilizers contain no organic matter and must therefore be used at recommended rates to avoid burning the plants.

Nearly all new plantings will benefit from a generous application of organic fertilizer (for example, compost) mixed directly into the planting hole, and subsequent applications of a high-phosphorus transplanter-type fertilizer during the first growing season. Once established, however, most shrubs are neither fussy nor heavy feeders, and a yearly spring application of a general-purpose fertilizer with a 1-3-2 or similar ratio is generally adequate. Some plants may benefit from an additional light application in mid summer, but late summer or early autumn feedings should be avoided, since they encourage late-season growth that can easily be damaged by frost.

Because each plant responds individually to fertilization, only experience will show the gardener what modifications may be necessary in the regimens outlined above.

WINTER PROTECTION Most shrubs that are hardy in your area do not need winter protection. However, for shrubs that are only marginally hardy, prune back severely before the winter, and mound up soil or mulch around the base of the plant. In the spring, remove the mounds of earth and cut off all winter-killed tips. Roses need winter protection in many areas.

TRAINING A VINE

There are nearly as many ways to grow a vine as there are vines themselves, and though most have a natural urge to clamber skyward, nearly all benefit from some initial training. Vines usually flower and fruit better when they are trained. The sooner you start the vine on its desired path, the sooner you achieve your goal. With the exception of those grown as ground covers or used to soften the sides of containers, vines usually require a structure on which to start their clambering. Whether that structure is a trellis, pergola, wooden fence, lattice work, or masonry wall depends largely on the vine's method of climbing (see list at left). Plants like *Ampelopsis* and passionflower have slender tendrils that usually coil easily around string, wire, or the stems of other plants. Twiners like wisteria and morning glory, on the other hand, send their stems around supports such as trellises and arbors. Clinging vines climb by rootlike holdfasts that attach themselves, with great stubbornness, to masonry or tree bark. Finally, there are procumbent vines, like jasmine, and vinelike plants, like Egyptian bean, that will not clamber upwards at all unless planted very close to or anchored directly to a support. However, these vines are effective in softening containers or the sides of raised beds.

For twiners, the best structures have horizontal crossbars, placed at 8- to 12-inch intervals, to help support the vine's weight and relieve stress on the anchored branches. They are also helpful in training stems in a horizontal fashion, which is beneficial in developing a visual screen. Structures include trellises, crisscrossed wires, and fences. Aluminum and plastic trellises offer the advantage of low maintenance, and some are even adjustable, expanding, accordionlike, either horizontally or vertically. Wood has an undeniable aes-

COMPOST

In forests and prairies, swamps and backyards, an amazing process is continuously taking place. Plant parts and animal leavings rot or decompose with the help of fungi, bacteria, and other microorganisms. Earthworms and an assortment of insects do their part digesting and mixing the plant and animal matter together. The result is a marvelous, rich, and crumbly layer of organic matter we call compost.

BENEFITS OF COMPOST Compost encourages the growth of earthworms and other beneficial organisms whose activities help plants grow strong and healthy. It provides nutrients and improves the soil. Wet clay soils drain better and sandy soils hold more moisture if amended with compost.

HOW TO MAKE COMPOST A compost pile keeps organic matter handy for garden use and, as an added advantage, keeps the material from filling up overburdened landfills. To make your own compost, start with a layer of chopped leaves, grass clippings, and kitchen waste like banana peels, eggshells, old lettuce leaves, apple cores, coffee grounds, and whatever else is available. Keep adding materials until you have a 6-inch layer, then cover it with a 3- to 6-inch layer of soil, manure, or finished compost.

Alternate 6-inch layers of organic matter and 2- to 3-inch layers of soil or manure until the pile is about 3 feet tall. A pile that is 3 feet tall by 3 feet square will generate enough heat during decomposition to sterilize the compost. This makes it useful as potting soil, topdressing for lawns, or soil-improving additives.

COMPOST CARE Keep your compost pile in a semishaded area to keep it from drying out too much. But if your compost pile is near a tree, turn it frequently to make sure tree roots don't grow into it. Make an indentation in the top of the pile to hold water and sprinkle the pile with a garden hose when it looks dry. Keep the compost moist, but not wet. Beneficial organisms cannot survive in soggy conditions.

USING COMPOST When your compost is ready, it can be mixed into the soil before planting, or applied to the surface of the soil as a soil-enriching mulch.

QUICK COMPOST If you need compost in a hurry, speed up the process by turning the pile with a pitchfork once a week for a month. Mixing the compost allows oxygen into the center of the pile, where it encourages the growth of bacteria and fungi. A pile that is turned regularly will become finished compost in 4-8 months.

MAKING A COMPOST BIN As illustrated below, many elaborate compost bins are sold. Some of these have devices for turning the compost and for removing it from the bin. Although these store-bought bins don't do the compost pile any harm, they are really not necessary. An enclosure made from chicken wire or from 5 wood pallets (one on the bottom, and four wired together for the sides) does the job just as well.

WHAT TO COMPOST
- kitchen waste
- lawn clippings (in thin layers so they do not mat down)
- chopped leaves (large leaves take a long time to break down)
- shredded branches
- garden plants
- shredded paper
- weeds (but be sure to use before they go to seed or weeds may sprout in the garden)
- straw or hay

WHAT NOT TO COMPOST
- orange and other citrus peels
- meat scraps, fatty trash (to avoid rodents and animals)
- excessive wood ashes

thetic appeal, especially if the vine has an open habit, but in the interest of upkeep choose a decay resistant variety like cedar or redwood and if possible leave the wood unpainted. (You can extend the life of the wood with a clear sealer or colored sealer stain, but remember that the color will fade, and it will be difficult to restain the wood after a perennial vine is established on it.) For wire supports, the best choice is thin stereo speaker wire, or you can use thin-gauge plastic-coated electrical wire, which comes in a variety of colors (the darker the better) and it won't heat up like bare metal.

To encourage the vine to climb, you'll need to secure it occasionally to the support (once every week or two during the spring season is a good rule of thumb). For tying, any stringlike material–preferably green, for the purpose of camouflage–will do, as will bread-wrapper twist-ties, but don't tie them too tightly or leave them on for more than a season, since the wire inside can do damage to the expanding vine. If you're training the vine to a wooden fence, you can thread the string through nonrusting cup hooks (C-shaped hooks mounted on screws available at most hardware stores). Or you can add matching horizontal wooden lattice boards for support. This makes for an interesting architectural effect during the winter season, when annual or herbaceous perennial vines leave the support largely uncloaked.

To train a vine to grow up the sides of a pergola or arbor, you can simply use galvanized nails 12-18 inches apart (depending on the vine; add more nails if you think they're necessary) and/or strings that match the color of the structure attached with nails or wrapped around the boards. On white stone pillars, clear fishing line is very effective, since it is virtually invisible. Another approach is to wrap the posts with a thin strip of wire or plastic netting or, for twining vines, to stretch three or four single wires from top to bottom spaced

Helping vines grow. *Top:* Trellis. *Above:* Invisible fishing wire. *Far right:* Wire mesh. *Right:* Twist-tie anchors.

An espalier is a shrub or vine trained to a flat surface. This procedure was devised in Europe many years ago to save space. Most plants with flexible limbs can be espaliered. Choose a container-grown plant, and place the container near a training surface, such as a wall or trellis, that accepts anchors. Stretch several branches to their desired position and anchor them with nails or wire. You will have to prune your espalier consistently to maintain its shape, cutting off unwanted branches.

about 6-12 inches apart. Avoid expanded metal since it cuts down on air circulation, which is essential for keeping the vine cool and for dissipating fragrance. It can also be difficult to remove annual vines from this in winter.

Though many climbing vines are relentless ascenders, nearly all benefit from some initial training, especially to keep them in aesthetic bounds. For brick and limestone structures there are brick- or limestone-colored hooks, equipped with wires for loosely twisting around the vine's stems. These attach with heavy duty glue or resin (don't twist the wires too tightly, since they have a tendency to break).

PEST MANAGEMENT

The best time to begin a program of pest management is *before* you plant. Carefully sited, well-tended plants require a minimum of intervention; weak or stressed plants, however, will be predisposed to the ravages of opportunistic insects and diseases. In fact, a whole host of horticultural disorders are caused not by living organisms but by poor cultural practices or environmental problems. Known as physiogenic diseases, these disorders commonly result from winter injury, poor drainage, air pollution, road salt, nutritional deficiencies, mechanical injuries, improper application of herbicides—even lightning and strong winds. Their symptoms—including stunted growth, yellowing or spotted leaves, and twisted stems—often resemble those of organically afflicted plants. The good news for gardeners is that, once identified, these physiogenic diseases can usually be corrected, or at least accommodated.

To keep organic pests and diseases at a minimum, begin by practicing proper hygiene; a clean garden is usually a healthy garden. Fallen leaves weeds, and other litter are more than just unsightly; they provide the per-

Aphid

Japanese beetle

fect breeding ground for disease. Of course, given the daunting list of potential pests (which includes insects, mites, nematodes, fungi, bacteria, viruses, and, of course, mammals), even the most carefully tended plant can succumb. To detect problems at an early, manageable stage, you'll need to monitor the garden on a regular basis. Make it a habit to stroll through the yard at least every two weeks, carefully examining plants for signs of trouble; don't forget to check the undersides of leaves, where pests and diseases often hide. Many insects, including aphids, beetles, scales, and caterpillars, are easy to spot, but you'll need a magnifying glass to detect smaller pests like mites and thrips. Borers and leafminers, which spend most of their life cycle inside stems and leaves, are difficult to see, but the damage they cause is obvious. Keep a record of the trouble you encounter: With experience, it's possible to anticipate problems on specific host plants.

For many gardeners, the words *pest* and *insect* are synonymous; rare is the rose that never served as supper for a Japanese beetle, or the late-spring landscape untrammeled by aphids. Some insects can do serious, life-threatening damage; others are simply unsightly. Every gardener has to determine for him- or herself an appropriate and tolerable level of infestation. When control is deemed necessary, there are a number of choices, including soaps, oils, and synthetic chemicals. Whatever the product selected, it's essential to follow label instructions carefully, both to ensure the method's efficacy and to protect the health of the plant and the environment. One of the most promising new areas of insect management is biological control, which enlists the services of natural predators like parasites, diseases, and other insects. (Ladybugs, for example, prove to be voracious afficionados of the aphid.) In controlled environments like greenhouses, these natural methods have proven highly successful; their efficacy in the backyard is still haphazard, though, since they tend to have date-limited applications. Another common pest is the mite, a tiny spiderlike creature that sucks the juice from tender leaves and stems and causes stunted or abnormal growth in affected plants. There are several types, and most thrive under hot, dry conditions. While small, they can often be detected by the fine, gray webs they create. Chemical controls are available, and simply syringing with cold water will help check their spread.

Nematodes, on the other hand, are virtually impossible to control. These microscopic worms attack roots, causing them to appear stubby, knotted, or covered with lesions (leaves are sometimes a target as well). The roots soon lose their ability to function effectively, which results in wilted or stunted growth in leaves and stems. Alas, nematodes are very difficult to detect, and infected plants must be removed and burned or discarded. Since many nematodes are soil borne, it's unwise to place susceptible plants in the same location.

Fungal diseases are among the most common in the garden, affecting leaves, stems, flowers, and roots. Spread by spores borne on air currents, water, or gardening tools, they can cause wilting, cankers, lesions, galls, blights, and leaf spots. Fungal infection is highly plant-specific and weather-dependent, spread generally during warm, wet, humid conditions. The most effective way to control fungi in the garden is to plant new resistant cultivars. If this isn't possible–or if your garden is established–you can prevent many fungal infections by keeping both garden and gardening tools as clean as possible. Prune plants regularly to maintain effective air circulation, and never water in the late afternoon or evening. If a plant does become infected, the application of fungicides may be your only recourse. Preventative in nature rather than curative, fungicides will protect uninfected tissue but do nothing to restore areas already penetrated by the fungi. Gardeners must therefore be vigilant and apply fungicide at the first hint of infection. Repeat applications are usually necessary during the growing season to protect new growth and replenish whatever fungicide has been depleted by rain.

Spider mite

Often spread by insects or gardening tools, bacteria are microscopic organisms that can cause foul-smelling rots, wilted or scorched leaves, and galls. Given the right conditions, they multiply and spread at a prodigious rate. Because no chemical controls exist, gardeners can fight bacterial infections only indirectly, controlling possible insect vectors, removing and destroying infected plants, and replanting resistant cultivars.

As in humans, the ultra-microscopic organisms known as viruses can wreak serious damage in the garden. Affecting a wide variety of plants, they cause a host of symptoms, among them stunted growth, leaf spots, and mosaics. Like bacteria, viruses are spread by a variety of mechanical means, and chemical controls are nonexistent. Once again, proper hygiene and resistant cultivars are the most practical means of prevention for home gardeners.

Anyone who lives in rabbit country knows how deleterious mammals can be to the garden. Some animals, like moles, wreak their destruction in a search for insects; you can minimize this kind of damage by eradicating the insects. Other animals are strictly vegetarian and often have selective appetites. You can try cultivating only those plants that don't appeal to your marauders, but in the case of deer, for instance, this could leave you with a fairly barren landscape. Among the general controls for mammalian pests are exclusion from the garden by fencing or live trapping, the application of taste or odor repellents to selected plants, and the use of cages and other mechanical barriers to prevent browsing. Normally, some trial and error is required to determine which combination of methods is effective and appropriate.

Above: Hopbush (*Dodonea viscosa*), an evergreen Arizona native that can be used as a hedge or fence planting.

SHRUBS AND VINES IN THE DESERT

In the low desert, all woody plants are best established in fall plantings. Fall is long and is still an adequate growing season; winters are mild and short. For this reason, the root systems of woody plants establish very well, and when the short spring and long warm to hot summer arrives, the plants are well equipped to tolerate those very rugged conditions.

All woody plants, whether desert plants or not, should be watered regularly and thoroughly for their first 2-3 years. This is best done with a drip system or a slow hose that soaks the entire root zone thoroughly but does not allow surface run off. Sprinklers do not supply enough water, and too much is lost.

HEDGES Humans use hedges to mark their boundaries as naturally as they breathe. In the desert, looming oleander hedges take the place of privet hedges, making not a boundary but a wall. Unshorn and used with a restrained hand, oleander is a wonderful summer-blooming shrub. It produces profuse flowers ranging in color from red, pink, and salmon to cream and white. But hideous pruning, thoughtless placement, and dreary overuse have made this most drought-tolerant desert plant a pariah among desert gardens.

The misuse of oleander points out one of the first principles of good hedges—scale. Hedges are a feature of the garden and should fit both in size and form to whatever else is happening within the gardenscape. Gargantuan, hulking plants in areas only 10-12 feet wide are grotesque, gulping up every other thing. Large properties can accept large hedges, smaller ones plead for something more to their size.

There are many other excellent boundary plants for desert gardeners:

Texas ebony (*Pithecellobium flexicaule*), when left to grow naturally, is a wonderful evergreen hedge. Texas ebony can reach a mature height of 15 feet, enough to hide almost anything. Arizona rosewood (*Vauquelinia californica*) is an under-appreciated plant that can be pruned into a handsome tree, or without such shaping grows into a rounded, evergreen shrub. Sugarbush (*Rhus ovata*), like rosewood, a plant of the chaparral of Arizona, is a gorgeous evergreen shrub. Both rosewood and sugarbush easily reach 10 feet and can be nearly as big around. Hopbush (*Dodonea viscosa*), Texas olive (*Cordia boissieri*), Texas ranger (*Leucophyllum candidum*), and desert hackberry (*Celtis pallida*) all reach at least 8-10 feet in height and make excellent boundary hedges.

More moderate-size properties call for more modest-sized plants. Texas ranger (*Leucophyllum frutescens* and its numerous cultivars) and jojoba (*Simmondsia chinensis*) work well as hedges. Bee bush (*Aloysia gratissima*) offers an entirely different approach to hedging; its cascading foliage and luscious fragrance make this plant a novel choice for garden definition.

Tapestry hedges, which are composed of numerous species, are a wonderful idea for desert gardens with the rich assortment of colors, leaf size and shape, and bloom color that desert shrubs provide. Tightly planted desert sumac (*Rhus microphyllum*), Texas ranger, quailbush (*Atriplex lentiformis* or *A. canescens*), and barberry (*Berberis haematocarpa*) would be an interesting combination. An imaginative hedge can include plants with different bloom times, variously-colored fruit, and striking foliage in different shapes and textures.

Some other shrubs desert gardeners should consider:

Creosote (*Larrea tridentata*) is a very common shrub in Arizona, and ornamental as well. There is probably no more drought-adapted plant on earth than creosote; its ability to wrench water from dry soils is legendary. The plants are lovely, open and airy, and offer a wonderful light shade for smaller plants. In spring, they are coated with small yellow flowers that are followed by hairy white fruit. Dark green in spring, creosote acquires a yellow cast in summer; it looks beautiful when backlit by the summer sun. Its slightly pungent aroma is one of the most nostalgic remembrances of the desert.

Bush dalea (*Dalea pulchra*) is a beautiful late winter/early spring blooming shrub, up to 6-8 feet tall. It is characterized by tiny gray-green leaves. In late winter, the plant blooms with a profusion of lavender blossoms, set in a head of light plumes; the overall effect is of a slight purple powderpuff. The plant blooms for almost two months, from February until May. The long bloom season and great drought and heat tolerance make this a great plant for the desert.

Arizona yellowbells (*Tecoma stans*) is tall (up to 8 feet) but light, with long serrated green leaves on tall wands of stems, and loose heads of large, intensely yellow tubular flowers that remain on the plant from May until December. This plant thrives on heat; it is best in a western exposure.

Texas mountain laurel (*Sophora secundiflora*) is a dense, dark green evergreen shrub that can reach 10-12 feet in height. In March, it puts outs a large hanging panicle of violet purple blooms that is followed by dark pods with bright red seeds inside. Although somewhat slow growing, it is a beautiful shrub, blooms very young, and always looks its best.

Littleleaf cordia (*Cordia parviflora*) is a very drought-tolerant ornamental with very small, deeply veined gray-green leaves. The bush can reach 8 feet in height over time and is a loose, somewhat lanky-looking shrub. In summer it blooms profusely with papery white blooms, about an inch in diameter. Blooming will continue throughout the summer in response to deep irrigation or a summer rain. Its relative Texas olive (*Cordia boissieri*) get much larger over time and has large, olive-colored leaves. Its blooms are almost 2½ inches across, in dense heads, pure white with a yellow throat.

BY MARY IRISH, DESERT BOTANICAL GARDEN

SOME VINES FOR THE DESERT

Macfadeyena unguis-cati (catclaw vine) will easily cover a telephone pole and is extremely dense. It has yellow flowers and long fruit pods. Beware–it can take over your yard.

Antigonon leptopus (queen's wreath) has heart-shaped, papery thin green leaves and nearly ball-shaped flowers in delicate pink. It is most attractive when growing up a tree or large shrub. It is a bit cold-sensitive, but recovers quickly.

Hardenbergia violacea, a tough evergreen vine from Australia, is a dense, fast grower and requires little supplemental water. It produces profuse, intensely purple, wisteria-like flowers.

Mascagnia macroptera (yellow orchid vine) is an outstanding vine for the desert, with small but interestingly formed intensely yellow flowers and fluted pods. It is frost-sensitive and will die with the first frost, but will recover well.

Maurandya antirrhiniflora (snapdragon vine) is a small, delicate vine, but it has loads of dark purple flowers that look like miniature snapdragons. It is aggressive and reseeds from year to year rather than resisting frost.

Merremia aurea (yucca vine), a magnificent member of the morning glory family, has attractive, wide green leaves and very large (up to 3 inches) deep yellow flowers that are continuous throughout the summer. They are followed by teardrop-shaped pods. Although frost-tender, this vine produces massive roots that allow it to come back year after year.

Above: Clematis growing in a stone container. *Right:* Oleander in clay pots

SHRUBS AND VINES IN CONTAINERS

There are many good reasons to grow shrubs and vines in containers. Planting in a container allows you to choose your own soil and so to grow plants that will not thrive in the soil of your region. Container shrubs add a lovely touch to decks and patios. Some invasive plants remain "contained" only if planted in a container. A small containerized plant can be brought indoors in winter, allowing you to grow plants that are not cold-hardy in your zones. And the containers themselves add an architectural note to the garden.

Any container will work, so long as it provides drainage through a hole in its bottom. Avoid containers that will crack (such as clay) if you are in a cold region. Before planting, place a few pottery shards over the hole, and cover with and inch or two of gravel; this keeps the hole from becoming clogged. Soil for containers should be light but rich; amend with generous amounts of compost, and add some perlite or vermiculite. Fill the container with this mixture so that the top of the rootball of your plant will come rest about 2 inches below the rim of the container.

For best results, purchase containerized plants for your own containers. Tease their roots slightly before placing in the new container; if the plant is potbound, cut the roots with a knife. Place the plant in the container and cover with topsoil; tamp down the soil to remove any air pockets.

Containerized plants need some extra care; their roots cannot seek nutrients throughout the garden, so you must be sure to provide plenty of fertilizer and water. If the plant becomes too large for the pot, remove it to a larger pot, or divide it. You can grow plants that are not hardy in your area if you place them in a sheltered area and make sure they are not subjected to frost or strong, desiccating winds.

ORGANIC GARDENING

Few gardeners today are unaware of the devastating effect pesticides and other chemicals used in the past have had on our environment. Rachel Carson's searing exploration of the subject, *Silent Spring* (1962), exposed the "needless havoc" wrought by products designed to promote healthy plants. Not only were the chemicals poisoning our environment, they were also killing the natural predators of the pests we were seeking to destroy, making it impossible for nature to come to its own defense.

In the past few decades a vast and successful effort has been made to find new ways to garden without using harmful chemicals. The approach is directed at the soil and at the measures taken to control pests.

The soil is built up through the addition of organic materials, especially compost. The addition of compost, homemade or store-bought, and other organic material such as peat moss, green cover crops, and bone meal makes the soil so fertile and productive that petrochemicals are not needed.

Pest problems are handled through a practice called Integrated Pest Management (IPM), developed by the Council on Environmental Quality. IPM is defined as "maximum use of naturally occurring pest controls, including weather, disease agents, predators, and parasitoids. In addition, IPM utilizes various biological, physical, chemical controls and habitat modification techniques. Artificial controls are imposed only as required to keep a pest from surpassing tolerable population as determined from accurate assessments of the pest damage potential and the ecological, sociological, and economic costs of the control measures." In other words, gardeners must make reasonable assessments of how much damage a particular pest will do. If the pest is just munching on foliage, let it be. If controls must be taken, nonharmful ones should be tried first. Only in extreme cases is chemical warfare waged—and then in the most nonharmful ways possible.

The weapons in the IPM arsenal include:

• Careful monitoring to identify problems before they become widespread.

• Beneficial insects, such as ladybugs, praying mantises, and some nematodes, which feed on garden pests. Some of these reside naturally in your garden; others can be bought and placed there.

• Bacteria such as Bt (*Bacillus thuringiensis*) that attack garden pests. These bacteria can be bought by the pound and dusted on the plants; strains have been discovered that breed and attack many common pests.

• Insecticides such as rotenone, pyrethrum, and sabadilla and insecticidal soaps.

• Pest-repellent plants such as marigolds, which repel bean beetles and nematodes, and garlic, which repels whitefly.

• Hand-picking pests off foliage wherever they are seen in small numbers.

See pages 203-205 for more information about pest control.

SHRUBS IN THE GREAT PLAINS

Lying in the rain shadow cast by the Rocky Mountains, the Great Plains is a relatively dry region, experiencing 12-32 inches of precipitation annually. The greatest challenge to growing shrubs, vines, or other ornamental plants in the Great Plains is the climate. To properly grow in the Great Plains, plants must not only be able to endure dryness, cold winters, and hot summers, but also occasional rapid daily changes in temperature and recurring cycles of drought.

These wide fluctuations in short-term and long-term climactic conditions are particularly stressful. Plants from more northern climates may be well-adapted to cold temperatures, but they may be unable to endure the rapid changes in temperature (as much as 60° F. in 8 hours) that sometimes occurs.

Wind is a given in most of the region. It can be a detriment to plant growth during both summer and winter by causing desiccation of plant tissues. Broadleaf evergreens like holly, rhododendron, and boxwood normally do not perform well for us.

Soil is another factor. Soils in the Great Plains are primarily neutral to slightly alkaline in pH. They often have a rather high percentage of clay, which can inhibit good water drainage. Incorporation of organic matter is a common practice to improve plant growth in these clay soils.

While a surprising number of shrubs and vines can be grown in the Great Plains if care is taken to meet their cultural requirements, the average gardener will want to find plants that are well-adapted to the rigors of our climate. Increasingly, we look to our native species and those from other parts of the world with similar climates.

JIM LOCKLEAR, DYCK ARBORETUM OF THE PLAINS

SHRUBS AND VINES IN COLD CLIMATES

Since shrubs and vines are expected to last for a long time, it is crucial to ascertain their hardiness—which is defined as their ability to tolerate the coldest temperatures of a region's winter, as well as early winter freezes and spring thaws—before planting them. Plants adapt to cold weather by entering a dormant stage during which they reduce all activity. Plants that are able to enter this dormant period early are more effective in cold climates; those that begin the process later (such as *Hedera helix*, English ivy) are less hardy.

Locating the shrub or vine in a sheltered area will help some marginally hardy plants survive. Try to find an area that is protected by a wall or large trees, creating a microclimate that is warmer and less exposed than the rest of the garden. If your property is large, you will note that there are several microclimates within it—hilltops, valleys, and open areas will usually be the coldest, areas protected by trees and walls will be the warmest. But don't allow your protective device to block out sunlight. Exposure to southern currents is advantageous.

A plant will have less trouble adapting to cold if it is well-nourished in other respects; northern gardeners should pay particular attention to soil maintenance, supply sufficient water, and monitor diseases and pests. A plant that is already weak because of moisture or nutrient deficiencies or infestations will be the first to die in the event of a cold spell.

A variety of devices has been developed to help the cold-climate gardener. Black plastic mulch is very effective at warming the soil at the beginning of the season and will reduce weeds if left on all summer. But if you find it unsightly—and it is—other mulches will work almost as well. Protective devices—floating and permanent row covers, hot caps, cloches, and shades—protect new seedlings in the event of a cold snap.

Shrubs can be protected by a winter mulch of bark chips, straw, or Christmas-tree branches; remove as soon as threat of frost is over. Fertilize only lightly, if at all, at the season's end, as tender new growth is easily killed by early frost.

It is important to purchase only plants grown in colder regions, or to exchange with neighbors. Plants grown from seeds or seedlings that originate in warm regions are often less adapted to cold weather—even if they are the exact same species.

In addition to cold temperatures, most plants in northern climates must contend with desiccating winds that speed up evaporation of moisture from plant tissue; strong sun can also dry out a plant. Many broad-leaved evergreens are not able to survive these winds; narrow-leaved evergreens (conifers) have adapted to this problem by reducing their leaf structure to a small size.

A deep layer of snow actually benefits many shrubs and vines, providing an insulating layer under which the roots can survive. A continuous layer of snow is actually the best protection that a plant can be given.

GROWING SHRUBS IN THE SOUTH

The South is the perfect place for extending the zones of many plants, especially if you attempt to grow plants that are borderline for the zones at both ends of the spectrum. Many tropical plants can be grown in the middle of the South if winter protection is provided, and many northern plants can be coaxed to thrive in spots where summer afternoon heat can be reduced. Camellias are a wonderful example of shrubs growing outside their normal range; *Camellia japonica* varieties will grow in many areas often believed to be too cold. The trick is to grow early and late varieties. The early varieties bloom before the onset of cold weather, and the flower buds of the late-bloomers remain tightly closed and protected until warmer weather arrives.

In most areas of the South, the soil is very poor–predominantly red clay in mid South and sandy soils along the coasts in most of Florida. When confronted with clay, prepare soil adequately with *washed* sands of various types to encourage drainage of water away from shrub roots. When working with sandy soil, encourage water-holding capacity with hightly organic materials, especially compost.

With the ever-increasing cost and decreasing supply of water, southern gardeners need to use water to their best advantage, including selecting drought-resistant species of commonly used plants, such as *Cotoneaster glauca, Rosa chinensis, Cytisus,* and *Buddleia.* Although there has been some controversy as to whether native plants are in fact more tolerant of drought, many attractive native plants can be used in predominantly ornamental plantings with fine results (for example, *Myrica, Lonicera, Cornus, Callicarpa, Kalmia, Rhus*). The timing of when to water has been hotly debated over the years, but my preference is to use water when it can be utilized by the plants when they need it most–in the late afternoon. Watering a few hours prior to sunset replenishes plant's water supply and permits the leaf surface to dry before nightfall, thereby significantly reducing the growth of disease organisms. It is best to water thoroughly. A saturating watering is far superior to frequent shallow waterings because it encourages roots to become established deeper in the soil.

Because southerners spend more time outside in comfortable temperatures than our northern friends, I encourage a continuance of bloom throughout the season and suggest striking bark patterns and colors for interest in winter (*Lagerstroemia indica* 'Natchez', *Acer griseum, Corylopsis*). More importantly, southern gardeners plant a wide variety of plants with fragrance (*Osmanthus, Camellia sasanqua, Clethra, Gardenia, Lonicera, Viburnum, Daphne*). Carefully planned locations–near outdoor entertaining areas, like deck foundations, rocking chair porches, or along garden paths–of delicately fragrant shrubs are a welcome delight.

Throughout the southern states, we are besieged with birds flying to their winter breeding grounds. Plants with persistent fruit (*Ilex, Cotoneaster, Pyracantha,* and *Ligustrum*) are a wonderful and natural way to feed these birds on their trip and to encourage return visits. ROBERT BOWDEN

SOME SOURCES
American Horticultural
Therapy Association
 362A Christopher Avenue,
Gaithersburg, Maryland 20879
800-634-1603

Canadian Horticultural Therapy
Association
c/o Royal Botanical Garden
PO Box 399, Hamilton,
Ontario, Canada, L8N 3H8
416-529-7618

ENABLING GARDENS

Being forced to stop gardening is one of the worst fates that can befall a gardener, but the inability to get down on one's hands and knees owing to arthritis, a bad back, a heart problem, the need to use a wheelchair—or the normal aches, pains, and fatigues of advancing age—is no reason to stop gardening. By using a few different gardening techniques, modifying tools, following new criteria in plant selection, and tapping into the many resources for information and help, no one ever has to stop gardening.

Begin by thoroughly and frankly assessing your situation.
•How much time can you devote to gardening?
•Do you need crutches, a cane, or wheelchair to get around?
•Can you get up and down from the ground without assistance?
•How much sun or heat is wise for you?
•Can you bend at the waist easily?
•Is your coordination impaired? balance? vision? ability to hold tools?

Consult your doctor, occupational or physical therapist, and most importantly speak to a horticultural therapist.

Horticultural therapists are specially trained in applying horticulture in therapeutic programs for people with disabilities and older adults. They have developed specialized gardening tools and techniques that make gardening easier for every situation.

Once you've decided how much you can and want to do, the garden can be planned. For example, people with relatively severe mobility impairments should have firm, level surfaces an easy distance from the house and should use containers or raised beds to bring soil up to a comfortable working height—usually somewhere around 2 feet high with a maximum width of 30 inches if worked from one side and 60 inches if both sides of the container or bed are accessible. People with more mobility can work with easily worked, light soils mounded to 8-10 inches above grade and should use lightweight, long-handled tools. Smaller containers can be hung within easy reach on poles or fences, and an overhead structure can be used to support hanging baskets on ropes and pulleys so the baskets can be lowered for care and then replaced to an out-of-reach position.

Important considerations when planning the garden layout include:
•Start small: keep it manageable
•Use or create light, easily worked soils so less force is required to work them either by hand or with tools
•Keep all equipment and tools in accessible places
•Arrange for a nearby water source—soaker hose or drip irrigation, perhaps—to minimize the difficulties in watering
•Use mulches to cut down on weeding

Shrubs fill an important role in the enabling garden. Shrubs that need to be deadheaded should be placed near a pathway; dwarf varieties are valuable because they stay in bounds. Vines are particularly useful because they take up little ground space and climb to comfortable harvest heights.

Acid soil: Soil with a pH level below 7

Alkaline soil: Soil with a pH level above 7

Annual: A plant whose life cycle comprises a single growing season

Anther: The part of a flower that bears pollen

Axil: The angle formed by a stem and a leaf stalk

Balled-and-burlapped: Describing a plant that is ready for transplanting, with a burlap-wrapped soil ball around its roots

Bare-root: Describing a plant that is ready for transplanting, with no protective soil or burlap covering around its roots

Bract: A modified leaf below a flower, often showy, as in dogwood

Broad-leaved evergreen: A nonconiferous evergreen

Calcaceous: Containing calcium or calcium carbonate (lime), as soil

Candle: On a conifer, the new budlike shoot that sends out young needles

Cane: A long, often supple, woody stem

Capsule: A dry fruit having more than one cell

Catkin: A long flower cluster comprised of closely spaced, generally small flowers and prominent bracts, as in pussy willows

Chlorosis: A yellowing of the leaves, reflecting a deficiency of chlorophyll

Clay soil: A soil, usually heavy and poorly drained, containing a preponderance of fine particles

Clinging vine: A vine that climbs by attaching itsself to a structure

Coiling vine: See *Twining vine*

Cold frame: A boxlike structure, set out of doors, in which seedlings, cuttings, and plants are grown; often used to extend the growing season

Compost: Decomposed organic matter, usually used to enrich the soil

Conifer: Cone-bearing plant, usually evergreen

Container-grown: Grown as a seedling in the container it is to be sold in

Corymb: A flat-topped flower cluster in which flowers open successively from the outside in

Creeping: Trailing along the ground

Cross-pollination: The transfer of pollen from one plant to another

Crown: The site on a plant where root joins stem

Cultivar: A variety of plant produced by selective hybridization

Cultivate: To work the soil in order to break it up and/or remove weeds

Cutting: A severed plant stem, usually used for the purposes of propagation

Deadhead: To remove spent blossoms

Deciduous: Losing its leaves at the end of the growing season; nonevergreen

Dieback: Death of part or all of the woody portion of a plant

Dioecious: Having both male and female flowers

Division: The removal of suckers from a parent plant, for the purposes of propagation

Double: In flowers, having an increased number of petals, produced at the expense of other organs

Drupe: A fruit with a fleshy covering over a hard-coated seed

Dwarf: A shrub whose mature height is under three feet

Ericaceous: In the heath (_Erica_) family

Espalier: To train a plant to grow flat against a structure, usually in a decorative pattern

Evergreen: Retaining foliage year-round

Exfoliate: To self-peel, as bark

Family: A group of plants sharing common features and distinctive characteristics and comprising related genera; the biological category above genus and below order

Fertile: Having the capacity to generate seed

Foundation planting: A massed planting designed to mask, disguise, or enhance the foundation of a house or building

Friable: Ready for cultivation, easily cultivable, as soil

Genus: A group of related species

Germinate: To develop a young plant from seed; to produce a seedling

Glaucous: Blue-hued; covered with a bluish or grayish bloom

Graft: To insert a section of one plant, usually a shoot, into another so that they grow together into a single plant

Groundcover: A plant with a low-growing, spreading habit, grown specifically to cover the ground

Habit: A plant's characteristic form of growth

Harden off: To mature sufficiently to withstand winter temperatures

Hardpan: Soil sufficiently clogged with clay or other particles that draining is impossible

Hardwood cutting: Cutting taken from a mature woody stem for the purpose of propagation

Hardy: Able to withstand winter temperatures

Herbaceous: Without woody tissue

Holdfast: The rootlike part of a clinging vine that adheres to a support

Humus: Soil composed of decaying organic matter

Hybrid: A plant produced by crossing two unlike parents

Indumentum: A massing of fine hairs, glands, or prickles

Insecticidal soap: Soap formulated to kill, repel, or inhibit the growth of insect pests

Integrated pest management (IPM): A philosphy of pest management based on the idea of using escalating methods of pest control, beginning with the least damaging; incorporates the selection of resistant varieties, the use of biological and nontoxic controls, and the application of pesticides and herbicides only when absolutely necessary

Invasive: Tending to spread freely and wantonly; weedy

Layering: The development of roots on a stem while it is still attached to a parent plant, for the purposes of propagation

Leaf mold: A form of humus composed of decayed leaves, often used to enrich soil

Lime: Calcium carbonate, often added to the soil to reduce acidity

Loam: A generally fertile and well-drained soil, usually containing a significant amount of decomposed organic matter

Microclimate: Climate specific to a small area; may vary significantly from that of surrounding areas

Mulch: An organic or inorganic soil covering, used to maintain soil temperature and moisture and to discourage the growth of weeds

Named cultivar: A cultivar that has been given a recognized horticultural name

Naturalize: To "escape" from a garden setting and become established in the wild

Neutral soil: Soil having a pH of 7   neither acid nor alkaline

Node: On a plant, the site at which the leaf joins the stem; the area where most rooting activity takes place; see Ail

Organic: Derived naturally, from living or once-living matter

Panicle: A branched raceme

Peat moss: Partially decomposed sphagnum moss, often added to soil to increase moisture retention

Perennial: A plant that lives for more than one growing season (usually at least three)

Perfect: Having stamens and pistils; bisexual, as a flower

Petal: Part of a flower's corolla, outside of the stamens and pistils, often vividly colored

pH: An expression of soil alkalinity or acidity; the hydrogen ion content of soil

Pioneer: A plant that flourishes in disturbed soil, as after a fire

Pistil: A flower's female reproductive organ

Pollen: The spores of a seed-bearing plant

Pome: A fleshy fruit

Procumbent: Trailing along the ground; prostrate

Propagate: To grow new plants from old under controlled conditions

Prostrate: See *Procumbent*

Prune: To cut back, for the purposes of shaping a plant, encouraging new growth, or controlling size

Raceme: An elongated flower cluster in which the flowers are held on small stalks radiating from a single, larger stalk

Ramble: To grow freely, often over another plant or structure

Rejuvenation pruning: The practice of cutting all the main stems of a shrub back to within ½ inch of the ground during winter dormancy; renewal pruning

Remontant: Able to rebloom one or more times during a single growing season

Renewal pruning: See *Rejuvenation pruning*

Root cutting: A cutting taken from the root of a parent plant for the purpose of propagation

Root pruning: The act of removing a portion of a plant's roots to keep top growth in check

Rootstock: The root of a grafted plant

Runner: A prostrate branch that roots at its joint

Scarify: To sand, scratch, or otherwise disturb the coating of a seed in preparation for its germination

Self-pollination: A plant's ability to fertlize its pistils with its own pollen

Semidouble: Having more than the usual number of petals but with at least some pollen-producing stamens

Semievergreen: Retaining its leaves for most of the winter, or in warm climates

Semihardwood cutting: A cutting taken from a stem that has just begun to develop woody tissue, for the purpose of propagation.

Sepal: The part of a flower that is circularly arranged outside the petals

Single: In flowers, having only one layer of petals

Softwood cutting: A cutting taken from a green, or immature, stem of a woody plant, for the purpose of propagation

Species: A subgroup of a genus, composed of reproductively similar plants or animals

Specimen: A plant deliberately set by itself to emphasize its ornamental properties

Spreading: Having a horizontally branching habit

Stamen: The male organ of a flower carrying the pollen-bearing anther

Staminoid: A pollenless stamen

Sterile: Unable to generate seed

Stolon: An underground shoot

Stratify: To help seeds overcome dormancy by cleaning and drying them, then maintaining them for a period of time under generally cool and moist conditions

Subshrub: A shrub that is woody only at the base

Sucker: A shoot growing from the root or base of a woody plant

Tap root: A strong, vertical-growing, central root

Topiary: The art of trimming or training plants into decorative three-dimensional shapes

Truss: A flower cluster set at the top of a stem or branch

Twining vine: A vine that climbs by coiling around another plant or structure

Understock: The stock or root plant onto which a shoot has been grafted to produce a new plant

Unisexual: Having either stamens or pistils

USDA hardiness zones: Planting zones established by the United States Department of Agriculture, defined by a number of factors, including minimum winter temperatures

Understory plant: A plant whose natural habitat is the forest floor

Variegated: Characterized by striping, mottling, or other coloration in addition to the plant's general overall color

Vine: A plant that trails, clings, or twines, and requires support to grow vertically

Weeping: Having long, drooping branches

Winter kill: The dying back of a plant or part of a plant due to harsh winter conditions

Woody: Forming stems that mature to wood

Xeriscaping: Landscaping with the use of drought-tolerant plants, to eliminate the need for supplemental watering

NOTE: Inclusion on this list does not imply a recommendation, and there are many fine nurseries that do not appear on this list.

Antique Rose Emporium
PO Box 143, Route 5
Brentham, Texas 77833
409-836-9051

Appalachian Gardens
PO Box 82
Waynesboro, Pennsylvania 17268
717-762-4312

Carroll Gardens
PO Box 310
Westminster, Maryland 21157
301-848-5422

Cascade Forestry Service
Rte. 1
Cascade, Iowa 52033
319-852-3042

Clifford's Perennial and Vine
PO Box 320 Route 2
East Troy, Wisconsin 53120
414-968-4040

The Cummins Garden
22 Robertsville Road
Marlboro, New Jersey 07746
Rhododendrons

Eastern Plant Specialties
PO Box 226
Georgetown, Maine 04548
207-371-2888

Forestfarm
990 Thethrow Road
Williams, Oregon 97544
503-846-7269

Foxborough Nursery, Inc.
3611 Miller Road
Street, Maryland 21154
410-836-7023

Girard Nurseries
PO Box 428
Geneva, Ohio 44041
216-466-2881

Gossler Farms Nursery
1220 Weaver Road
Springfield, Oregon 97478-9663
503-746-3922

Greer Gardens
1280 Goodpasture Island Road
Eugene, Oregon 97401
503-686-8266

Heronswood Nursery
7530 288th Street Northeast
Kingston, Washington 98346
206-297-4172

Lamtree Farm
PO Box 162, Route 1
Warrensville, North Carolina 28693
919-385-6144

Louisiana Nursery
PO Box 43, Route 7
Opelousas, Louisiana 70570
318-948-3696
Magnolias and other shrubs

Mellingers, Inc.
2310 W. South Range Road
North Lima, Ohio 44452

Musser Forests, Inc.
O Box 340, Route 119 North
Indiana, Pennsylvania 15701
412-465-5685

Owen Farms
PO Box 158, Route 3
Ripley, Tennessee 38063
901-635-1588

Pacific Tree Farms
4301 Lynwood Drive
Chula Vista, California 92010
619-422-2400
(Shrubs for warm climates)

Powell's Gardens
PO Box 21, Route 3
Princeton, North Carolina 27569
919-936-4421

Roslyn Nursery
211 Burrs Lane
Dix Hills, NY 11746
516-643-9347

Stallings Exotic Nursery
910 Encinitas Boulevard
Encinitas, California 92024
619-753-3079
(Shrubs for warm climates)

Twombley Nursery
163 Barn Hill Road
Monroe, Connecticut 06468
203-261-2133
Conifers

Wavecrest Nursery
2509 Lakeshore Drive
Fennville, Michigan 49408
616-543-4175

Westgate Garden Nursery
751 Westgate Drive
Eureka, California 95501
707-442-1239

Weston Nurseries
30 Phipps Street, Route 135
PO Box 186
Hopkinton, Massachusetts 01748
508-435-3414

White Flower Farms
Route 63
Litchfield, Connecticut 06759-0050
203-567-0801

Whitney Gardens and Nursery
PO Box F
Brinnon, Washington 98320
206-796-4411

Woodlanders, Inc.
1128 Colleton Avenue
Aiken, South Carolina 29801
803-648-7522

Yucca Do Nursery
PO Box 655
Waller, Texas 77484
409-826-6363

Periodicals

The Avant Gardener
PO Box 489
New York, NY 10028

Flower and Garden Magazine
4251 Pennsylvania Avenue
Kansas City, MO 64111

Horticulture
300 Mass Avenue
Boston, MA 02115

Organic Gardening and Farming
Organic Park
Emmaus, PA 18049

CONTRIBUTORS

MAIN GARDENS

Ethan Johnson
The Holden Arboretum
9500 Sperry Road
Mentor, Ohio 44060

Chris Graham
Royal Botanical Gardens
PO Box 399
Hamilton, Ontario Canada l8N 3H8

Galen Gates
Chicago Botanic Garden
Lake Cook Road
Chicago, Illinois 60022

CONSULTING GARDENS

Dorthe Hviid
Berkshire Botanical Garden
PO Box 826
Stockbridge, Massachusetts 01262

Mary Irish
Desert Botanical Garden
1201 N. Galvin Parkway
Phoenix, Arizona 85008

James Locklear
Dyck Arboretum of the Plains
Hesston College,
Hesston, Kansas 67062

Anne Richardson
Huntington Botanical Gardens
1151 Oxford Road
San Marino, California 91108

Richard Isaacson
Minnesota Landscape Arboretum
3675 Arboretum Drive
Chanhassen, Minnesota 55317

Rick Lewandowski
Morris Arboretum of the University of Pennsylvania
9414 Meadowbrook Avenue
Philadelphia, Pennsylvania 19118

Wayne Cahilly
The New York Botanical Garden
Bronx, New York 10458

Claire Sawyers
The Scott Arboretum of Swarthmore College
500 College Avenue
Swarthmore, Pennsylvania 19081-1397

PHOTO CREDITS

LEAF SHAPES

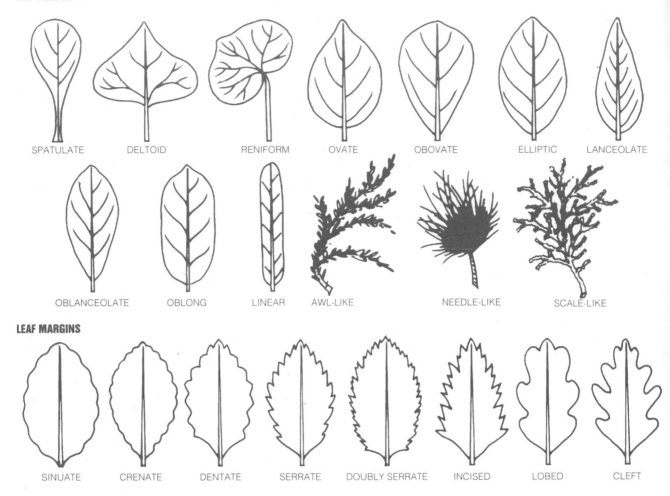

SPATULATE DELTOID RENIFORM OVATE OBOVATE ELLIPTIC LANCEOLATE

OBLANCEOLATE OBLONG LINEAR AWL-LIKE NEEDLE-LIKE SCALE-LIKE

LEAF MARGINS

SINUATE CRENATE DENTATE SERRATE DOUBLY SERRATE INCISED LOBED CLEFT

LEAF ARRANGEMENTS AND STRUCTURES

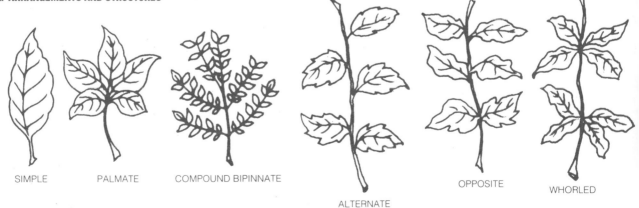

SIMPLE PALMATE COMPOUND BIPINNATE OPPOSITE WHORLED

ALTERNATE